LAW AT THE MOVIES

LAW AND LITERATURE

The Law and Literature series publishes work that connects legal ideas to literary and cultural history, texts, and artifacts. The series encompasses a wide range of historical periods, literary genres, legal fields and theories, and transnational subjects, focusing on interdisciplinary books that engage with legal and literary forms, methods, concepts, dispositions, and media. It seeks innovative studies of every kind, including but not limited to work that examines race, ethnicity, gender, national identity, criminal and civil law, legal institutions and actors, digital media, intellectual property, economic markets, and corporate power, while also foregrounding current interpretative methods in the humanities, using these methods as dynamic tools that are themselves subject to scrutiny.

LAW AT THE MOVIES

TURNING LEGAL DOCTRINE INTO ART

STANLEY FISH

For Mark — thanks you very much for getting me a job in my old age — Stanley Feb. 2025

OXFORD
UNIVERSITY PRESS

OXFORD
UNIVERSITY PRESS

Great Clarendon Street, Oxford, OX2 6DP,
United Kingdom

Oxford University Press is a department of the University of Oxford.
It furthers the University's objective of excellence in research, scholarship,
and education by publishing worldwide. Oxford is a registered trade mark of
Oxford University Press in the UK and in certain other countries

Published in the United States of America by Oxford University Press
198 Madison Avenue, New York, NY 10016, United States of America

British Library Cataloguing in Publication Data
Data available

Library of Congress Control Number: 2023945425

ISBN 9780198898726

DOI: 10.1093/oso/9780198898726.001.0001

Printed and bound in the UK by
Clays Ltd, Elcograf S.p.A.

Contents

Introduction

It's Against the Law

In this book I am interested in movies that take legal doctrine seriously and regard it, not as a footnote or as an appendage to substance, but as a primary generator of both plot and character. Here is an example. In the penultimate scene of Sydney Pollack's *The Firm* (1993), the protagonist Mitch McDeere (Tom Cruise) explains a piece of legal doctrine to the FBI agent who has forced him to spy on the firm he had joined just out of law school. Earlier, the FBI confirmed what McDeere had begun to suspect: Bendini, Lambert, & Locke is a front for laundering the dirty money of a Chicago crime syndicate. Agent Wayne Tarrance (Ed Harris) and his colleagues tell McDeere that, if he does not cooperate with the bureau, he will be swept up in the charges that will be brought against the firm in the near future. But McDeere knows that, if he does cooperate, he is in danger of his life: four members of the firm have died under suspicious circumstances. He is thus between the proverbial rock and a hard place: threatened with jail by one party and with bodily harm, or worse, by another. And in the background lurks the specter of the Morolto brothers, Mafia bosses who will do anything to anybody in order to protect their interests.

The plot question is, how does McDeere extricate himself from this mess and avoid the dangers that await him on every side? The somewhat surprising answer is the doctrine of mail fraud, which says that it is a felony to use the mails in furtherance of an attempt to defraud. McDeere discovers, more or less accidentally, that Bendini, Lambert and Locke has been overbilling its clients in a way that indicates intention (not just a one-time mistake) and therefore

Law at the Movies. Stanley Fish, Oxford University Press. © Stanley Fish (2024).
DOI: 10.1093/oso/9780198898726.003.0001

a conspiracy. He secures copies of the mailed billing invoices along with the records of the transactions involved, and he then persuades the Moroltos to authorize giving the invoices to the government by assuring them—and this is another lesson in doctrine—that the documents will be used only as evidence of mail fraud and that in "any other area of the attorney–client relationship" he remains bound by oath to maintain "full and complete confidentiality." In a stroke, the firm is removed as a threat because its members will now be prosecuted and convicted. The threat posed by the Moroltos is at least mitigated, because they now have a stake in keeping McDeere alive: should he die, the files might fall into the hands of persons under no pledge of confidentiality. McDeere does not quite say that, but he more than implies it when he frames a simile: "I am like a ship carrying a cargo that will never reach any port; as long as I am alive, that ship will always be at sea." And, to tie a bow around the package, the FBI now has what it asked him to get—proof that Bendini, Lambert and Locke is a criminal enterprise. (His wife had earlier remarked that he is running a three-ring circus, and at this moment he succeeds in keeping all the balls in the air.)

Agent Tarrance, however, is not satisfied. He has two related complaints. First, mail fraud seems small potatoes given the crimes the firm and the Mafia have committed—murder, blackmail, extortion. "Overbilling, mail fraud," Tarrance exclaims sardonically: "that's exciting!" "It's not sexy," McDeere replies, "but it's got teeth . . . ten thousand dollars and five years in prison for each act." But, responds Tarrance (and this is his second complaint), while you may have nailed the firm, "you let the Mafia off the hook." Why limit what the government sees to the invoices? Why not turn over the full record of the Moroltos' suspect transactions? "They're my clients," McDeere explains. "They're the crooks," Tarrance retorts. These statements mark the gulf between the two men. For Tarrance, punishing wrongdoers by any means available is everything. For McDeere, hewing to the law is everything. There may be a greater good in bringing down the Mafia, but McDeere is not in the greater-good business; he is in the lawyering business, and its rules dictate his actions and provide a safe harbor neither the firm, nor the gangsters, nor the FBI can offer. That is what he has learned in the crucible of his travails: "I discovered the law again; you actually made me think about it." Only by attaching himself to the law and respecting its limits—it speaks to some things, not to everything—can he carve out a space no one can penetrate: "I won my life back; you don't run me, and they don't run me." The law runs him in the sense that it is what he consults. Doing the greater good or advancing the general cause of justice may be the long-range effect of what he does, but it is not the reason he does it. His reasons from now on will always be legal ones. When he gives Tarrance a tape of a conversation between them in which his cooperation is clearly being coerced, the agent asks why he didn't make it public. The simple answer: "It's against the law." (In some states, it is illegal for someone to tape-record a conversation without the permission of the other party.)

This small scene (it goes on for a little more than two minutes) contains a deep reflection on the law, but the deep point is never explicitly made (although I have teased it out in the preceding paragraph). It emerges by implication from the detailed, inside-baseball, unpacking of mail fraud. It is moments like this, when the dry as dust soil of legal doctrine flowers into something truly substantive and dramatically compelling, that interest me in the movies I consider in this book. *The Firm* isn't one of them (it has no chapter of its own), because the discussions, first of attorney–client confidentiality and second of mail fraud, take up only eight or so minutes of a movie over two and a half hours long. For the rest of the time, we are watching a Tom Cruise caper movie complete with extended chase and the death of at least one man; and, when Mitch isn't running or setting up his three-ring circus, he is dealing with the fallout from having cheated on his wife in the Cayman Islands at the instigation of his "mentor" Avery Tolar (played with his usual brilliance by Gene Hackman); and when he's not in Memphis or the Cayman Islands, he's at a prison visiting his incarcerated brother (David Strathairn) and devising a plan to get him out of jail with the FBI's help. And, as if all that weren't enough, there's the subplot in which Tammy Hemphill (Holly Hunter), secretary to a private detective murdered by the firm's "security" force, teams up with Mitch's wife Abby (Jeanne Tripplehorn) to copy the files in Tolar's possession before sailing off (for life, it seems) with the aforementioned brother. That's a lot to be going on, and, while legal doctrine certainly plays a role, it is as a plot device (especially at the end), not as the linchpin and very foundation of the plot.

The reverse is true of the movies that receive a full analysis. In those movies, legal doctrine is not waved at on the way to more "sexy" issues; rather, legal doctrine and thematic substance are inextricable; the latter grows out of the former. In *Absence of Malice*, the transformation of libel law in the wake of *New York Times* v. *Sullivan* (1964) is not merely noted in passing; it is the film's subject and generates everything that happens. Questions of property law are not merely raised in *Amistad* while the larger issue of race is explored; by insistently asking what is and is not property, lawyer Roger Baldwin (Matthew McConaughey) forces an inquiry into the relationship between freedom and the right not to be owned; the narrow issue, when plumbed, leads to an understanding of the larger issue. The line between law and violence is not merely declared in *The Man Who Shot Liberty Valance*; its indistinctness is reaffirmed in every scene, as is the necessity of maintaining it even while it shimmers and blurs. The negotiation of the conflicting demands made by God's law and man's law is the task everyone works at in *Inherit the Wind*, *The Crucible*, and *A Man for All Seasons*. The lawyerly problem of fitting a fact situation into pre-existing legal categories is not simply a feature of *Anatomy of a Murder*; it is the whole movie. In *Judgment at Nuremberg*, the classical opposition of natural law to positive law—the law that is on the books—is stated, debated, and dramatized but never resolved in either the courtroom scenes or the scenes set in bars, restaurants, and private homes. The indifference of law as a closed system to the person caught in its toils—a byproduct of the aspiration to generality—informs every bleak moment in *The Wrong Man* and *Billy Budd*. The interaction of privilege, misogyny, and culture—together mandating obedience to the way things are—hems in the thoughts and actions of every character in *North Country* until a lawyer, for professional not moral reasons, opens things up by extending, for the first time, the concept of class action to workplace sexual harassment. Law's inadequacy in the face of aesthetic questions produces a trial where no question is ever answered in *Howl*. In all of these films, a level of political and moral reflection is not the starting point; it emerges from a patient attention to what one of the characters in *Amistad* terms "legal minutiae."

The obvious heterogeneity of themes in these movies militates against any one of them becoming this book's thesis. In a way, then, the book has no thesis. Many important social and political issues surface and receive extended attention, but in the end the issues take a back seat to the legal machinery brought to bear on them; they are grist for the law's mills, and it is the law's mills that provide the energy and focus of my analyses. There is, however, one topic to which I repeatedly return, because in many respects its parameters and concerns are isomorphic with the parameters and concerns of Anglo-American law.

That topic is liberalism, a form of government that dislodges from the position of authority a God or a king or a central committee and elevates to a central place the autonomous, rights-bearing individual who, in the absence of an antecedently established ruler or guide, must fashion a way of living that somehow achieves generality in a brave new world of diversity and independence. The chief location of that fashioning is the law, and, before proceeding to a consideration of that fashioning in the movies I have chosen, I will say something about the difficulties—largely intractable—of the task.

1

Liberal Heroism and Reasonable Doubt

12 Angry Men

Whenever I teach "Law at the Movies," my code name for the course (only revealed to the students late in the semester) is "Jurisprudence in Disguise." By that I mean two things: (1) movies are the Trojan horse that allows me to introduce jurisprudential questions students might find off-putting were they posed directly, and (2) those questions are the real content of the movies we study, questions such as "What is law?," "How is law established?," "What is the source of legal authority?," "What is the relationship between law and morality?," "What compels obedience to the law?" There are many answers to these questions, but one that is almost never offered, and is resisted whenever it surfaces, denies the distinction between law and violence and asserts that obedience to the law is compelled by nothing more than force. In his magisterial essay *The Concept of Law* (1961), H. L. A. Hart strongly rejects this thesis. He insists that, whatever law is, it must be very different from the scenario in which a gunman "orders his victim to hand over his purse and threatens to shoot him if he refuses."[1] Were law merely a matter of "orders backed up by threats" (the "command theory" of law elaborated by nineteenth-century legal theorist John Austin), none of the features we prize in law—its settled nature, its impartial execution, its independence of bias and interest—would be present, and it would be less a refuge from injustice than a vehicle of it.

We have a number of ways of making this point. We say that Justice is blind. We say that law is the "impartial third" that hearkens to

Law at the Movies. Stanley Fish, Oxford University Press. © Stanley Fish (2024).
DOI: 10.1093/oso/9780198898726.003.0002

neither side in a dispute but delivers a disinterested judgment. We say that law is "no respecter of persons"; for the verdicts it issues would be the same whether the defendant was rich or poor, powerful or lowly, white or black, a man or a woman, straight or gay. We say that "ours is a government of laws, not men"; for, if ours were a government of men, the rules of entitlements and sanctions would track the preferences of this one or that one; but general rules—rules that have the form "all citizens can or cannot do X" rather than "Dick and Jane and Harry cannot do X, but you can"—intersect with personal preferences only incidentally and accidently. It is rules of that kind that constitute the justice system (or so the standard story tells us) and make ours a government of laws.

But where do these general rules/laws come from? The question is urgent, because the problem of partiality returns if the source of general laws is not itself general but is instead identified with a particular ideology or theology or morality. If law is identified with the dictates of a religion, non-congregants will have no reason to follow it. If law is identified with a political philosophy (utilitarianism, libertarianism, communitarianism, socialism), those who find its goals unappetizing or even pernicious will chafe against it. If law is identified with a moral vision—even one so basic as "Do unto others as you would have them do unto you"—the content of that vision will be endlessly debated, as in fact it is.

But, once you set aside theology, ideology, and morality as the possible sources of law, what is left? The answer given by liberal democracy—that form of government whose (paradoxical) claim is to be apolitical—is process. If laws could be made without reference to substantive concerns, if laws could be entirely formal—without hostages to disputable contents—no one could claim that they were tainted by partisan interests, and you could obey them without committing yourself to anything. Are there such laws? What would they be like? Well, they would be like the law commanding you (and me and everyone else) to drive on the right side of the road (or on the left in the United Kingdom), or like the rule in a supermarket line or in a line to purchase a train ticket that you must wait your turn; you don't get to go to the front of the line because you are wealthy or virtuous or good-looking or have a high IQ, although it might be that exceptions, generally agreed on in advance, are made for the very old and the infirm. Such laws and rules are indifferent to persons, and take no notice of status other than the status conferred by the formal mechanism, the road's dividing line or the queue.

To be sure, it would be possible, if you tried hard enough, to discover a latent ideological content in the most formal of rules—Thomas Hobbes remarked of geometry that its definitions are not disputed only "because men care not, in that subject, what be truth, as a thing that crosses no man's ambition, profit, or lust"[2]—but, apart from a special effort, mounted typically by political and epistemological revolutionaries, to uncover the biases hidden beneath apparently neutral surfaces, there does exist at any moment a category of merely procedural rules adherence to which signifies fidelity to law and nothing else. The project (and claim) of political liberalism is to order civic life (private life is left untouched by the liberal state, which has no interest in what's in your heart) by such rules. Of course, there is still the problem of figuring out what they are, given that by the first principle of liberal thought no God, king, dictator, or wise man will tell you. In fact, nothing will tell you; in the absence of an external authority such as a king or a pope (exiled from liberal thought at the outset), authority can emerge only from the search for it. The establishment of a regime of process—of laws that incline to no one's interest because they affirm nothing substantive—is itself a process. With nothing anchoring it from the outside, the liberal state must engineer its foundations from the inside. You begin with core examples like the example of driving on one side of the road and strive to fashion laws that display the same indifference to race, class, gender, sexual orientation, educational level, wealth. You won't get it right the first time or the second or the third, and so you keep on refining your formulation in response to the claims made by some (and there will always be some) that this latest version of law is unfair to them. It is through the trial and error of legislative outcomes and judicial decisions that the law strives to realize the liberal ideal of a regime that treats each and every one of its citizens as equal before the law. The ideal cannot be achieved at a single stroke; it is the endless work of generation after generation, as the law, in a phrase favored by many legal theorists, works itself pure. It is the political process that promises to deliver, in the long run, an apolitical jurisprudence independent of both partisan interest and the exercise of force, gunman-style.

In the previous paragraphs, I have rehearsed what might be called the standard story of law as it is presented in our textbooks, proclaimed by our courts, pledged allegiance to by our politicians, by and large believed in by our citizens. It is the story of a legal system that, despite its fault lines and occasional stumbles, more often than not affords guidance, protection, and justice to everyone who puts his trust in it and lays down his arms in the confidence that his fellows will do the same. That, however, is not the story told in many of the films that take up law as their subject. Instead, we find a law that is absent, a law that is corrupt, a law that is politicized, a law that is inadequate, a law that is instrumentalized, a law that breaks down at exactly the moment it is most needed. To be sure, this is exactly what would be expected: drama thrives not on things running smoothly, but on things gone awry. It would be hard to make drama out of a process that turns out just as it should. That, however, is the unlikely achievement of Sidney Lumet's *12 Angry Men* (1957), a movie that has been celebrated as the perfect law-centered movie, although I shall argue that it is also perfectly dishonest.

But, before I make that argument, let me remind you of the arc of the film's plot. Twelve jurors are charged with determining the guilt or innocence of a boy (probably Puerto Rican) who has been accused of murdering his father. He was heard saying to him, "I'll kill you." As deliberations begin, it appears that everyone thinks the boy is guilty, but, when a preliminary vote is taken, one juror, identified only as Juror #8 (played by Henry Fonda), votes not guilty. In the course of the discussions (some very heated) that follow, the other eleven jurors, one by one, change their minds until, once again, there is a single holdout, this time for conviction. He finally relents, and the jurors file out of the room.

As viewers we are encouraged to understand the narrative as a vindication of liberal political values and as a demonstration of those values in action. Clouds of prejudice, bias, and ignorance are dispelled by rational deliberation supported by evidence that emerges from careful measurement and disinterested observation. In short, enlightenment occurs. The field of enlightenment is the minds of the jurors, minds, when we first encounter them, filled by petty preferences ("I'd rather be at the ball game"), personal grievances ("My son hates me"), racist sentiments ("You know what they're like"), xenophobic fears ("You come here and right away start telling us what to think"), false propositions ("The knife is unique"), and a complacent confidence in the legal process ("Even his lawyer didn't make much of a case for him").

The work of the give and take of dialogue, occasionally escalating into a shouting match, is the removal from the jurors' minds of attitudes and errors that stand in the way of clear judgment. Clear judgment is judgment that proceeds from intellects dedicated to the discovery of truth and to nothing else.

The problem, of course, is that human intellects are prone to various unfortunate tendencies—the tendency to overvalue one's own opinions, the tendency to prefer evidence that supports one's already-held convictions (known as "confirmation bias"), the tendency to be moved by flattery or fear or both, the tendency to identify what is true and valuable with self-interest or the interest of one's family and tribe. (An influential catalogue of these inherent weaknesses is provided by the seventeenth-century jurist and scientist Francis Bacon in his discussion of the "idols of the mind.") Given liberal thought's relocation of authority from fixed, unimpeachable sources (God, the king) to the deliberative powers of the individual seeker of truth, it is imperative that the mind, newly elevated to a place of prominence, be made—or rather make itself; there's the rub—into the proper kind of instrument. That's the work of a mandated and ongoing conversation conducted under the assumption that nothing can be taken for granted and everything must be examined and questioned, especially those things (or sentiments) that seem to us to be incontrovertibly true. Liberalism equips itself with various devices designed to prevent resting complacently in widely accepted assumptions—in the political realm, the checks and balances celebrated in *The Federalist Papers*; in the psychological realm, the practice of consciousness-raising, a technique for bringing to light the exclusions and distortions that are part and parcel of any perspective tenaciously clung to; in the epistemological realm, J. S. Mill's insistence in *On Liberty* (1859) that no belief, however securely based in evidence it may seem to be, can be allowed to stand without challenge; if no challenges currently exist, they must be invented.

In *12 Angry Men*, Juror #8 is the embodiment of Mill's imperative. He says he votes not guilty because the unanimity of his fellow jurors, rather than swaying him, makes him uneasy. Here is playwright Reginald Rose's description of him in the notes prefatory to the script: "A quiet, thoughtful, gentle man—a man who sees all sides of every question and constantly seeks the truth."[3] Every word of this description rewards analysis. Being quiet, Juror #8 does not thrust his opinions on the world in a loud, aggressive manner. Being thoughtful, he considers matters before he decides to speak or act. Being gentle, he courteously attends to arguments he initially finds unpersuasive. Committed to seeing all sides of a question, he resists being rushed to premature judgment. A seeker of truth, he will settle for nothing else. And he is a man, that is, a being capable of sustained concentration and abstract thought—not superficial or frivolous or impressed by surfaces; he is serious. Early on Juror #8 is offered a piece of chewing gum. He politely declines. It is a small moment, not lingered on, but it signifies. In the 1950s chewing gum was something that wise-cracking, finger-snapping teenagers did; it was part of the package of delinquency and displayed a disrespect for traditional decorums and an unconcern with the conventions of politeness. It is something Juror #8 would never do. (Later he accepts a cough drop, but that is quite another matter.) Nor would he make much of not doing it. He has no need to advertise his virtues and wouldn't think of them as virtues at all, just as forms of action that follow naturally from upright—manly—behavior. Although Juror #8 is thoughtful, he is not introspective; that is, he does not spend time inventorying his views or the events of his life. In fact, he doesn't seem to have any views, except for the view that decisions, especially life-and-death decisions, should be arrived at deliberatively and with a determination dispassionately to consider every piece of evidence. A resolve to do that can be maintained without any reference to his preferences or political allegiances or religious affiliations or domestic arrangements or professional activities. Indeed, we know nothing of any of these, of what he likes, of what he believes, of what he aspires to, of what he desires or of what he fears. The only thing we know about him is that he is an architect, a designer of structures whose parts, we can assume, hang together and combine to produce a stability based on rationality and physics. His buildings, like his arguments, don't fall down.

Juror #8 stands alone in this absence of a personal history. His fellow jurors lead much richer lives: they have businesses, jobs, and bosses; they have estranged children; they have hobbies and obsessions; one is timid, another is a bully, a third is a bigot, a fourth is a glad-hander; the youngest is reluctant to speak; the oldest speaks from the perspective of someone who has lived too long. In the course of the debates these men have, their very different personalities shape their arguments. Juror #8 has no personality, and his arguments don't proceed from anxieties and hopes he doesn't have; they are merely arguments, offered for the sake of the effort to get things straight and for nothing else. (He is a member in good standing of Jürgen Habermas's ideal speech community.) It is only a slight exaggeration to say that he has nothing inside him except the capacity for deliberative thought. He performs the act of subtraction imagined by political philosopher John Rawls when he asks us to go behind the "veil of ignorance" and reason as we would if we knew nothing about our "race and ethnic group, sex and gender and [our] various native endowments such as strength and intelligence."[4] Juror #8 is Liberal Man incarnate.

If his fellow jurors are to follow him (as they eventually do), they must imitate his emptying of self. They must confront and set aside the insecurities and fears that stand between them and a clear sight of the evidence they are charged to consider. Juror #10 must be forced to see his racism, as he does when the others turn their backs on him. Juror #3 must realize that his anger at the young defendant is a projection of the anger (and anguish) he feels toward his son. Juror #4 must relax the severity of his judgment and acknowledge that he too exhibits the frailties he scorns in others. Juror #2 must push through his tendency to be manipulated by the last person who spoke to him and find his own voice. Each juror in turn detaches himself from his habitual motives for action, and after doing so stands equipped only with his reasoning powers and nothing extraneous to them. At that moment, he sees what Juror #8 saw from the beginning—reasonable doubt all over the place—and votes to acquit.

It is a very neat story, and it presents itself as the record of the triumph of logic and evidence over rhetoric and unsupported opinion. That self-presentation has achieved the status of orthodoxy. Here is Christopher Falzon's quite representative account: *12 Angry Men* is "accurately seen as one man's heroic stand for the truth in the face of others whose views are clouded and distorted by interest and prejudice."[5] But this, I would contend, is not accurate at all. Despite its surface stigmatizing of rhetoric in favor of cool deliberative process, the film performs rhetorical manipulation at every moment, and this is especially true of its interactions with the viewer, who is, after all, the ultimate juror. The manipulation begins with the casting. The viewer wishes to be aligned with Juror #8 before he says a word because he is played by Henry Fonda. It may be hard for those under 50 to appreciate the cultural significance of Fonda, an actor whose iconic roles include Abraham Lincoln, Tom Joad, Wyatt Earp, Mr Roberts,

Clarence Darrow, and Clarence Gideon, all men of uncommon dignity, at least as he portrayed them. If Fonda was the lead actor in a film, you knew that his character would be morally upright, totally honest, and inflexible in a good way. (The bad guys he occasionally portrays—in, for example, *Firecreek* and *There Was a Crooked Man*—are slightly distorted versions of the usual Fonda hero.) Fonda is the only star in *12 Angry Men*; he is the tallest of the jurors, and he wears a white suit. Although he is, like the others, uncomfortable in a very hot room, the heat doesn't seem to bother him. He remains cool in several senses of the word. The one time he speaks in an aggressive manner turns out to be a ploy: he wants the juror he is taunting to say, "I'll kill you," and thereby demonstrate that those words, spoken by the defendant to his father, are often uttered without serious intent. He performs anger and incivility only in order to make a rational point.

As viewers we are not surprised by this behavior, because it is exactly what we expect from a Henry Fonda character, a character whose actions we approve of in advance. We follow his lead before he offers it, and, when he votes not guilty in the initial ballot, we become his advocates and accomplices, eager to affirm any argument he makes. The fact that his arguments are "scientific"—they involve the careful marshaling of physical evidence—fits perfectly with the liberal ethos he exemplifies. The scientist, like the responsible liberal citizen, sets aside his personal preferences and devotes himself to disinterested observation. (Scientific Man is Liberal Man.) If the conclusions he reaches are valid, they must be conclusions anyone following the same method would reach, no matter what his or her political party or religious affiliations or tribal allegiances. Scientific work must be replicable—capable of being repeated by anyone possessing the requisite knowledge and rigor. Let's look at the evidence together, Juror #8 urges. Is it really the case that the knife the defendant admits to owning is unique? Is it really the case that the old man who reported seeing the defendant run away from the scene of the crime could have gotten to a window in fifteen seconds? Is it really the case that the woman who claims to have seen the killing could have done so in the moment of waking before she had time to put on her glasses? The answer to each of these questions turns out to be no or probably not, and the once apparently unassailable proof of guilt collapses when the props supporting it are removed one by one. Reason triumphs, mere opinion and prejudice are sent away.

Or so it seems. There are counterarguments to be made. The fact that there is more than one knife of the kind that was used doesn't mean that the young man didn't use it. The old man may have been wrong in his estimate of the time that elapsed between his hearing an argument and seeing the son run away, but so what? The woman who looks through her window without her glasses may have been farsighted. Those holding out for a guilty verdict try to make these arguments, but they don't register strongly, because the case for acquittal has acquired an irresistible momentum, a momentum carried forward by the disqualification as biased of the very voices that now say, "Stop." "You're twisting the facts" is the plaintive and ineffectual cry of those who see their majority slipping away. They are right, but the film's narrative steamrolls them, as all the points are awarded to the opposition, more secure in its virtue with every moment. The movie is a liberal set-up. The film that celebrates impartial, rational process and derides rhetorical manipulation is itself supremely manipulative. Of course, it might be said that all films are manipulative, but not all films present themselves as briefs against manipulation and for the unfolding of a purely rational deliberation.

Another way to put this is to observe that the movie is saturated. Every little thing about it sends a message, and it is always the same one. The fact that the jurors are known only by numbers—by a formal designation, a designation without content—tells us that the judgment they are asked to deliver should be independent of their identities; the more those identities affect what they think and say, the further they are from the ideal of deciding on the basis of logic and evidence and nothing else. The fact that Juror #8 is not Juror #1 or Juror #12 or Juror #6 completes his (non)profile: he isn't first, he isn't last, he's not exactly in the middle; he's just there, randomly placed. He is a hero without armor or a white horse (although he does have a white suit), or an army or a grand title; he's just an everyman, or, more precisely, he is what every man, endowed with no special powers, could be if he set his mind—his rational mind—to it.

A rational mind is a mind that operates steadily and calmly; it is without heat, and it stands firm against the appeal of overheated rhetoric. In *12 Angry Men*, this metaphor is made literal. From the moment the jurors file into the room to the three-quarter mark, no topic is more commented on than the heat. A locked door, no air conditioning, a fan that doesn't work, a smallish, shabby room dominated by a long table, windows that open onto a steamy summer late afternoon, a perfect incubation dish for Juror #3's burgeoning cold. Soon, jackets come off (except for the jacket worn by uptight broker Juror #4), ties are loosened, sweat darkens shirtfronts and underarms (again except for Juror #4), already frayed tempers become more frayed; in short, the worst possible conditions for a cool examination of a complex fact situation. And yet—and we are encouraged to understand this as a testimony to the liberal faith in the dispassionate weighing of evidence—in these most inhospitable of physical circumstances, experiments are conducted, arguments are made and refuted, convictions once fiercely held are dislodged, and unanimity is achieved.

Well, not quite. Juror #7 (Jack Warden), a marmalade salesman who boasts about his income, joins the new majority only because he wants to get to a ball game and sees where the wind is blowing; he switches sides for reasons unrelated to the issues as they have been teased out and debated. You can't do that, another juror tells him. "We want to hear your reasons." My reason, he says feebly, is that I don't think he's guilty. Earlier, Juror #7 rudely walks away as Juror #9 (the old man) is making a point. The old man protests, but Juror #8, overhearing the exchange, says, "He can't hear you; he never will." This is the severest judgment Juror #8 issues; he is declaring that Juror #7 is incapable of participating in the rational process he hopes to initiate; he's a lost cause. And how does he know this and why do we agree with him? In part because of Juror #7's clothes. He wears a loud, flashy jacket and a pork-pie hat (associated with "hipsters" and pool-hall denizens). His appearance practically shouts "not serious," and Juror #8 says that he never will be. He's just too colorful. In the liberal palette, colors, especially red, the color of passion, are suspicious; the preferred hues are white, silver gray, and mild earth shades; the preferred tone of voice is low, soft, and subdued. The moment glad-handing, gum-chewing Juror #7 comes on the scene, we dismiss him. The moment the white-suited Juror #8 refuses Juror #7's offer of gum, we embrace him. Every second of every scene pressures us to make small judgments that in time (and almost imperceptibly) flower into the large judgment demanded of us as putative jurors. The movie that privileges deliberative choice doesn't give us one. We haven't got a chance.

The stages of our seduction are marked by the weather. When the vote tally reads 6–6, the rains come, as if to say, the air is clearing, opinions are evenly divided, rationality can proceed in what we all now see as the proper direction. Because the rain makes the room dim, the lights are put on, and when the lights are put on, the fan works. (Even Juror #7 says, "Things are looking up.") Soon after, the pace accelerates. Juror #4 (E. G. Marshall) finally sweats when he cannot remember some details of the movie he saw a few days ago. Juror #5 (Jack Klugman) insists with authority that a boy who was familiar with switchblades would never stab downward. Juror #4 declares himself persuaded of the boy's innocence after it is pointed out to him that the "eyewitness" was probably not wearing her glasses when she looked out the window. Juror #10 (Ed Begley), rejected by his colleagues when they turn their backs on his racist rant, mutters, "Not guilty." Juror #3 (Lee J. Cobb), finally realizing that his desire to convict is really a desire to punish his son, follows suit, sobbing. "We're ready now," says the foreman (Martin Balsam). The jurors exit the room quickly. Jackets are taken from the coatrack, which fills the forefront of the shot. The last jacket belongs to Juror #3, who remains slumped at the table. Juror #8 taps him on the shoulder and helps him put the jacket on, a gesture that underscores what we already know: here is a man so secure in his own identity that he can be generous to his adversaries.

There's one more piece of business. As the jurors leave the courthouse (we never see them formally render a verdict), Juror #9, the old man, approaches Juror #8, and asks, "What's your name?" Not "what's your number?" but "what's your name?" If we expect to learn something substantive, something more informative than a number, we are disappointed. "Davis" is the answer. Not Greenberg or Alvarez or Polansky or even Riley, but Davis, as uninformative a name as you can imagine. Juror #8 walks down the courthouse steps just as he entered the jury room, less a man of flesh and blood than a representative of an ideal type. As he nears the bottom of the steps, he raises his head slightly and the sun comes out. Of course.

The movie is so confident of the force of its arguments that the counterarguments are provided in plain sight. I inventoried them earlier, and, just before he gives in, Juror #3 rehearses them in tones of outrage: Every single thing, he thunders, says the boy is guilty. The woman testified in open court, didn't she? The eyeglasses? Maybe she was farsighted. And why didn't his lawyer say something? The old man, what's the difference if he's a few seconds off in his judgment of how much time had elapsed? The knife, so there's another knife, so what?

That story he told about the movies, give me a break. Everything's been twisted and turned, the crime is being committed right here, in this room. The mechanism of what he calls the crime is the isolating of particular moments as if each stood alone. In an essay titled "Did *12 Angry Men* get it wrong?" Mike D'Angelo points out that each piece of evidence is interrogated individually "in a vacuum," as if it bore the entire burden of determining guilt or innocence.[6] Lost sight of is the overarching story within which single pieces of evidence have a place: a man was murdered and the prime—the only—suspect is his son. ("It seems pretty clear" is a general refrain as deliberations begin.) That story functions as an assumed background enabling the jurors to make sense of what they hear, and it is that background that is dismantled piece by piece, with every little bit of deconstructive analysis. The action is largely but not wholly negative; for, as the supports for one structure are being taken away, another one is rising in its place. It is, however, a curious structure, for it has no center and no content. The new evidence generated by Juror #8's efforts does not add up to a new account of what happened; it merely empties out the narrative space that had been occupied by the general understanding everyone began with. Now there is only the understanding—voiced repeatedly by jurors on both sides—that nothing is certain, everything can be doubted, and no one really knows anything. A theory of knowledge—or rather of knowledge's impossibility—has replaced the search for specific knowledge. What's the point of making a case for a certain sequence of events if any case you make can be immediately discredited by a skepticism so general that nothing can survive its corrosive touch? What Juror #3 is trying to do is bring his fellow jurors back to that earlier moment when at least some things could be assumed, but it's too late. The facts he rehearses so desperately can hardly find a receptive audience now that the very notion of fact has been put into serious question.

Once again, the movie is ahead of me, for the analysis I have just offered is anticipated and foreshadowed by a small exchange in the bathroom between Juror #8 and Juror #7. "You a salesman?" Juror #7 asks. No, an architect, is the reply. Juror #7: "You know what the soft sell is? Well, you got it, believe me." The soft sell is a persuasive technique used by salespersons; it is low pressure, indirect, non-aggressive (at least on the surface), patient, quiet, and (relatively) subtle. The hard sell, in contrast, is upfront, insistent, loud, and quick-hitting. Juror #7 is a hard-sell practitioner who lists his methods: "laughs, drinks, jokes, tricks." The two strategies differ in the effects they seek. The hard seller pushes for an immediate decision; he deploys his entire bag of tricks right away, risking everything in the hope of sealing the deal. The soft seller holds his marks on a long leash, allowing what he says to make its way into their minds to the point where they believe they have been self-persuaded. When the soft seller succeeds, those he has brought along don't think they have been sold anything; they just think they have come to the right conclusion with the help of a disinterested, honest interlocutor. That, of course, is exactly the pose Juror #8 assumes. He says he is not trying to change anyone's mind; he doesn't declare that the boy is innocent; he just says, again and again (repetition is part of the soft sell), that it's possible. The only thing he wants to do is talk, and what could be wrong with that?

What, then, is the soft seller selling? The answer is doubt. A doubt here, a doubt there, and pretty soon doubt everywhere. But is it "reasonable doubt" in the sense required for an acquittal? A reasonable doubt cannot be a theory-generated doubt, a doubt entertained simply because, on a very general level, everything is subject to doubt. Rather, it must be a doubt that emerges from a consideration of the totality of the circumstances as presently understood and can be tested against those circumstances. A reasonable doubt, said the US Supreme Court in *Hopt* v. *People* (1887), is "reasonable in view of all the evidence."[7] It's not a doubt you manufacture in obedience to Mill's directive to allow nothing to stand unchallenged. It can't be just possible; it must be relevant and the appropriate object of questions. Is this doubt so strong that it threatens to undo the conclusions so far reached? Can we give it credence and still affirm the basic shape of the argument? Is it a doubt at the margins, or does it hit at the center? If saying of a doubt that it is possible—a criterion every proposed doubt will meet—is enough to accord it serious attention, its path forward will meet with no resistance, and, in the company of its lighter-than-air confederates, it will proliferate unchecked, like a virus. The distinction I am making is made succinctly and powerfully by the Court in *Hopt*. "Persons of speculative minds may in almost every such case suggest possibilities of the truth being different from that established by the most convincing proof. The jurors are not to be led away by speculative notions as to such possibilities."[8] The jurors in *12 Angry Men* are led astray in exactly that way. And, as the thirteenth juror, so are we.

That's what I meant when I said that the movie is dishonest. Is it knowingly so? Do Lumet and Rose self-consciously contrive to fool viewers into thinking they are partners in a rational exercise while deploying every manipulative trick in the book? I don't think so. For his part, Lumet seems not to be focused on the moral or philosophical content of his films at all. On the evidence of his writings and the extensive interviews he gave, his interests are technical. He explains at length and with great enthusiasm the extraordinarily complex tasks of coordination required for the making of a film. The director must find a script and a writer and secure the necessary funding. He must choose an assistant director and a cinematographer. Together, he and his team must scout locations, work out camera angles and lighting, decide which lens will be employed in which scenes, consult with the set designer and the costume designer, select the music—either a stand-alone score or a collection of commercial recordings—and match the narrative themes with musical signatures. It is these things (and many more not listed) that excite Lumet when he talks about *12 Angry Men*, when he tells us, for example, "I shot the first third of the movie above eye level, and then, by lowering the camera, shot the second third at eye level, and the last third from below eye level."[9] He did it that way, he tells us, in order to heighten and accentuate the claustrophobia of a single small set. When, in the final third of the movie, the ceiling of the room appears, we are made to feel as if "not only were the walls closing in, [but] the ceiling was as well." And all this is in preparation for the final wide-angle shot of the courthouse steps, whose effect is "to let us finally breathe."[10] This is a brilliant analysis of a brilliant technique, but it is not conceptual. I'm not saying that Lumet is unconcerned with the message his movies send. We can presume that he would not have signed on had he found the material repellant. But one senses when reading and listening to him that, as long as the project is something he can relate to sympathetically, he will marshal his considerable skills in the effort to realize it on the screen.

In the case of *12 Angry Men*, the project is Reginald Rose's, the author both of the original teleplay (1954) and of the screenplay. Rose seems not to have left us any extended commentary, but we can assume that he would agree with critic Jeff Saporito, who describes the play and movie as "a love letter to the American judicial system." Saporito quotes another commentator who calls *12 Angry Men* a "public service announcement . . . in reminding the public that our democratic system renders someone innocent until proven guilty beyond a reasonable doubt."[11] That is surely how the public has received it over the years. The movie is shown and taught in public schools; the play is performed in innumerable small towns. It is as American as the Declaration of Independence, isn't it? Rose is not on the record repudiating this account of his work as an act of patriotism celebrating the virtues of the American legal order.

But, if neither Lumet nor Rose is the architect of the film's duplicity (at least as I see it), who or what is? The answer once again is liberalism. Liberalism as a meta-author produces a drama that at every moment pushes us toward a predetermined conclusion while presenting itself as the passive recorder of the discovery of fact. This is not a criticism of liberalism, but an analysis of the paradox built into every narrative informed by liberal principles: the story can get started, but there is no legitimate way to end it, to cut it off. This follows from the key liberal assumption that authority and conviction issue from the back-and-forth deliberation engaged in by autonomous rational agents who should not be prevented from turning over one more stone. Closing off debate is always an illegitimate act if one believes, as Millian liberals do, that all the evidence is never in and no voice should ever be silenced. On the other hand, business, especially legal business, must be done; verdicts must be handed down, closure must be performed. Closure, however, can never be achieved if law is faithful to liberalism's principled refusal to shut inquiry down. There comes a point—not really the endpoint (liberal analysis, like psychoanalysis, is interminable) but an endpoint the system requires—where you put together a few things out of the many things at your disposal and announce, as the jury foreman in *12 Angry Men* does, that "we're done," always an announcement that is arbitrary.

This does not mean that justice is never achieved; it does mean that we often don't know whether it has been. Perhaps that is the movie's lesson. Perhaps *12 Angry Men* is more profound and more honest in its way than even the author or director (or critic) knows, for it simultaneously displays a large confidence in its narrative and provides a counternarrative—breadcrumbs dropped along the way, should anyone want to follow them. The movie, as I have said, cheats, driving toward a resolution that has not been honestly earned, but, as I have also said, it cheats in plain sight, making it possible to piece together a story other than the one that apparently wins. That story in which a boy is saved from the death penalty by Henry Fonda sits side by side with the story of a jury talked by Henry Fonda into letting a murderer go free. (Juror #6 raises this possibility early on.) Which is it? It's impossible to tell—Juror #8 repeatedly refuses to say anything like "I know that this is what happened"—and perhaps that impossibility is what the movie (like liberalism) affirms. The nice thing about this reading is that it grants me my negative analysis but gives it a positive twist: *12 Angry Men* practices the manipulation it disdains, but, because it provides opportunities for the detection of its manipulation, it can be said to be honest in its dishonesty.

2

The Law as Blind Machine

The Wrong Man

One year before *12 Angry Men* was released, Henry Fonda starred in another legal drama, *The Wrong Man*. It was directed by Alfred Hitchcock, and no one would be tempted to describe it as a love letter to the American judicial system. Quite the reverse. *The Wrong Man* is the true story of Christopher Emmanuel Balestrero, a bass player in the Stork Club's house band, who was detained by New York City police shortly after he had stopped in at an insurance agency to ask whether he could borrow money on his wife's policy. Clerks at the agency were certain that he was the man who had robbed them twice before. After asking Balestrero to show himself at other victimized places of business, the police arrested him and charged him with the commission of several robberies. He was arraigned and released when his family raised the money for bail. He and his wife Rose then tried to find witnesses who could testify that he was miles away from New York City at the time one of the robberies occurred. But two of the potential witnesses had died, and the third was nowhere to be found. Balestrero was then put on trial, and the judge declared a mistrial after a juror made an inappropriate remark. Distressed and discouraged, Balestrero resigned himself to the ordeal of a second trial, but was exonerated when the real thief was caught in the act of attempting another robbery. The clerks who had identified him so firmly now just as firmly identify the other man, the right man. Balestrero rushes to tell his wife (played by Vera Miles) the good news, but she is deep in a state of depression and paranoia and is unable to respond. An epilogue tells viewers that Rose Balestrero recovered her mental equilibrium two years later and moved with her husband and sons to Florida.

Law at the Movies. Stanley Fish, Oxford University Press.
DOI: 10.1093/oso/9780198898726.003.0003

In at least one respect, *The Wrong Man* and *12 Angry Men* are mirror versions of one another. In both films, all the evidence points to the accused, and in both films the original assessment of guilt is overturned. The difference is that, while in *12 Angry Men* the reversal occurs at the end of a lengthy, attenuated deliberative process in which pros and cons are weighed and debated, in *The Wrong Man* the reversal follows upon an accident: the "right" man might well have gotten away with his most recent robbery, and it is sheer serendipity that one of the detectives who had originally interrogated Manny (the name Balestrero is known by) happened to be there when the actual thief was brought in; indeed, the resemblance between the two men does not register on him until after he has left the station and something clicks in his mind. It is because of this difference—the difference between an acquittal generated by argument and the examination of evidence and an acquittal that falls from the sky—that *The Wrong Man* could not possibly be seen as a vindication of the justice system. Manny has done nothing wrong and cooperates fully with those who arrest and incarcerate him, but the machinery of the law grinds inexorably toward an apparently predetermined finding of guilt. Not only is Manny saved by the last minute and wholly unearned (the police weren't searching for anyone else) discovery of the true criminal, but the justice system is saved from what would have been the successful unfolding of its own procedures. The lead detective twice says that "An innocent man has nothing to fear." Nothing, it turns out, could be further from the truth. The more innocent you are, the more likely it is that you will be crushed by a process eager to fix blame. Except for a miracle—for which Manny prays and which he arguably receives—he hasn't got a chance.

Rose sees this before anyone does. Indeed, she sees it before anything happens. Some critics fault *The Wrong Man* for falling in-artfully into two pieces when in its second half Rose's paralyzing fears, rather than Manny's legal travails, become the focus of the narrative's concern. The criticism is spectacularly in error: Rose's anxieties and the view of the world they imply are on prominent display from the very beginning when Manny comes home from the Stork Club and finds her deep in worry. That afternoon she had been told by a dentist that it would cost \$300 to remove four impacted wisdom teeth. She says it's always something: "We borrow money and for years we pay out on the installment plan; it keeps us broke." The installment plan method of paying for durable goods was introduced in the nineteenth century and became popular and respectable in the first two decades of the twentieth century. As a teenager in the 1950s, I worked part time in the credit department of a large store, and my job was to accept installment payments. Men and women approached my window holding out their payment books and a few dollars. I registered the payment and gave them back the record of their continuing, and often perpetual, bondage. That's Rose's complaint. Once you are in the installment plan world, your days are haunted by the shadow of an obligation that seems never to end; especially when, as is often the case, the payment cycle finishes just as another unforeseen disaster puts you back on the treadmill. Rose: "Every time we get up, something knocks us right down again." For Rose, impacted wisdom teeth are just the latest in a series of setbacks that, she is sure, will only be added to as the months and years pass. Her anxieties are not specific—although specific happenings are their vehicle—but general. She believes that the world is out to get her, to trip her up, undo her, frustrate her plans, endanger her family, undermine her well-being. When she finds out that Manny has been accused of a crime, she says, "I knew it was something like that." She doesn't mean that she knew he harbored criminal tendencies. She means that she knew something completely unexpected and out of the blue was always in the wings waiting to pounce. There is no escape, nothing to do, except perhaps to find an enclosure and immure yourself in it and shut out everything else, a strategy she proposes later in the movie when her paranoia is full blown.

Or is it paranoia? True, Rose exhibits the classical signs—feeling powerless, increasing isolation, depression, insomnia, low self-esteem, global suspicion, undifferentiated fear, mistrust of everything and everyone. The doctor Manny consults tells him, "Her mind is in an eclipse. She sees great lurking dangers everywhere, she's living in another world from ours, a frightening landscape that could be on the dark side of the moon." Our world, the doctor is saying, is the real one; hers is a paranoid fantasy. But the strength of this diagnosis depends on the availability of evidence that contradicts Rose's dark views. There is no such evidence in the movie. Manny thinks he has provided some when, in response to Rose's saying, "Sometimes I'm so frightened waiting for you to come home," he reminds her, "I always do come home, don't I?" And then, the very next day, he doesn't.

He doesn't come home because he is in police custody. From the moment he visits the insurance agency to ask for a loan, Manny is the living confirmation of Rose's vision of a hostile, implacable universe always closing in on you. Long before he is literally behind bars, bars hem him in. He is hemmed when he leaves the Stork Club to go home. Two policemen fall into step with him and flank him as he walks along the street. The configuration lasts only for a moment and then Manny descends the staircase of a subway station, a dark narrow passage that leads to the narrow space of the platform and a door that opens onto the even narrower space of a subway car partitioned into narrow rows of seats. The two policemen have disappeared, but their place has been taken by the subway's confining architecture, an architecture that doubles the architecture of his own small house, a narrow hall with doors that open onto small dark rooms, the frame of the shot bounded on the left by a steep-pitched narrow stair case (it's not clear that it goes anywhere), the steps of which look like bars.

Bars are everywhere in the scene in which three insurance agency clerks (in one shot looking like the witches at the beginning of Macbeth) finger Manny as the man who has twice before held them up. The door Manny enters has open blinds on the inside (as does the door to his house). The same blinds adorn the office's windows. They are not literally bars, but they have the appearance of bars. In between the door and the windows are the actual bars of the partition separating the office staff from the customers. These vertical bars—echoed by the vertical stripes on the blouses of two of the clerks and by the radiators glimpsed at the back of the room—frame Manny as he approaches the counter and pretty much hug him as he asks about the possibility of a loan. Manny exits after an apparently pleasant and low-key discussion, but the visuals of the scene place him where he will soon be—behind bars.

The policemen who take him there flank him as he is led to their car, just as the two policemen he fell into step with the night before had, but with a difference. This time it's for real. In the car he sits between two of the policemen; one of them, in tandem with the policeman who is driving, lobs apparently softball questions—what do you do? do you take your wife to the Stork Club?—but the very blandness of the interrogation contributes to the menace breathed by the situation: a man literally shanghaied into a car with no explanation of why he is there and where he is going. He is, of course, going to the police station, where he is taken to a room barely larger than the car and takes a seat while the three policemen hover over him. Finally, he is told of the accusation made against him and offered an opportunity to clear himself; he need only visit a few of the stores that had been robbed. (At this point, members of the audience will be thinking, or calling out, don't do it, ask for a lawyer, but these were pre-*Miranda* warning days.) He says, sure, if it will help, and they get back in the car and stop at two locations, where Manny is asked to walk up and down the narrow corridors of a liquor store and a deli, watched by nervous proprietors. Then it's back to the station, where the same overhead lights we saw in the stores cast a glare, but no illumination. (Overhead lights are ubiquitous in the movie; they don't aid sight, they obscure it.)

Ostensibly, what we are viewing here is a process by means of which the true facts are made to emerge; but the look of each frame tells a different story, the story of alternative perspectives being shut down even before they are offered, the story of walls closing in, the story of narrow corridors leading to even narrower corridors, the story of a man being shuffled around from place to place while the point of the exercise is withheld from him, the story of a man whose agency has been taken away, not by any one person or a single office, but by a constellation of jailors, some animate, some inanimate—cells, paddy wagons, fingerprint pads, desk clerks, magistrates, handcuffs, photographers, bail bondsmen, courtrooms, prosecutors, juries, each and every one intent only on reinforcing a designation and status the entire system has conferred on him from the very first moment. The cumulative effect of all these structures of confinement and labeling registers in a famous shot. Manny is taken to a cell. The door slams shut. He looks out on bars looking out on bars. More bars cast barlike shadows on the floor. He walks the few steps around the room, sits down, looks at his hands, impotent, and, as he leans back, the camera circles around him clockwise, ever faster, until his head takes on the aspect of a Ferris wheel car, going round and round in a motion he cannot control. All the while Bernard Herrmann's music gets louder and louder, rising to a crescendo only a bit less insistent than the crescendo he was to reach four years later in the shower scene of *Psycho*.

After that it's more of the same. The next morning we see a momentary glimpse of the sun as Manny is brought out and put in a paddy wagon. There is a brilliant shot of the wagon going over a bridge—black vehicle, the bridge's struts, a gridlike floor, again a narrow enclosure being traversed by a narrow enclosure. Ushered into another stolid official building, Manny is arraigned. Before he is called to the front of the room, he stands framed in a doorway, bars to the side, bars above. He is unshaven and his cheeks are hollowed out. He climbs to a stage and stands in front of a white board inscribed with horizontal lines measuring his height. Needless to say, the lines look like bars. And then it's back to the station where for a second we see a staircase that is the double of the staircase in Manny's house, except that it is on the right side of the screen. (The prominence of doubles in the movie will be considered in a moment.) Another stint in a cell and suddenly his name is called. He's made bail. He embraces his wife, stumbles in an apparent half-faint, and says, "You never know." The second half of the movie begins.

The relentless feel of the first half—the feel of everything (accusers, policemen, cells, handcuffs, magistrates) closing in on Manny—is replaced by something even more debilitating, the serial disappointment of hope. Manny and Rose find a lawyer, but the first thing he says to them is "I have little experience with criminal cases," and he then predicts (correctly, as it turns out) that he will likely be overmatched by experienced prosecutors. He advises them to become their own detectives and seek out witnesses who might testify that Manny was somewhere else on the days the crimes were committed. They dutifully trek out to the country inn where they had vacationed, but its proprietors have trouble remembering anything. A register yields the names of two guests. Manny and Rose eagerly set out to find them, but then are told—first by a pair of giggling preteen girls who seem to be in another movie and then by a non-English-speaking housekeeper—that they are dead. In response, Rose laughs maniacally: "There's our alibi; it's perfect; it's complete." Even Manny is beginning to catch on: "It's like someone is stacking the cards against us."

Who is that someone? In other Hitchcock movies, there is an answer to that question. The villain, often shadowy, but ultimately revealed, is arranging events in order to frustrate the hero's efforts to get at the truth and clear his name. In *North by Northwest*, Roger Thornhill (Cary Grant), mistaken for a man named Kaplan, is kidnapped and taken to a large suburban mansion where he is made drunk and placed in a car that seems certain to go out of control and kill him. He survives and tells his story to disbelieving detectives. He leads them to the mansion and, confident that his story is about to be confirmed, rings the doorbell. He is ushered into the room where he was forcibly intoxicated and triumphantly points to the sofa where bourbon was spilled by the men who assaulted him. But there is no bourbon stain and no liquor at all in what he identifies as the liquor cabinet. Only books. A gracious, attractive woman enters, embraces him by name, and talks quickly of the evening before and of her concern that he might not get home safely in his "tipsy" condition. Obviously (at least to the viewer and Thornhill) the stage has been elaborately set in a way that entirely discredits Thornhill. Even his mother doesn't believe him. He exits the mansion fully embedded in a reality that has been manufactured by hostile forces that remain mysterious and hidden. In *The Wrong Man*, there is no mysterious worker behind the scenes, no stage settings, no deep manipulator of deceptive surfaces, no stacker of the cards. There are just the cards, the successive but not purposive moments of ordinary uncaring life, a randomness that in its indifference to human plans and aspirations derails and disappoints them with a devastating casualness. As Manny said earlier, "That's life."

With their evidentiary cupboard bare, Manny and Rose go back to their ineffectual lawyer, who urges them to find the ex-boxer whom Manny, but no one else, remembers. "We're going to win this case," the lawyer declares, but the words ring hollow. At home, Manny finds Rose has been sitting up all night. You don't seem to care what happens to me, he complains. Her answer gives voice to the conclusion the movie has been moving toward: "Don't you see, it doesn't do any good to care? No matter what you do, they fix it so that it goes against you. No matter how innocent you are, they'll find you guilty." The immediate referent of "you" is Manny, but the referent is more general: Manny, Rose, you, I, everybody. We are all trapped in a world that either intends us ill or goes its merry and destructive way without any concern or solicitude for our hopes and aspirations. The only thing we can do, she reasons, is to stay home, lock our doors, and "keep them out." Her strategy is inadvertently realized when Manny, on the advice of her doctor, institutionalizes her. As the doors of the sanatorium close and Manny drives away, she is finally safe: "they" have been kept out.

Now Manny has nothing, no evidence, no witnesses, no wife. His last hope is the trial. In most films centered on the law, the trial is a centerpiece. In *The Wrong Man*, it is a small and paltry thing. The prosecutor trots out the two insurance agency clerks who had identified Manny as the robber. They do it again. Manny's lawyer attempts to discredit their testimony by asking them nitpicking questions. No one in the courtroom seems interested in his cross-examination, not even Manny's sister. The opposing attorneys are joking around and not paying attention. A few of the spectators leave. Everyone appears bored, especially one juror, who rises to ask if "we have to listen to this?" His interruption (implying that Manny is obviously guilty) leads immediately to the declaration of a mistrial, and Manny is told by his lawyer that they'll have to do the whole thing over. That evening Manny says to his mother, "I think I could have stood it better if they found me guilty." Even a decision that went against him would be better than prolonging the nightmare he has wandered into, a nightmare that now threatens to be extended in a second trial that won't take place for some time. "Once isn't enough, they've got to do it to you again." (He's sounding more and more like Rose.) Only one thing can break the cycle, the discovery of the real robber, but there is no suggestion that this will happen. The focus of the movie, like the focus of the justice system's machinery, has been entirely on Manny. The camera follows him around obsessively; it doesn't look at anyone else, just as the police don't look at anyone else. In many crime films, the last-minute revelation of the villain's identity prompts an "ah" from viewers who retroactively tumble to clues they had missed. Here there are no clues to be missed. Were any such revelation to occur in *The Wrong Man*, it would be experienced either as a miracle—an event that is inexplicable because it has no antecedents and follows no laws—or as an arbitrary, tacked-on ending to a plot that was unable to achieve an earned resolution. Manny doesn't expect it, even though he gives voice to the hope: "Somebody committed those holdups. Where is he?"

The answer arrives immediately in a sequence that has been much commented on. Manny goes into the bedroom to dress for work. As he puts on his shirt, he looks at a framed portrait of Jesus and moves his lips, presumably in prayer. (His mother has just urged him to pray.) As he prays and dresses, his face fills the screen, and behind it we see a figure walking down the street wearing as Manny always does a long coat and a hat. Is this just Manny going to work? Manny's face continues to occupy the forefront of the screen, and the figure in hat and coat moves toward him until the faces of the two merge; they fit into each other—Manny literally and cinematically dissolves into the other who resembles him in almost every detail. Now there is only one man, and we begin to realize that he is the right man, the somebody who committed those holdups, and now attempts to commit another. He fails, is overpowered and taken away by the police. Happy ending, right?

But what does it mean? What lesson are we to draw from this modern instance of peripeteia, Aristotle's term in his *Poetics* for a reversal from one state of affairs to its opposite? Are we to see this as a miracle, a response by a higher power to Manny's prayers? Jean-Luc Godard certainly thinks so and credits Hitchcock with being one of the few directors who brought off the task of cinematically presenting a miracle. Daniel Morgan elaborates the point. Noting that, in a Hitchcock film, "nothing lies outside narrative, there is no space for free action," he concludes that "the superimposition [of the two faces] in *The Wrong Man* is a miracle precisely because it breaks the metaphysical conditions that define the world of the film: Manny is allowed to go free despite having been caught up in the inexorable narrative machine."[1] In short, it's a miracle because it comes out of nowhere.

But so does everything else in the movie, beginning with Manny's detention and incarceration. No one saw *that* coming. The unexpected and unprepared for appearance of the right man is not an anomaly; it is of a piece with everything else in the movie. Manny's dictum, "You never know," applies to good things that happen as well as to bad things that happen. In a way, Manny's rescue is as distressing as his arrest: neither makes sense; neither points to a world in which events have traceable sources and come tagged with plausible explanations. Sabrina Negri is right to see this moment in the film as an instance of "Hitchcock's uncertainty toward the possibility to pursue knowledge through a well-defined path, be it rational or transcendental." "The fact," she says, "that it is a happy resolution is hardly significant;" what is significant is the "unintelligibility of fate"—you never know—and the movie's "celebration of chance disguised as a miracle."[2] It could have gone the other way, and will, perhaps, go the other way tomorrow.

Let's linger on this moment and slow it down. What just happened? Manny's troubles begin when he is mistaken for someone else, and now the mistake is corrected when the someone else turns up, looking just like him. This would be reassuring if the real robber looked nothing like Manny or just a little like Manny, for then the identities of the two—innocent man and miscreant—would have been distinct; one could be told from the other. The fact that he looks a lot like Manny acts to clear him (who?) in the moment, but the fact that he *still* looks like Manny means that it could happen again. If doubleness is both a sign of innocence and a sign of guilt, it can be of no help in the effort to get and keep things straight. The merging into one another of the two faces is at once the occasion of Manny's salvation and a repetition of the confusion that undid him. If you have a double, the singular identity that makes you you is always in peril. You are always in danger of being mistaken for him (or her), and there is always the possibility that the mistake will become part of an official record, and you will be in the position of having to prove that you are you and not the other. Recently I received a notice from the Delaware traffic system showing a car going through a toll booth without paying. The license plate was clearly visible, and it was the same as the license plate attached to a car of mine that had never been out of Florida. So my license plate has a double, and it's out in the world doing things that will be attributed to me, have already been attributed to me. Rather than getting into an argument with a state agency about who I was and wasn't, I paid the $4 fine (and thus changed places with my double) and hoped that whoever is driving the car with my license plate sticks to the letter of the law. If he doesn't, who knows what I'm in for.

David Humbert calls this anxiety about whether one thing or person can be distinguished from another the "crisis of undifferentiation,"[3] the inability of identities to remain stable. If you can't tell a this from a that, or person X from person Y, if one can turn into the other in an instant, making your way in the world with confidence in a design or purpose becomes nearly impossible. Things may fall into place occasionally, but always by way of accident. As Rose says, you may think you're ahead, finally in the clear, but something will always come in to knock you down again.

This is a lesson Manny is slow to learn, and he still hasn't learned it as he hurries to bring Rose the good news. He triumphantly brandishes a newspaper with a headline that should have given him pause. "Suspect in Holdups Cleared By Double." *Cleared?* By a double? The fact that you have a double makes things more clear? vindicates *you*? Could it not also vindicate the other guy? Freed of doubt (another meaning of "clear") by a double? Doesn't the existence of a double engender doubt? While Manny thinks he's carrying a passport to a better world where everything is once again in its proper place, he is in fact carrying a message that should tell him, but doesn't, that the present configuration of things is only temporary. Rose knows. When Manny declares the nightmare over, and says, "We can start our lives all over again," Rose replies (twice of course), "That's fine for you." In other words, don't read too much into a turn of fortune's wheel that momentarily seems propitious; it will soon turn again with results less pleasing. Manny asks, doesn't this reprieve from conviction and prison help you? Her answer is a simple "no." The nightmare is not just this unhappy episode; the nightmare is all of life. You can't start all over again with a clean slate and expect things to run smoothly just because one obstacle has been removed; new obstacles and dangers are always waiting in the wings, ready to spring when you least expect them. "You can go now," Rose tells Manny. She's no fool; she knows what's what, and she is staying right here, not moving, not acting, not talking, just lying low in the hope that the world will not notice her.

Directors often speak through a character who is in effect their spokesperson. In *The Wrong Man*, Hitchcock's spokesperson is Rose. It is her vision of the world that the movie affirms. The strength of that vision—the strength of the film's relentless narrative, the machinery, in Godard's words "grinding inexorably on"—is such that the tacked-on epilogue cannot be taken seriously, at "face" value.[4] A superimposed text tells us that in two years Rose was completely cured (false) and that the Balestreros moved to Florida (true). As Manny and Rose's nurse walk down the dark, narrow corridor of the sanatorium, the scene dissolves into the bright expansive landscape of a Miami street, and for a brief instant we see Rose, Manny, and the two boys strolling along a boulevard, a restored family unit. Of this moment Godard says dryly, "Draw your own conclusion."[5] The only conclusion is that this cannot be the conclusion. It's at best a fantasy and at worst a concession to Hollywood's preference for a happy ending, even when the narrative preceding it is a dark one.

In this respect, it is instructive to compare *The Wrong Man* with Henry Hathaway's *Call Northside 777* (1948), another movie based on a true story. In both movies a man is wrongly accused and declared guilty by the justice system. In both movies a mother believes in the innocence of her son, and a wife is ambiguously supportive. In both movies witnesses for the defense are either unavailable or dead. In both movies exoneration is effected out of the blue by a kind of miracle; in *Call Northside 777*, by the then new technological magic of photo-enlargement that provides evidence contradicting the testimony of the key prosecution witness. And in both movies the passive, ineffectual "hero" is returned at the end to his family as either a screen-message or a voiceover reads a benign lesson. "It's a good world outside and Frank Wiecek is free." Those are the last words spoken in *Call Northside 777*, words that blithely disregard and gloss over the fact that Frank Wiecek served eleven years while his wife divorced him (at his urging) and his mother scrubbed floors on her knees night and day so that she could offer a reward to anyone who could prove his innocence. An upbeat benediction ("It's a good world") doesn't wipe that fact away any more than the image of a family promenading in Florida wipes away the fact of what happened to Manny and Rose. The real ending of *The Wrong Man* takes place in Rose's small room as she turns away from Manny and the world that will always betray her.

In an irony so delicious that no scriptwriter would dare use it, the real Manny Balestrero appeared in 1957 on a TV quiz show where the panelists were asked to identify the real Manny Balestrero. The name of the show was *To Tell the Truth* (it's still going), and the truth that was to be told was a truth about identity. Three men stood at adjoining podiums, each claiming to be Manny Balestrero. (The nightmare of the double is enhanced by one.) The panelists were instructed by the master of ceremonies, Bud Collyer, that only the real Manny Balestrero was pledged to answer their questions truthfully; the other two could lie at will. Before the game formally began, Collyer asked the panelists—Hildy Parks, Polly Bergen, Dick Van Dyke, and John Cameron Swayze—to introduce themselves, and after they did so he declared, "I can attest that these people are telling nothing but the truth." (How do we know? Why should we take his word for it?) After several rounds of questioning, a vote was taken, and the panelists split 2 to 2. So, with the real Manny Balestrero standing right in front of them, four literate, sophisticated men and women—eyewitnesses, as it were—couldn't distinguish the real one from the fake. Neither the three Mannys nor the panelists and Collyer seemed to be aware that what they had just done was re-enact the movie's key and unresolved dilemma—the difficulty if not impossibility of telling the right man from the wrong man. I hope that Hitchcock, a television star himself, got to see this.

Now that we have two movies under our belt, what can we say? They share a star, and it's worth taking a minute to note the differences in Fonda's two performances. In *12 Angry Men* his character is confident, imperturbable, commanding (in a quiet way), and without self-doubt or anxiety. In *The Wrong Man*, he is increasingly off balance, befuddled, full of self-recrimination ("I've been an idiot"), and largely passive. When things go bad, he says it will all work out, and when it doesn't, he seems to have no resources to call on, no strategies or devices that might move matters in a better direction; he seems unable to take hold of a situation and bend it to his advantage, as Juror #8 does and as Roger Thornhill (*North by Northwest*), Jeff Jefferies (*Rear Window*), and Charlie Newton (*Shadow of a Doubt*) do, in their different ways. It is odd to say this of a Fonda character, but, aside from his interactions with his children, he is a sad sack.

The difference between the two Fondas reflects a difference in their relation to the justice system. Juror #8, it might be said, is acting out the pronouncement of the detective who says to Manny, "An innocent man has nothing to fear." Why? Because the process, if it is not blocked, as it threatens to be by the eleven "guilty" voters, will ensure a full deliberation in the course of which fact will be separated from mere hearsay and a just verdict will be delivered. That, at least, is the story *12 Angry Men* tells about itself: if you are careful enough, and consider every possibility, no matter how far-fetched it may at first seem to be, the path to the truth will reveal itself. (That is, as I have argued, a misrecognition by the movie of its own dynamics; but it is a misrecognition widely shared.) Manny's experience is the reverse: the longer the process goes on, the greater the amount of information it yields, the more he is entangled in its self-regarding web, in its procedural concern to dot every "i" and cross every "t" on its way to condemning a man it never really looks at. The policemen who interrogate him are always engaged in constructing the character demanded by the machinery of which they are the agents: a high-flying compulsive gambler, who lives far beyond his means. In his opening statement, the prosecutor at Manny's trial goes on about the New York gamblers Manny is in debt to, a debt that, it is presumed, provides a motive for the robberies he commits. But there are no New York gamblers (one wonders if Manny's lawyer ever objects to this fabulation; probably not), no large debt, and of course no Manny-committed robberies. It's all made up by the same justice system that pretends to be fair to him. (The lead policeman says twice, "We want to be fair to you Manny.") That system does not interact with him; instead it substitutes for him a criminal type it has at the ready. (Rose: "No matter how innocent you are, they'll find you guilty.")

I'm not saying that in *The Wrong Man* the justice system is corrupt. *The Wrong Man* is not . . . *And Justice for All* (1979), a Norman Jewison movie featuring a lone honest lawyer, Arthur Kirkland (played by Al Pacino in an Academy-nominated performance), surrounded by venal colleagues, self-serving prosecutors, and judges who are either criminal or insane. In the film's climactic and over-the-top scene, Kirkland declares to the court that his client (a judge no less) is guilty and should go "straight to fucking jail," and when he is declared out of order, he tells the judge, "You're out of order," and then he turns and says the same thing to everyone in the courtroom: "You're out of order, you're out of order, you're out of order." There is nothing out of order about the justice system in *The Wrong Man*; it is in perfect order, but that order unfolds without so much as a side glance at the man enmeshed in its toils. It is not corruption but indifference that undoes Manny. The system doesn't care about him and cares only that his body—and if not his, then the body of his double, it doesn't matter which—fills a slot (the criminal identified and punished) its logic requires.

3

The Law Emerges from Violence

The Man Who Shot Liberty Valance and *High Noon*

These three films, then, present three disparate versions of the justice system: in one (*12 Angry Men*) it is benign, at least if it is allowed to run its course; in a second (*. . . And Justice for All*) it is a marketplace in which the imperative to make a deal has replaced the search for truth; and, in a third (*The Wrong Man*), it is a self-executing machine that runs its own routines and looks neither to the left nor to the right as it ingests everything that comes its way. In whatever version it assumes, the justice system in these films is fully articulated, with all its moving parts in place, however smooth functioning or disordered they may be. No one remarks on or inquires into its origin. No one asks how the legal system—good, bad, or indifferent—came into being. What preceded it? How was it established? On what does it rest? Such questions return us to the first pages of Chapter 1 of this book and the desire of government actors and political theorists to ground law by distinguishing it from the exercise of violence performed by a gunman. The fragility of that distinction is a frequent theme in one important genre—the western. And, of the western films that meditate on that fragility, perhaps the most searching is John Ford's *The Man Who Shot Liberty Valance*. (Although, as we shall see, landmark films such as *High Noon* and *Shane* participate in this exploration.)

The main narrative of *The Man Who Shot Liberty Valance* is a flashback framed by scenes that occur in the future. We first see a small train coming into the town of Shinbone, state unidentified. United States Senator Ranse Stoddard (James Stewart) and his wife Hallie (Vera Miles

Law at the Movies. Stanley Fish, Oxford University Press. © Stanley Fish (2024).
DOI: 10.1093/oso/9780198898726.003.0004

again) alight from the train and are greeted by the portly figure of Link Appleyard (Andy Devine), formerly the town sheriff. News of Stoddard's arrival comes quickly to the attention of Maxwell Scott, editor of the *Shinbone Star*, who asks the senator why he is here. To attend a funeral, is the answer. An old friend of Stoddard and his wife has died, and they have come to pay their respects. The friend's name was Tom Doniphon (John Wayne), a person entirely unknown to the editor or his young reporter. Scott demands to know the story, and Stoddard agrees to accompany him to the paper's office, where they will be more comfortable. Stoddard suggests that Link take Hallie around in his buckboard so that she might see the changes that have occurred since they left the town. So, when Ranse begins his narration, Hallie is not in the room, a fact that becomes worthy of note later. The story he proceeds to tell opens with his arrival in Shinbone many decades earlier. He travelled by stagecoach, and outside of town the stagecoach is robbed by the local, known to everyone, bandit—Liberty Valance (Lee Marvin). When Stoddard attempts to intercede on behalf of a fellow passenger who doesn't want to hand over a brooch her husband had given her, Valance whips him and contemptuously throws his law books on the ground. Valance sneers, "Law, huh, I'll teach you law, western law." Before the beating, Stoddard had drawn himself up and declared, somewhat pompously, "I'm an attorney at law," an announcement obviously without force in the present circumstance.

So the movie's basic opposition is immediately established: western law, the law of the gun and the whip, versus formal law, a body of rules designed to prevent and punish the violence that is for Valance a way of life. Valance is a one-dimensional allegorical figure whose name fixes his essence: he stands for force wholly unconstrained, force at liberty; it is no accident that Valance and violence share an initial consonant and the ending "nce." Rendered unconscious by Valance/Violence, Stoddard is found on the road by Tom Doniphon, who takes him to town, where he asks his girlfriend Hallie to minister to him. The remainder of the story is structured by a set of interlocking relationships: between Valance and everyone he victimizes, the editor, the coroner/doctor, the sheriff, basically the entire town; between Valance and Ranse, starkly contrasting representatives of the gun and the book; between Valance and Tom, each of whom believes he is the toughest man in the territory; between Tom and Ranse, who compete silently and without much overt drama for Hallie's affections (Hallie's drift toward Ranse is gradual and marked by small, apparently insignificant gestures); and the more abstract, but governing relationship between those who desire statehood and the stability it brings and those committed to maintaining the free and open ways—the liberty, to be precise—of a West that is largely untamed. (This, of course, is the theme of countless westerns; Kevin Costner's *Open Range* (2003) and Tom Selleck's remake of *Monte Walsh* (2003) are recent examples.) The master opposition, which informs each relationship in the subset, is between a vaguely Rousseauian state of nature where man is free to do as he pleases (he is at *liberty*) and there are a minimum of ties that bind, and the modern town/city/state with its rules, boundaries, fences, zoning laws, contracts, banking systems, all combining at once to secure an individual's safety and to constrain him. Whatever gifts civilization imparts, the price you pay for them is the acceptance of constraints you did not choose.

Not only are the constraints imposed; they are artificial. They do not flow naturally from the basic needs and actions of life—food, drink, sex, mobility. They are imported from some form of socially organized life that holds itself out as natural and declares that its ways are the ways all should follow. In a word, these constraints are *conventional*; fidelity to them is a matter of custom, not right. Two small moments in *The Man Who Shot Liberty Valance* illustrate both the force of convention and its fragility. As Hallie, a waitress in the family restaurant, approaches newspaper editor Dutton Peabody's table, he says to her, "Please, the proprieties concerning the cutlery. How many times do I have to tell you that the fork goes to the left of the plate and the knife goes to . . ." She interrupts him: "What's the matter with you; are you superstitious or something." Or, in other words, what does it matter where the knife and fork are placed? This is Shinbone, and the fact that some people in Chicago or St Louis (imitating people from Paris and London) do it this way is beside the point, which she immediately identifies: "Well, what are you going to have to eat?" Eating is what's important; its technology is a matter of indifference. Later, after the classroom Rance had set up to teach reading and civics is shut down by Tom's news that Valance and his men are on the rampage, Hallie bustles into the kitchen of the restaurant and says, "Mr Peabody is drunk as a skunk in the Mexican joint, he ain't eating tonight." Ranse, stepping right into the Peabody role, immediately corrects her. "Hallie, he *isn't* eating tonight remember?" Again she is on the mark: "Isn't, ain't what difference does it make? Ain't going to be no school any more anyway." Note that she repeats her grammatical error and adds another, "no" for "any." Her first transgression had been involuntary, a bit of backsliding; but her second is deliberate and provocative. She is saying to Ranse, as she said to Peabody, that grammatical conventions and table manners have about as much efficacy as law books. When it comes to eating, just get the food into your mouth. When it comes to communicating, just get the point across. And, when it comes to protecting what's yours, just get a gun—exactly the advice given by Tom to Ranse when they first meet. The proprieties of cutlery, the rules of grammar, and the codification of laws all go together; they are ineffectual (or so several of the characters declare) in a world where force is the only real rule. As Hallie says to Ranse after he has discovered that she can't read or write, "What good has reading and writing done you? Look at you in an apron."

Hallie is the hinge figure in the movie. Her body and mind are the terrains on which the material and cultural battles are fought. Will she remain illiterate and marry Tom Doniphon and live the elemental life of a frontier woman? Or will she move with Ranse into the modern, cosmopolitan world where she will dine with silver forks and knives (properly placed), speak the King's English, read poetry, and support her husband while he makes the laws? In a landscape where alternatives are starkly opposed, she is the location of ambiguity, the text on which two different narratives are inscribed.

Her passage from one narrative to another is marked by her learning to read. It is difficult for most of us to remember what it was like before we could read. As young children, we received our knowledge of the world through our senses as they were mediated by some primary structures of understanding—time (present, past, future), space (close, far, above, below), cause and effect (who did what to whom). What mattered to us were the experiences of our local habitation and the persons who lived with us or near us. Books, as it has often been remarked, transport us into realms we have never even imagined and introduce us to ways of thinking (about politics, ethics, philosophy) far removed from the basic give-and-take of everyday life. The vocabulary that describes this passage from the immediate to the distanced and represented contains words like "transformative," "eye-opening," "mind-expanding," and "revelatory," and leads to exclamations like "I never thought of that before." Once this process has begun, there is no going back, no return to the closed but comfortable security of what we knew immediately from the intimacies of our unexamined surroundings. And the thing spreads. When people learn how to read—learn how to enter narratives and paths of argument that extend the boundaries of their understanding—they want to share the good news. Reading turns out to be a communal activity, and the community that engages in it moves away from the narrow concerns of raising a family and scratching out a living to the larger concerns of the kind of world we want to live in.

That is what happens in the pivotal scene of instruction that takes place in the makeshift schoolroom adjacent to Dutton Peabody's office and printing shop. The first thing to note is the diversity of the gathering. There is racial diversity: whites, Mexicans, and one black (Pompey, Tom's "boy"). There is age diversity: young, old, and older. There is social diversity: restaurant workers, ranch hands, a sheriff, a classically educated newspaper editor (listening at the door), and a lawyer. And there is gender diversity: Hallie is now (in only three weeks) a co-teacher as well as a pupil. The division of interests and obligations according to social identity has been superseded by a unifying interest in connecting up with and participating in the nation's history and primary values. (Pictures of Washington and Lincoln adorn the walls.) Instruction in reading and instruction in "our country and its governance" (Ranse's words) go hand in hand. That is precisely the message written on the blackboard: "Education is the basis of law and order." It is only when we are transported by reading and discussion from the parochial confines of our usual practices to the abstract corridors of political philosophy that we see what is founding and essential in the democratic way of life. The limited roles each "student" occupies in his or her daily life have been replaced by the single, all-encompassing role of citizen. In the liberal ideal, the category of citizenship is marked by no gender, race, wealth, or educational differences. All men and women belong to it because, as Pompey (Woody Strode) says, after much prompting from Ranse, all men and women are created equal.

Pompey's rehearsal of that sentiment is not without its ironies: he attributes the words he speaks to Thomas Jefferson, who owned many slaves and fathered children with one of them, and he speaks them as a man totally subservient to another. That man, Tom Doniphon, bursts into the room and chides Pompey for neglecting his proper duties: "No sashes or doors yet? What have you been wasting your time here for? Get back to work! Your schooling's over." In Tom's eyes, sitting around and talking about democracy and the like is an exercise in frivolity, not unlike worrying about table manners or grammar. It is not real work, and it stands in the way of getting real work done. All this talk about universal equality and the leveling force of democracy (one man's vote counts as much as the vote of his social or economic superior) is of no account when there's a house to be built or homesteads to defend.

Tom's rebuke is meant, not just for Pompey, but for everyone in the room. Liberty Valance and his men are headed this way and will certainly arrive by the time a regional delegate to the territorial conference considering statehood is to be chosen. Ranse reminds him that there are more votes south of the picket wire, but Tom retorts, "Votes won't stand up against guns." Ranse surrenders to that judgment and tells Hallie to dismiss the school. She demurs—"but Ranse, you said . . ." His reply is devastating. "You heard what Tom said. When force threatens, talking's no good anymore." That is, education's no good anymore. Ranse erases "Education is the basis of law and order" from the blackboard and drives his buckboard out of town to a place where he can practice drawing and shooting. It would seem that his own lessons have been lost on him, as he falls into the role of so many western heroes who, in the end and after many speeches about the futility of violence, strap on their guns.

It is tempting to say that Tom was wrong; votes *do* stand up against guns. Ranse and Peabody are chosen to be delegates; they go on to the territorial convention, and Ranse wins office and after that a succession of offices, higher and higher, with the vice presidency beckoning. But his success has little to do with his words and everything to do with his reputation as the man who shot Liberty Valance in the street after he had been called out. This is the movie's major irony: the triumph of law and order over a regime of violence is effected by an act of violence, the shooting of Liberty Valance by (or so it seems) Ranse, who apparently bests him in a showdown. Robert B. Pippin points to the moral, which, as he suggests, is a general one: "there can be no law unless the lawless are eliminated . . . but given what the lawless are willing to do, this violent elimination cannot itself be just or fair, cannot play by the rules . . . Violence before there is law is unavoidably lawless," and that includes the violence involved in inaugurating the law.[1] One moment there is a form of law—as Liberty says, the gun and whip are forms of law, western law—and in the next there is a new one. When and how was the change effected? Not with the agreement or cooperation of the law being superseded, but despite it, against its resistance. The new law just announces itself in a *coup de force* (verbal or material or issuing from the machinery of a process that is conjured out of thin air) and labors to make the announcement stick. As the philosopher Jacques Derrida explains, "Since the origin of authority, the foundation or ground, the position of the law, cannot . . . rest on anything but themselves, they are themselves a violence without ground,"[2] or, more precisely, without a ground that will stand up under interrogation; the ground the new order rests on is finally no different from the ground that it has replaced.

That is just what Major Cassius Starbuckle (John Carradine), called by Peabody the cattle barons' mouthpiece, points out when he challenges Ranse's credentials at the territorial convention. After Peabody has praised Ranse as someone not packing a gun but carrying instead a bag of law books, Starbuckle retorts that his "only claim to office is that he killed a man." He presents himself as an attorney at law, an officer of the court, but he "usurps the functions of both judge and jury." "The mark of Cain," he concludes," is on this man . . . with blood-stained hands." (The mark of Cain was often conflated with the curse of Cain and associated by segregationists with the blackening of Cain's face; Cain's descendants, they believed, are marked by their dark skin for servitude.) Ranse takes Starbuckle's accusation to heart and leaves the room, saying to Tom, who has followed him out, "Isn't it enough to kill a man without trying to build a life on it?" Ranse sees that whatever good effects his political efforts might have will be tainted by the act that made them possible. He announces, "I'm going back East where I belong." He won't embark upon a career that rests on the ground of a violence he has always abhorred.

Tom saves him from that dilemma only to deliver him to another one. "*You* didn't kill Liberty Valance," he says, and, in a flashback within the flashback that is Ranse's narrative, tells him what really happened when Valance called him out. "Think back, pilgrim," he admonishes, and as he says those words, we are returned to the scene where Ranse and Valance face off, but with a crucial cinematic difference: where before the encounter was foregrounded, with Ranse at bottom screen in the shadows and Liberty at top screen in the light, the curtain is now drawn back to afford a wide-shot panoramic view and we see that the true foreground—the position of perspectival authority—is occupied by Tom, who is stage-managing from the other side of the street, pulling the strings and, literally, pulling the trigger. Like a good director, Tom orchestrates the moment so that his shot—fired from a rifle Pompey has tossed to him—coincides with Ranse's. There is one loud sound, and a body, Liberty's body, falling. The desired result is achieved: everyone, including Ranse, various spectators, and the movie's viewers, believes that Ranse has shot and killed Liberty Valance. When Tom tosses the rifle back to Pompey and walks away, he is in effect saying, "Cut, that's a wrap."

The moment reminds us of how much we are at the mercy of those who get to tell the stories. We have been at the mercy of Ranse, but now Tom's flashback, which rewinds the story, erases Ranse's narrative (at least on this crucial point) and substitutes for it a truer one. Or does it? Where before we had Ranse's word for what happened, now we have Tom's. But, of course, what we really have is Ford's. He has controlled the perspective and determined what information will be conveyed by whom, to whom, and at what time. Who's to say what revelation might come next, necessitating still another revision of our understanding? With so many narratives in play, how do you decide which one to authorize?

The answer to that question is given by the most famous line in the movie. Seconds after Tom sends Ranse back into the convention ("You taught her how to read and write, now give her something to read and write about"), the main flashback ends, and we are returned to an older Ranse sitting in the office of the *Shinbone Star*, where he has been talking for more than an hour. "You know the rest," he says, and then editor Scott obligingly rehearses the highlights of Ranse's career. But, as he does so, he picks up the notes he has been taking and rips them in half. "You're not going to use the story?" asks Ranse. The response is immediate and without apology: "This is the West sir; when the legend becomes fact, print the legend." If you were in the East where things are settled, boundaries firm, hierarchies fixed, decorums in place, attention to literal fact might make sense; the institutions are long established; the routes of access are known; the steps to success are written down in manuals and company directives; there is not so much room or need for legend. But the West depends on legend, *is* a legend, always telling stories about itself, in songs, dime novels, Wild West shows, and movies like this one. The truth about the West is the sum of the phrases and images associated with it—wide open, ever expanding, lawless, without limits ("Don't fence me in"), intensely masculine, individual, and independent (the Marlboro Man), the land of opportunity, the land of second chances, the last frontier, the road to the pot of gold ("California, Here I Come"). The story of the mild-mannered, bookish tenderfoot who, pushed to the wall, shoots the villainous Liberty Valance and goes on to become a political icon fits perfectly into the West's project of imagining and constructing itself. In fact, it is easy to imagine *The Man Who Shot Liberty Valance* without the flashback and the revelation that Ranse didn't. It would still work. Barely a line would have to be changed. Ranse would be just like any number of western movie heroes who, in a moment of courage, expel the guns from the valley (the reference is to *Shane*) and clear the space for civilization to flourish. It's the story that editor Scott decides to affirm, even though he knows it is false, and he decides to affirm it because it is the story the West, and those who see themselves as westerners need to believe in. It is the legend that has been responsible for the fact that is the modern Shinbone. Were the legend to be debunked and discredited, who would benefit?—not Ranse, not the town, not even Tom, who would, it is true, finally get the credit for what he did, but it would be the credit for being, in his own words, a cold-blooded murderer. Everything conspires to demand that the legend be maintained and, once again, printed. (The need for legend is quite literally illustrated by Willie Nelson's *Barbarosa* (1982), a western in which the title figure is finally killed by a member of the family he has been at war with for decades; but victory and closure are not what the family wants; it wants Barbarosa as a mythical figure around whom its members can organize their lives, and it gets him back when Barbarosa's young sidekick, played by Gary Busey, steps into the role and reincarnates the legend.)

By refusing to correct the record, Scott creates unhappy futures for both Tom and Ranse. Tom, of course, has no future. He is dead. But now he is doubly dead, because the editor has killed the story of his role in bringing law to Shinbone and beyond. That story of what really happened in a West that never moved beyond violence is now interred with him in a box that has kept him out of sight from the beginning. When that box is buried (something neither we nor Ranse and Hallie see), all memory of Tom and the life he lived in a de-sanitized Shinbone is erased. Meanwhile Ranse is left with a double burden. He will still be known as the man whose life's work rests on a foundation of violence, and now he will be known—at least to a few—as the man who for decades has been living out a lie. The alternatives are not pretty: either be celebrated for having killed a man (Starbuckle's accusation) or be exposed as someone who has been trading on and profiting from a killing he did not commit. It seems significant that Ranse does not protest and insist that the true facts be made public. Perhaps the legend has for so long been indistinguishable from him as a public figure that he has no other identity. Perhaps at this late stage in his career and life, he's past caring; he could go either way. Perhaps he thinks that, having offered the world (in the persons of the editor and his associate) the correction it did not seek, he has done enough, and if the world declines to take note, so be it.

The ambivalence of the moment follows Ranse and Hallie onto the train, where they engage in a conversation marked at every point by inconclusiveness. Ranse asks Hallie whether she would mind if they left Washington and returned to Shinbone to live; perhaps he could open a law office. She replies with marked enthusiasm: "If you knew how often I have dreamed of it. My roots are here. I guess my heart is here. Yes, let's come back!" In another movie, those would be the closing words. The return home after many years of wandering is always satisfying. ("There is no place like home.") Cue embrace, swelling music, and "The End." But Hallie continues with what she considers a rhetorical question. She looks out the window and says, "Look at it, it was once a wilderness, now it's a garden. Aren't you proud?" Again, in another movie, this could be the coda. Two young people with few resources start out on a journey, and years later, after many obstacles overcome, they create a lasting legacy. But Ranse barely glances out the window at the garden for whose flourishing he is supposedly responsible. Does he think it's a garden or is he less taken with the new sanitized Shinbone than Hallie assumes he is? His expression gives little away; he seems a bit surprised by the alacrity of Hallie's reply to his proposal and, instead of answering her question, poses one of his own. "Hallie, who put the cactus rose on Tom's coffin?" Earlier Ranse had told Hallie that if she ever left Shinbone she would see real roses, but, after having led a cosmopolitan life, she still prefers the cactus rose. It would seem that the only thing Ranse has heard Hallie say is "I guess my heart is here." Does she still love Tom? Does she regret the choice she made many years ago? Is her eagerness to return to Shinbone a rejection of the decades she has spent with Ranse? A bit defiantly, she says, "I did" (of course he knew that). Ranse looks down and swallows and fingers his watch. An awkward domestic moment is interrupted by the busy return of the conductor Jason, who brings a new spittoon and boasts of having the railroad hold the express so that Ranse and Hallie can board it and get back to Washington quickly. (Want to bet that's where they stay?) This bit of self-promotion gives Ranse the opportunity to switch back into pompous statesman mode. He promises to write the railroad a letter of thanks, and, as if to punctuate the promise, he strikes a match preliminary to lighting a pipe. Jason says, "Think nothing of it. Nothing's too good for the man who shot Liberty Valance." Ranse's jovial manner disappears, the match goes out, the pipe remains unlit, and through the entire sequence Hallie looks slightly down with no expression on her face except for a slight parting of her lips at the words "the man who shot Liberty Valance." And that, finally, *is* the end as the train goes around a bend.

What is remarkable about this scene is the number of things we don't know when it's over. We don't know if Hallie knows who really killed Liberty Valance. We don't know if Ranse and Hallie will really return to Shinbone. We don't know what their marriage will be like. We don't know when or where Tom was buried. We don't know what he did all those years. We don't know whether Pompey will manage to live on the "pork chop" money Ranse gives him. Were there no double flashback, if we saw Ranse kill Liberty and that was the end of it, these points wouldn't amount to much, just the kind of loose ends found in any movie. But the fact that the deception is revealed less than six minutes before the movie ends casts a shadow over everything that precedes it. We thought we were watching one movie, and now we discover we were watching another, and the investments we had formed in nearly two hours of viewing are in jeopardy. In an instant Ranse is no longer the unlikely David who slays Goliath. Tom is no longer the straight arrow who fights tough but fights fair. Liberty is no longer just a malevolent force; he is also the victim of a cold-blooded murder. (Starbuckle had it right but accuses the wrong man.) Everything and everyone shimmers. For most of the film, its title is descriptive; at the one-hour-and-fifty-seven-minute mark, it becomes a question.

However the question is answered—Rance Stoddard did it or Tom Doniphon did it or they jointly did it—the victim of the killing is the myth of the taming of the west by straightforward, honest frontiersmen who brought law, order, and civilization to a landscape previously ruled by force. In this movie, force is not tamed; it is triumphant, and, as we have seen, the mark of its triumph is its erasure from the history it founds. The garden that is modern Shinbone grows from the soil of a murder and a lie, twinned instances of what Derrida calls "originary violence,"[3] a violence that is now forever hidden and expunged from the record. "Print the legend" is not only the line viewers remember, it is what the movie does; but, by surrounding the legend with the facts it must occlude in order to flourish, it disallows the audience the usual patriotic good feeling with which so many examples of the genre end. *The Man Who Shot Liberty Valance* is a western to be sure, but, unlike, for example, *How the West Was Won* (also released in 1962 and starring Jimmy Stewart), it does not encourage elegiac reminiscences of a past that never was. The movie at once presents the legend—the story before Tom's flashback—and explodes it, and then re-presents it as the effect of the editor's act of censorship. The legend lives on in the mind and words of Jason the conductor and others, but those few who, like Ranse and now countless movie viewers, know what really happened cannot hear its recital without wincing. *The Man Who Shot Liberty Valance* is not a revisionist western; it is worse than that; it's a western that sullies its own narrative and renders everything it touches and presents hollow to the core.

It is a wonder that John Wayne didn't see this and recoil from it, especially since he famously objected to *High Noon* for presenting a less than celebratory "picture of the American west." What true westerner, he complained, would go around begging for help from preachers and shopkeepers? (Wayne and Howard Hawks made *Rio Bravo* as a self-conscious response to *High Noon*.) But, compared to *The Man Who Shot Liberty Valance*, *High Noon* is a veritable valentine. Yes, the town in the movie does not support the hero, but the hero perseveres nevertheless and emerges as someone worthy of our unambiguous admiration. The law may be abandoned by those it serves, but the law, residing in the breast of one man, remains true to itself. As the movie begins, Will Kane (Gary Cooper), just married, is no longer the marshal of Hadleyville, but the new marshal has not yet arrived. In this small interval—less than an hour and a half of a Sunday morning—there is no law officially in place, and it becomes known that four gunslingers will descend on the town at noon. True, Kane proceeds to put the badge back on when he hears this news, but it's not clear with what authority. The judge who has presided over the marriage ceremony wants him to leave (and leaves himself), the mayor wants him to leave, the town selectmen (all his "good friends") want him to leave, his deputy wants him to leave, his old mentor wants him to leave, his new wife wants him to leave, and his ex-girlfriend wants him to leave. When pressed to explain why he insists on staying, he doesn't reply directly, but says things like "seems to me I've got to stay" and "I've never run from anybody before." The argument made repeatedly to him that it is no longer his job doesn't move him at all. The closest he comes to a response is, "I'm the same man with or without this [the tin star]." It is clear at least that the responsibility he feels has nothing to do with the office he no longer holds. It's something inside him. The full explanation is given in the famous song: "If I'm a man, I must be brave | . . . Or lie a coward in my grave." Not "I'm brave," but "I must be brave." *That* is his job, to be brave no matter what the circumstances or the audience. The fleeing judge mocks Kane for being concerned about what happens in "a dirty little village in the middle of nowhere." But it's not the stage or its size that's important. It is fidelity to what he thinks—no, "thinks" is too deliberative a word, the better word is "feels"—is right. He must remain the same man with or without a badge, with or without support, with or without the understanding of anyone else, including his wife. The moral is Polonius': "to thine own self be true . . . and thou canst be false to any man"[4] (It is also Kantian, as Christopher Falzon argues.[5])

It could even be said that the failure of his friends to support him is a gift to Kane; for, as they fall away, the fact of his bravery—not bravado; he is worried and fearful and asks for help—is highlighted against a background that is empty of anything except his isolated self. This is the point of the famous shot just before the gunplay begins when the camera draws back and high to show a small figure in the middle of the screen surrounded by a menacing street and buildings where everyone in the town is hiding. All the while the assumption has been that Kane will not be able to prevail against four killers, but he does in a sequence that is true to the unheroic nature of his heroism. Alerted to the killers' position by the sound of glass breaking (the most callow of his adversaries grabs a bonnet out of a store window), Kane gets behind them—not the usual posture for a hero in a showdown—and, after calling their leader's name, he gets off a shot and kills one of them.

That leaves three. The second is killed when he chases Kane into a barn where he is crouched in a loft. Kane shoots him from above. The third is shot in the back by Kane's new wife (Grace Kelly), who had gotten off the train that was to carry her away. The fourth, the notorious Frank Miller, drags Mrs Kane onto the street, forcing Kane to come out of hiding. As he walks out the door, his wife struggles with Miller and manages to push him away. Kane shoots him twice before he gets off a shot. So one from behind, one from above, one by his wife, and the last when his wife disarms his assailant. No face-off between a villain and the stalwart hero who lets him draw first. No wonder John Wayne didn't like it.

Only one minute and ten seconds elapse from this point to the end of the movie. Several things happen, but they happen in such rapid succession that there is no time to savor the moment of victory (if it is that). As Kane picks his wife up and embraces her, the townspeople pour into the street. Suddenly, from the right, a buggy appears driven by a boy who admires Kane and is one of two townspeople who offer him aid. (The town drunk is the other.) Before Kane steps onto the buggy, he looks with disdain and distaste at the men he had once sworn to protect, takes off his star, throws it, palm up, in the dirt, climbs in, takes the reins, and drives away. "The End," faster than it took me to type this paragraph.

The question, of course, is: What are we to understand by Kane's gesture. What is he saying? What is the film saying? The answer has already been given earlier by Kane's old mentor (played by Lon Chaney, Jr), who said: "People got to talk themselves into law and order before they do anything about it because maybe deep down they don't care." For the residents of Hadleyville, law and order mean women able to walk down the street without being afraid. This fact of physical security seems to mark the limit of their investment, of what they care about. (This is what Kane finds out as he seeks vainly for allies.) There is no acknowledgment of the law as the foundation and realization of a set of moral and philosophical values that are the content of democratic life. Nothing in their behavior corresponds to the inner compass that compels Kane to stay. They don't engage in a collective action that would count as an affirmation of the ties that bind them together in a genuine fellowship. They just run away or hide behind their wives or plead physical disability or mutter something about how the town doesn't want to get a reputation for violence.

Kane's friend Herb says, "I just live here, I have no stake in this." When Kane throws his star in the dirt, he isn't repudiating the law; he is just marking its absence from a population that equates it with personal safety and nothing more. The law is alive and well in his heart, and its residence there moves him to the actions he performs. When he leaves, it leaves with him independently of whether or not he is wearing a badge. ("I'm the same man with or without this.") Without an internal and sustained commitment by persons, there is no law, despite whatever formal machinery—a court, a jail, a judge—may be in place. Perhaps the most ironic moment in the movie occurs when the judge who is getting out of town as fast as he can packs an American flag, a small model of the scales of justice, and some law books. The action he is taking at this moment deprives these symbols and artifacts of any meaning; they are just the inert props of values he has no real connection with. He says he can be a judge in some other small town, but he can never be a judge in any serious way, even though he may wear a robe.

So that's the double-sided moral of the tale. Law can't really exist as a vital force if those it serves do not believe in it deeply. That's the bad part. The good part is that, even when a community fails to keep law alive and dies, as Helen Ramirez (Katy Jurado) predicts Hadleyville will die, law can still live in the person of a single just man.

No such moral can be drawn from *The Man Who Shot Liberty Valance*. Ranse is just until he decides to live out a lie. Tom is upright and strong until he shoots Liberty from the shadows. Hallie is compromised in ways we never fully fathom. Link Appleyard is a coward and a buffoon. The only person who exhibits an integrity that does not waver is Dutton Peabody (Edmond O'Brien). He may be bombastic and a drunkard, but he does stand up for the freedom of the press, even when he is beaten half to death for his principles. But, as Peabody himself says at one point, he is not an active participant in the town's political and moral drama; he is the recorder of the actions of others. For that reason, he cannot bear the burden of the film's meditation on law. That burden belongs primarily to Ranse and Tom, who crack, in different ways, under its weight. *High Noon* leaves us with the law ensconced in a single breast; he is the ark of the law's covenant. *The Man Who Shot Liberty Valance* leaves us with a piece of cynical political advice. "When the legend becomes fact, print the legend." Rhetoric, storytelling, and opportunism have taken the place of the search for justice and truth. The idealism of the short-lived classroom is nowhere in sight. There's no example to follow, no repository of a long-term hope, no hero we can unambiguously admire. *The Man Who Shot Liberty Valance* is half a step away from film noir.

4

The Law as the Object of Manipulation

Beyond a Reasonable Doubt and *Witness for the Prosecution*

Delayed revelation that rearranges everything you thought you knew is a film noir staple—think of *Laura*, *The Blue Dahlia*, *Farewell, My Lovely*, *The Third Man*, *The Woman in the Window*—and in no film is it more disruptive of assumptions and apparently firm judgments than in Fritz Lang's *Beyond a Reasonable Doubt* (1956), a nasty piece of audience manipulation that marked the end of Lang's Hollywood career. The plot is ingenious and somewhat preposterous. In the first scene, a state-administered execution is witnessed by newspaper publisher Austin Spencer (Sidney Blackmer) and his soon-to-be son-in-law and ex-employee, novelist Tom Garrett (Dana Andrews). Both men are troubled by what they have just seen and worry that the justice system as presently structured offers little protection against the possibility of an innocent man being sent, legally, to his death; a clever district attorney, Spencer observes, "can make a juror believe a thing is a fact when it isn't." But how to make the point in a way that will cause the public to take notice? Spencer comes up with the idea of framing an innocent man for a murder and then, just at the moment when he has been convicted and is about to be executed, revealing that it's all been a setup staged to make a point about the moral dubiousness of the death penalty. Garrett asks, but who can we get to be the guinea pig? And the answer Spencer gives, of course, is "you." "After you are convicted and sentenced, I'll reveal the details of our plan." They will build a case against Garrett so strong that no one could reasonably

Law at the Movies. Stanley Fish, Oxford University Press. © Stanley Fish (2024).
DOI: 10.1093/oso/9780198898726.003.0005

doubt it, and then they will provide proof so strong that no one could reasonably convict. What could go wrong?

All they need is a murder, and one turns up as if on order. A burlesque dancer named Patty Gray is found dead in a ditch. The police have no clues, but the team of Spencer and Garrett proceeds to provide them. They plant a cigarette lighter given to Garrett by his fiancée Susan Spencer (Joan Fontaine), Austin's daughter; they photograph Garrett buying a top coat of the kind and color worn by the murderer when he picked up Gray in a dark, late model car like the one Garrett also drives. They leave a single stocking in the glove compartment of the car. They rub body powder of the kind used by Gray into the seams of the car's seats. In effect, they are constructing a film noir plot while letting the audience in on the contrivance. We know that Garrett is innocent and we look forward both to the baiting of the trap and to Garrett's escape from it once it is revealed that it has been self-set.

All goes according to plan. Garrett turns up at the burlesque joint where Gray worked and comes on to one of the girls. He takes her to an upscale restaurant, where they are photographed. A gossip columnist features an "item" about the two, and, when she sees it, Susan Spencer breaks off the engagement. Garrett can only say, "You'll understand later," for he and her father have agreed not to tell her about the plan. She is the audience in the dark, while we are the audience in the know. Meanwhile the show girl Garrett is ostentatiously shepherding about becomes suspicious and contacts the detective in charge of the case. When Garrett drives with the girl to the same spot where Gray's body had been dumped, the detective follows. Garrett parks and reaches for the girl, who resists. At that moment the detective appears at the car's window. Garrett is arrested, taken to the police station, and booked for murder.

In the trial that follows, the planted evidence falls into its prearranged place. (It tells its own story.) Susan Spencer reluctantly testifies that she gave the incriminating lighter to Garrett. (The indifference of Garrett and her father to Susan's feelings and emotional wellbeing is appalling.) The stocking and the body powder are duly trotted out in addition to suspicious withdrawals from Garrett's bank account. In response to the District Attorney's many points, Garrett can only plead "coincidence." He is alternately diffident, irritated, and smug. Nothing he says makes him either likable or believable. A guilty verdict seems inevitable.

And then, just as we are happily anticipating the dramatic "reveal," the plot takes a turn we hadn't anticipated. As the jury deliberates, Austin Spencer leaves for court, the photographic evidence of Garrett's innocence by his side in an envelope. He has barely exited the garage when his car is hit by a truck. He is killed and everything inside the car is destroyed by fire. When Garrett's lawyer, Johnathan Wilson (another victim of the deception), tells his client what has happened, the reaction is immediate and much more emotional than anything we have seen from him before: "He's got to be alive. Austin is the only one who knows I didn't kill that girl . . . We planted all the evidence together after the girl was killed. It was all part of a plan."

Wilson attempts to have the trial reopened on the basis of the story his client has told him. But nothing backs up Garrett's claim. A frantic search for new evidence is conducted by Susan and an old beau (who happens to be the DA's assistant). They turn up nothing—no connection at all between Garrett and the victim. The only thing they find out is that the girl was a predatory character, out for her own, completely untrustworthy, and that her real name was Emma Blucher. Execution looms.

And then, just in the nick of time, still another surprise. The executor of Spencer's will and estate reports that, in the course of opening various vaults and safety deposit boxes, he has discovered a letter addressed to District Attorney Thompson. The background music swells to a crescendo, indicating that the drama is about to reach its denouement. The letter is produced and read. It completely exonerates Garrett, who is now seen, even by the District Attorney, to have been telling the truth all along. The District Attorney here achieves an understanding we viewers have long enjoyed; we've known from the very beginning that Garrett was telling the truth, and now the whole world will know. End of movie? Not quite.

Susan meets with Garrett and tells him the good news. He will be pardoned by the governor at 9 p.m. For his part, Garrett is less pleased than he is annoyed, even outraged, by District Attorney Thompson's single-minded effort to convict him. "He should have been trying to find out who really killed Emma." The music stops as Susan looks up, shocked. "How did you know the girl's name was Emma?" We too didn't know that he knew that the girl's name was Emma, a knowledge he could have only if he had known her before, despite his many protestations that he had never had anything to with Patty Gray. Technically, that is true: he did not know Patty Gray; but, as it turns out, he did know Emma Blucher, and for the purpose of the big question—did he do it?—the difference is beside the point. Susan sees this immediately: "You killed that girl didn't you?" That is, you killed "that girl," whatever name she went by. Cornered, Garrett confesses—he killed Emma, a former wife who had promised to divorce him and now turns up like a bad penny saying that they were still married—but tells Susan that he did it for her and for the life she and he could share once Emma was out of the way: "We had our whole life ahead of us." In response, Susan focuses on the deception visited on her: "I thought you were innocent." *We* thought he was innocent and were encouraged to think so by Lang at every moment. Where before our perspective dovetailed with Garrett's (or at least with what we took to be Garrett's), we are now allied with Susan as the victims of misdirection. Her victimhood is more consequential than ours: we have been mis-reading or mis-viewing; she has been mis-living, actively using the resources of the newspaper she now owns to drum up support for what turns out to be a guilty man. Garrett has no comprehension of the position he has put her in, and the thinness of his moral imagination leads him to misjudge her character no less than she has misjudged his: "You would have fought for me anyway if you knew why I did it." He assumes that she, like him, would put her interests ahead of any moral scruples. She replies with an honesty that is, quite literally, beyond him: "I don't know what I would have done."

She now has a chance to know. In the final moments of the movie, its focus shifts from Garrett's travails—manufactured by him—to hers, very real and demanding an immediate action. What will she do? For the first time, we encounter a real character. Everyone else is typecast and flat. Garrett is the suave man on the way up. Austin Spencer is the liberal do-gooder. Roy Thompson is the ambitious district attorney. Bob is the reliable and loyal old friend. Until this moment, Susan is the cultured, cool, and somewhat distant Hitchcockian blonde. (Fontaine was the only actor to win an Academy Award under Hitchcock's direction.) Now she is a woman faced with a terrible choice: either give up the man she loves (or used to love) to the death penalty or become complicit in a crime. It appears that she will take the second course when she is unable to complete a call to the state prison. (There's only a half hour until the execution.) The scene shifts to the prison, where the governor is about to sign a pardon. Garrett is jovial and, in answer to a reporter's question, says that he will return to writing: "It's the way I make my living." The governor's pen is poised when the phone rings. We hear only his side of the conversation: First, "Are you quite sure about this?" And then, "Is Miss Spencer with you now?" The governor puts the pen back in its holder, and says to the warden, "Have Mr. Garrett taken back to his cell. There will be no pardon." Fade out, the end, a tight shot on the unsigned pardon.

The trailer for *Beyond a Reasonable Doubt* promises "one of the most surprising climaxes ever filmed." The movie delivers, but to what end? What's the point? To a large extent the point is Lang's ability to pull it off. He constructs a plot in which knowledge of what is really going on is withheld from both the characters and the audience at the same time. (And we now have to consider the possibility, indeed probability, that the Spencer-Garrett scheme was cooked up after Garrett had already committed the murder or was planning to.). Within the general category of the misled, there are gradations. Austin Spencer knows more than his daughter or the District Attorney, but he doesn't know the crucial thing. Viewers know as much as Spencer does; with him they are constructors and consumers of the story as the narrative seems to present it. The showgirls are mere props in the plot hatched by Spencer and Garrett; and they are even more the objects of manipulation in Garrett's master plot: we are allowed to think that he wants them to implicate him in a crime he did not commit so that his subsequent exoneration will be that much more dramatic, but in fact he wants them to implicate him in a crime he *did* commit so that, when his manufacturing of the case against him is revealed, any evidence they might have provided points away from him. (Is your head spinning yet?) The District Attorney, the detectives, Garrett's lawyer, Susan's perennial suitor, and the dead girl (never seen) are barely placeholders; we don't care about them for a second. And, of course, all these strings are being pulled by Lang, who finally, in the last one and one half minutes, puts everyone on the same page and neatly exits from a film that offers as a reward for viewing it nothing but a skill exercised at our expense.

But what about capital punishment, the movie's ostensible subject? To be sure, the right man is sent to his death, but not because the justice system has worked as it should or because an argument about the death penalty has been persuasive. Had Garrett not made a mistake and let Emma's name slip, he would've gotten away with it and we would have been watching a movie with a conventional happy ending. The questions raised by Spencer remain unanswered; the movie does not address them, but sidesteps them, substituting its own structure of serial surprise for any serious inquiry into a legal issue. As viewers, we are left not with a point or a concern, but with a request for applause as a filmmaker demonstrates that he can do anything he likes with us. When John Ford in *The Man Who Shot Liberty Valance* disrupts our understanding of what's going on in a narrative we have been watching for almost two hours, he does it so that the lines between law and violence and truth and legend can be further blurred. Lang just does it to demonstrate his skill.

Witness for the Prosecution: Who's the Director?

Lang's skills at manipulation are more than matched the following year by another Austrian–Jewish refugee, Billy Wilder, who in 1957 directs a film version of Agatha Christie's play *Witness for the Prosecution* (1953). A key plot twist is telegraphed in the title. The witness is the wife (or so it seems) of accused murderer Leonard Vole (surprise #1). Christine Vole (Marlene Dietrich) testifies against her husband, who is in fact not her husband because her marriage to a German named Helm was never dissolved (surprise #2). She contradicts Vole's claim that he was home by 9:26 on the evening a woman friend who had bequeathed £80,000 to him was killed. He came in, she says, after 10 p.m. and had blood on his sleeve. It looks as if the defense has been dealt a severe blow, but then in chambers Vole's attorney Sir Wilfrid Robarts (Charles Laughton) receives a call from a woman who says that she has the goods on Mrs Vole. He goes to a train station, where a cockney slattern with a scarred face sells him a packet of letters written by Mrs Vole. In the letters, addressed to "my dear Max," Christine reveals (surprise #3) that she is framing her "husband" so that she and her lover can be together after he is executed. Sir Wilfrid recalls Christine to the stand, confronts her with the letters and forces her to admit that she wrote them (surprise #4), which in fact she did, although not with the purpose they state. Leonard is then acquitted by the jury. Besieged by hostile spectators, Christine seeks refuge in the courtroom, where Sir Wilfrid sits not enjoying his victory because he finds everything "a little too neat, too tidy altogether, too symmetrical." It is then that

Christine tells Sir Wilfrid that, although he won, he had help: *she* was the cockney woman (surprise #5) playing a role designed to discredit her prior testimony and gain sympathy for Leonard. You didn't have to do that, says Sir Wilfrid; you could have trusted me to prove his innocence. You don't understand, she tells him. "I knew he was guilty" (surprise #6). Leonard then comes in flush with plans for spending the money he will inherit from the woman he killed. His plans, however, will include not Christine, but a young woman who rushes to embrace him and identifies herself as his girlfriend (surprise #7). Christine can't believe it and demands to hear it from Leonard. He pushes her away and turns to leave with the girl, whereupon Christine picks up the knife he used to cut himself (it was on the evidence table) and stabs him to death (surprise #8). As she is led away by the police, Sir Wilfred announces that he will be appearing in her defense (surprise #9). The end.

As the credits roll, a voice implores the moviegoers "to not divulge to anyone the secret of the ending." It is as if the producers were saying, "The last few minutes of this movie are all that matters." If so, they sell their movie short, in part by misdirecting the audience as to what the film is really about. The key question is not whether Leonard Vole is innocent or guilty; the key question is will Sir Wilfrid be able to do it again, pull off an acquittal when conviction seems likely and imminent? The answer is, he will and he won't. We first meet Sir Wilfrid when he is newly home from a lengthy stay in the hospital and locked in mortal combat with his nurse (played by Laughton's real-life wife, Elsa Lanchester), who is determined to keep him away from stress, brandy, cigars, and the practice of law. What he wants above all is to be back in the game ("I never knew how much I missed it"), and, when a colleague with soon-to-be-defendant Leonard Vole in tow importunes him, he cannot resist the opportunity once again to participate in a high-profile trial.

The sequence that leads from his return home to his decision to take Vole's case is carried, cinematically, by a chairlift that had been installed so that he can go from his chambers upstairs to his bedroom without strain. Disdainful of the mechanism at first, Sir Wilfrid is soon delighted with its up-and-down, stop-and-go motion. Not only a new toy, the lift allows him to escape Nurse Plimsoll; he discovers immediately that he can stop it in mid-ascent and so evade her clutches. Wilder is able to use the lift to punctuate a succession of moments. After Sir

Wilfrid has told solicitor Mayhew he can't take the case given doctor's orders, he pushes the up button and achieves a height that gives him a view of Mayhew's vest pocket, where he spies two cigars. He immediately pushes the down button and rushes Mayhew into his chambers on the pretext that he should at least be able to offer his friend some advice; what he really wants are the cigars. Once inside he is drawn into the case and, at the end of a conversation with Vole, he signs on for the defense. Exiting his chambers, he once more mounts the lift, but pauses it halfway up to discuss with his associate the importance of Christine's testimony. Given that she is a foreigner and a woman and thus likely inclined to hysteria, it might be best, he says, to have smelling salts ready. Suddenly a clipped, precise, voice declares, "I do not think that will be necessary." Marlene Dietrich has arrived.

Sir Wilfrid powers down to greet her. He announces that his colleague will be appearing for the defense and prepares to ascend again. Disappointed, she provokes him by suggesting that her husband's case may be too hopeless even for the lawyer known to be the champion of hopeless causes. He seems not to take the bait, steps into the lift, and rides it up to the waiting Plimsoll. But once upstairs and in the course of preparing a bath, he turns around and rides down again, now fully committed. Throughout this sequence, the lift functions as Sir Wilfrid's narrative control. He powers it up and down anytime he wants to turn the story in a different direction. It is as if he, not Wilder, were the director, giving orders from his elevated chair.

The same sequence of scenes is tied together by another device—Sir Wilfrid's monocle, which he twirls obsessively and deploys as a test of prospective clients. He turns it so that it shines a light directly in Vole's eyes. Vole blinks and is obviously uncomfortable, but he keeps his composure, leading Sir Wilfrid to believe in his innocence. (So much for his presumed and assumed acuity.) Later, he exposes Christine to the same monocle test, but she responds by coolly walking over to the window and pulling the shade down, negating the intended effect. He is bested by her, but what he doesn't know is that he has also been bested by Vole. In fact, even though the movie is full of tributes to his sagacity and legal prowess, Sir Wilfrid's judgments are almost always wrong. He is wrong about Vole. He is wrong about the woman he first knows as Mrs Vole. He is wrong about the woman who brings him the evidence damning Mrs Vole. He scores a point or two in his cross-examination of the housekeeper Janet McKenzie, but he loses the momentum of that easy victory when his speculation that the voices she claimed to have heard came from the television set is punctured by her triumphant announcement that the set was out for repair that week. He is wrong to think he is fooling Nurse Plimsoll, who, as it turns out, knows exactly what he's doing when he pretends to be drinking hot cocoa but is actually drinking brandy. (To his credit he does come to appreciate her in the movie's last moment.) And, most important of all, he is wrong to believe that he is the center of the movie, a belief abetted by Laughton's charismatic screen presence (you can't take your eyes off him) and by the wonderful pieces of business—the lift, the monocle, the brandy-filled thermos, a truly appalling pair of Bermuda shorts—that adorn his performance. In fact, although he doesn't know it until the very end, Sir Wilfrid is not the lawyer–hero star of the piece, but a featured player in a melodrama crafted and scripted by the foreigner he condescends to. He's not in the movie he thinks he's in (the one we think we are watching), where his client's wife sabotages her husband's defense and tries to get him convicted because she doesn't love him and wants to be with someone else. He's in a movie where a loyal Christine creates a defense for her guilty beloved and by means of a clever theatrical diversion fools everyone, including Sir Wilfrid, his colleagues, the prosecuting attorneys, Nurse Plimsoll, the courtroom spectators, the judge, and us.

Perhaps the most impressive thing about Christine Helm–Vole's ingenious contrivance is that it has her at every moment telling the truth and nothing but the truth. No perjury is committed. It is true, as she says in her initial testimony, that Leonard came home after ten, disheveled and with blood on his sleeve. It is true that he confessed the killing to her and asked her to help him by providing an alibi. It is true, as she says in her second testimony, that she knows no one named Max (she invented him). It is true that she wrote the letters Sir Wilfrid triumphantly brandishes as if their discovery was his accomplishment. Unfortunately for her, it is also true that the man she commits perjury for her is the master of ceremonies, the true director presiding over still another narrative, another drawing-back of the curtain that reveals him pulling *her* strings; while she was duping Sir Wilfrid and the court, he was duping her. The heroic and loyal act of getting herself condemned in court is, in Leonard's story, the act of a foolish woman so blinded by love that she entirely misjudges its object. The multiple and swift revolutions in perspectives leave us with nothing to hold on to. At first we see the story from Sir Wilfrid's point of view, then we see it from Christine's point of view, and finally we understand it from the point of view so blithely introduced by Leonard when he says, in effect: "None of you knew what was really going on; I've been the one in charge all along, but don't be upset, I'll give each of you a bit of the money."

Not only are all of the other characters Vole's victims; the justice system, in all its ceremonial British grandeur, is his victim too, and his prop. Sir Wilfrid says as much: "You have made a mockery of English law." All of it—the high ceilings, the ornate furniture, the powdered wigs, the formal address, the archly polite back-and-forth, the high-in-a-chair magistrate who thinks *he* is the one in charge—is just a stage-setting enabling Vole to get away with a sordid, vicious, and petty (he is no master criminal) crime. There have been criticisms of Tyrone Power's performance: he's too old for the part; he exhibits no depth; he just smiles a lot. But he's perfect; that is, he perfectly captures the shallow motives and paper-thin personality of a good-looking man gone to seed (true of Power himself, known early on as "Beautiful Ty," but now at 43 more than showing his age and only months from death), at once totally charming and without a moral, or even an interestingly immoral, center. (Agatha Christie specialized in this type.) It makes perfect sense that, after it's all over, he's going to go on a cruise with a younger woman. How wonderfully banal!

But of course he doesn't go, for he doesn't get away with it; not because the justice system finally asserts itself, but because Christine won't let him. In contrast to all the layers of deception that precede it, her act, even though it is murder, is clean, direct, and refreshingly free of artifice. The only thoroughly honest moment in the movie, the stabbing, is a breath of fresh air that clears the table and gives Sir Wilfrid an opportunity to undo Vole's mockery of the law by defending Christine at a future trial. But we don't see that trial or that movie, and the movie we do see is without a redeeming last note, even though Wilder pretends to provide one in the image of Sir Wilfrid and Nurse Plimsoll leaving the courtroom with his arm around her shoulder (shades of Tracy and Hepburn). But, while their exit affords us a formal escape from the film's dark vision, the bad taste of a corrupt world where every surface is a lie lingers, as it does in other Billy Wilder productions—*The Apartment*, *The Fortune Cookie*, *Double Indemnity*, *The Lost Weekend*, *Ace in the Hole*, *Stalag 17*, *Kiss Me, Stupid*, *Sunset Boulevard*, and even *Some*

Like It Hot, which ends with the revelation of a deception—"I can't marry you, I'm a man"—cheerfully accepted and cynically embraced: "Nobody's perfect."

Witness for the Prosecution is to some degree a more serious movie than *Beyond a Reasonable Doubt*. Sir Wilfred's indignation on behalf of the law seems genuine enough. The dynamics of the marriage (if it is that) between Christine and Leonard are complicated: he expresses his admiration of her even as he announces he is leaving her. The relationship between Sir Wilfrid and Nurse Plimsoll is a nice mixture of light comedy and emerging affection. But the producers were not wrong to hang so much on the surprise ending or, to be more precise, endings. The successive revelations are what the movie is about. What Wilder aims for are the gasps provoked by each pulling-back of the curtain, which together produce a total surrender of the audience to the director's manipulative skills. And it must be added that the performances of the principals—Laughton, Power, Dietrich—are themselves worth the price of admission.

5

Natural Law versus Positive Law

Judgment at Nuremberg

Reflecting on *Witness for the Prosecution*, Billy Wilder said that Marlene Dietrich is "one of the greatest faces in the history of film." She is one of those people, he continued, who "don't look like ordinary humans."[1] A few years later, her remarkable presence is on display in a movie that couldn't be more serious, *Judgment at Nuremberg* (1961). Like *High Noon* a Stanley Kramer production, *Judgement at Nuremberg* acts out a perennial jurisprudential debate. Is law to be identified with the statutes that are written down and "on the books"? Is its pedigree entirely procedural? Or is law tied firmly to a morality that is universal and timeless? Are specific laws deficient or even invalid if they have no connection with true moral principles? These questions are debated repeatedly in the movie, by opposing attorneys, by presiding judges, by defendants, by ordinary citizens; and everyone who has a say regards his or her view as obviously right and the views of others as obviously wrong. A particularly succinct formulation of the positivist position—law is what has emerged from the in-place legislative and judicial processes and is not to be tested against some moral/philosophical measure—is given by defendant Friedrich Hofstetter, who declares, just before he is sentenced, that he has been faithful to the "highest concept" of his profession (the profession of judging), which is, he says, "to sacrifice one's own sense of justice to the authoritative legal order, to ask only what the law is and not to ask whether or not it is also just." Hofstetter is one of four Nazi-era judges on trial, not for violating the law, but, as prosecutor Tad Lawson (Richard Widmark) observes, for following a law no jurist who upholds the values of civilization should respect. Hofstetter's co-defendants do not echo

Law at the Movies. Stanley Fish, Oxford University Press. © Stanley Fish (2024).
DOI: 10.1093/oso/9780198898726.003.0006

his deference to procedure and pedigree. One declares that everything he did was justified by the overriding imperative to defeat Bolshevism. A second is confused and not in possession of his faculties. A third, Ernst Janning, turns against his former colleagues and his former self and speaks in tones that ally him with those, like Lawson and Chief Judge Dan Haywood (Spencer Tracy), who invoke a law higher than the law of any political jurisdiction.

Three years before the film's release, two celebrated legal theorists, H. L. A. Hart and Lon Fuller, debated the issues it takes up in the pages of the *Harvard Law Review.* Hart and Fuller ask whether Nazi Law was, in fact, law or something so debased that it was not worthy of being followed. They agree, of course, on the evil nature of the Third Reich, but divide on the question of whether a regime rooted in evil could nevertheless establish a legitimate legal system its citizens are obliged to obey. Hart says "yes" and Fuller says "no."

Hart goes first and he quickly identifies himself as committed to the distinction between "law as it is and law as it ought to be," between, that is, positive law and morality.[2] He follows the doctrine formulated by nineteenth-century legal theorist John Austin: "The existence of law is one thing; its [moral] merit or demerit is another."[3] Of course, the two systems more than occasionally interact; the laws as written and the moral law do converge; but to confuse them is to set up a situation in which moral disapproval of the law legitimates disobeying it. Stability and predictability depend on our affirming that "a law which actually exists is a law though we happen to dislike it."[4] The alternative view, firmly rejected by Austin (who attributes it to William Blackstone), is that "no human law which conflicts with the Divine law is obligatory or binding,"which means, Austin complains, that no human law that conflicts with the Divine law *is* a law.[5] Hart acknowledges the possibility of states instituting morally dubious laws, but he quotes approvingly Jeremy Bentham's argument that, if you think a law bad and immoral, obey it nevertheless but then labor to change it: "obey punctually . . . censure freely."[6] Hart then puts Austin and Bentham together and concludes that "it could not follow from the mere fact that a rule violated standards of morality that it was not a rule of law; and, conversely, it could not follow from the mere fact that a rule was morally desirable that it was a rule of law."[7] (That is why we sometimes say of a moral precept that it ought to be the law, but it isn't.)

Hart acknowledges that "[u]nder the Nazi regime men were sentenced by courts for criticism of the regime," often in order "to maintain the state's tyranny effectively."[8] Obviously, the purpose of the law was bad, but was it nevertheless a law? Yes, Hart answers, for a "decision on [its] grounds would be intelligent and purposive, and from one point of view the decision would be as it ought to be."[9] The "ought" here is not moral, but procedural: given that this was the law then in place, no matter what you might think of its moral status, the court was right to apply it, ought to apply it. Hart cites as an example the case of "a woman [who], wishing to be rid of her husband, denounced him to the authorities for insulting remarks he had made about Hitler." As a result the husband "was arrested and sentenced to death . . . though he was not executed but was sent to the front."[10] (Someone was recalling the Old Testament story of David and Bathsheba.) After the war the wife was prosecuted for "illegally depriving a person of his freedom," and she contended that "her husband's imprisonment was pursuant to the Nazi statutes and hence that she had committed no crime." A court of appeals affirmed a judgment against her, because the statute she cited in her defense "was contrary to the sound conscience and sense of justice of all decent human beings." Hart doesn't challenge that characterization, but finds the court's reasoning objectionable, because it amounted to "declaring a statute established since 1934 not to have the force of law." The better course, he says (although it is also problematic), is to acknowledge that the wife was convicted "pursuant to the introduction of a frankly retrospective law."[11]

No, says Fuller. The better course would be to acknowledge that the 1934 statute wasn't law, not because it was generated by an evil regime, but because its internal structure invalidated it. The statute began by declaring: "Whoever publicly makes spiteful or provocative statements directed against . . . the leading personalities of the nation . . . shall be punished by imprisonment." But, in the next section, "publicly" turns out to mean "privately." "Malicious utterances not made in public shall be treated in the same manner as public utterances when the person making them realized or should have realized they would reach the public."[12] "Should have realized" is so open a standard that no one accused under the statute could offer a defense. The third section removes another avenue of defense when it explains how the "leading personalities" of the nation will be identified: "The National Minister of Justice shall, with the advice and consent of the Representative of the Leader, determine who shall belong to the class of leading personalities for purposes of Section 1."[13] In other words, the list of those the law protects from "provocative" statements will not be identified, but will be compiled by the persons who feel themselves offended and are powerful enough to retaliate. This amounts to declaring that anyone who says something (not defined in advance) that a few important people (exactly who is not specified) don't like will be punished and possibly executed. Fuller declares that he can't share Hart's indignation that a postwar court "saw fit to declare this thing not a law."[14] The contempt in the phrase "this thing" is directed at a so-called law that is so porous and open-ended that no one the authorities wished to target could fail to be found guilty.

In Fuller's view this defect in the law is not an accident, but an inevitable consequence of the regime from which it issues. It would not be quite right to say of that regime that it stands for nothing; it stands for the maintenance and spread of its own power. Its laws, therefore, are animated solely by that purpose and exhibit no connection with any larger ideal or overriding spirit such as equality or impartiality or the rights of the individual. These laws need not be consistent with one another or even with themselves; they can be retroactively declared, withdrawn with no notice, be secret and unpublished (all features of the Nazi "legal system" at times). This extreme version of positivism—of the separation of law and morality—never, says Fuller, "gives any coherent meaning to the . . . obligation of fidelity to law." Its obligation "seems to be conceived as sui generis, wholly unrelated to any of the ordinary, extralegal ends of human life."[15]

So here, according to Hart and Fuller, are our choices: a fidelity to the laws that have been set down by particular powers in particular places, no matter what their moral content, or fidelity to a higher law that reigns, or should reign, at every time and in every place and therefore supersedes whatever positive laws happen to be in place. The advantage of making the first choice is that we will always know more or less where we are. We can say confidently and collectively: "That's the law." If we make the second choice, we ally ourselves, not with the rules and protocols of local precincts (a city or state), but with general, indeed universal, norms that underlie life and give it meaning. The problem is that the identification of those norms will always be controversial. Positive law, the law of what is written down, has the advantage of providing a common agreement about what is and is not permitted; just read the text narrowly and you can know with some confidence whether the act you contemplate is lawful. But, if the universal moral law is your lodestar, agreement is difficult, if not impossible, to secure. For no sooner is the moral law declared than innumerable voices will challenge it in the name of laws *they* believe to be universal. So what do you want? Stability, predictability, and the trains running on time, or the exhilarating, but precarious and radically uncertain, straining after what is eternally good and true?

Each of the characters in *Judgment at Nuremberg* must ask himself or herself that question and contemplate the consequences that attend either answer. The chief consequence of affirming the general over the particular and the local is the difficulty of fixing responsibility. As soon as we depart from the model of formally prescribed laws that name specific acts individuals are not allowed to perform and assign agency wider and wider, the question of responsibility becomes urgent and largely unanswerable. Lawson ends his closing remarks by declaring: "Responsibilities for these crimes must be placed in true perspective." In counsel with his fellow judges, Dan Haywood says to Judge Ives, "Curtiss, you were saying that these men were not responsible for their acts. You're going to have to explain it to me; you're going to have to explain it to me very carefully." The explanation (which we do not see) obviously did not take, for, in the course of rendering his judgment, Haywood concludes that "the men in the dock are responsible for their actions."

But this ringing declaration only raises a larger question that structures the back and forth of the courtroom scenes. What exactly were their actions? The actions for which they were indicted by the Nuremberg court are specific and local. One judge is accused of authorizing the forced sterilization of a man whose political views were suspect in the eyes of the state. Two others are jointly accused of sentencing an elderly Jewish man to death because he allowed himself to be kissed by a teenaged Aryan girl. However, these straightforward charges—straightforward because specific pieces of evidence can be brought forward to support or refute them—occupy the same narrative space as a much larger charge that is never formally made but hangs over every scene. Not who is guilty of this particular crime (if it is a crime), but who is guilty of the national crime of attempted, and partially successful, genocide? Genocide is not included in the bill of particulars brought against the defendants. Its specter is raised when Lawson shows films of the Allies entering the concentration camps at war's end and discovering emaciated survivors and mountainous piles of those who perished. (In 1961, most Americans would not have seen these films.) The films cry out for an explanation and an accounting. Who did this and what is or will be their punishment? The only candidates for punishment in the Nuremberg courtroom are the defendant judges, none of whom shot a prisoner or turned on the gas. Nevertheless, guilt attaches itself to them, if only because they were functionaries in the system that presided over these horrors. In short, they are the conveniently available receptacles of a vengeance that cannot precisely identify its object. They are scapegoats. They are judges in a corrupt and monstrous regime; they must be guilty of something, so let's make them guilty of everything. It is this reasoning—never explicitly announced but present the moment the films are shown—that draws the ire of defense counsel Hans Rolfe (Maximilian Schell), who exclaims that it is "wrong and unfair to show such films in this case against these defendants." It is unfair because these defendants are not on trial for genocide, so why should they be tarred with its brush? Rolfe is saying, let's do the legal business of considering the specific legal charges rather than accusing the defendants of everything under the sun.

However, when the specific charges are made and countered (by Rolfe), we as viewers, along with those in the courtroom, cannot help remembering the concentration-camp images. Even when particular points of positive law are being discussed, the very general issue of overall responsibility for everything that happened in the Third Reich never recedes into the background. The difficulty of separating the case at hand from the entire history of the war is accentuated by the poignant appearance of the two key witnesses, Rudolph Peterson and Irene Hoffman-Wallner. These two tortured souls are played by two famously tortured souls, Montgomery Clift and Judy Garland. Director Kramer counts on the sympathy they elicit before they utter a word. The combination of their star power and their well-publicized personal traumas serves to render them larger than life (as they in fact were) and to turn them into symbols of every injustice suffered by innumerable Jews and other victims of the Nazi horror.

On the stand, each is forced into a re-creation of the trauma that now defines his or her life: Peterson, sterilized by the state many years previously, is once again subjected to a test designed to measure his mental capacities, and Hoffman-Wallner is once again pressured to admit that her affectionate embrace and kissing of an elderly Jewish man amounted to the kind of sexual interaction forbidden by the racial pollution laws. The emotional turmoil portrayed by Clift and Garland is so moving and absorbing that the *legal* issues fade into the background, but, if we bring them to the foreground, it becomes clear that Rolfe's defense of the judges who found them guilty has merit.

Peterson was accused of being a mental defective and therefore subject to sterilization under the "Law for the Prevention of Genetically Diseased Offspring," which stipulated that "[a]ny person suffering from a hereditary disease be rendered incapable of reproduction if the experience of medical science shows that it is highly probable that his descendants would suffer from some serious physical or mental hereditary defect."[16] In the course of Rolfe's interrogation of him, Peterson acknowledges that (*a*) he didn't do well in school, (*b*) his father and every one of his many brothers were manual laborers (he is a baker's assistant), and (*c*) his mother was labeled "feebleminded," a designation he protests in anguish, as he takes her picture from his jacket and shows it to the court in a heartbreaking gesture. In response to a question, he says that the only test administered preliminary to his being sterilized required him to rehearse the birthdays of Hitler and other leading Nazis. (He could not.) Rolfe feigns surprise and recalls a test often given to those whose cognitive abilities were in question: make a sentence out of the words "hunter," "hare," "field." The task is to take words that are just items in a list—inert as it were—and embed them in a syntactical structure that makes an assertion or offers a description. The skill required is conceptual: you have to imagine a little world (that's what a sentence is) where the words, now part of a logic of relationships, name an action being performed, an actor performing the action, the manner (time, place) of the performance, and the object of the action. For example,

> The hunter chased the hare into the field.
> The hare escaped the field, running from the hunter.
> The field contained both the hunter and the hare.

The level of intelligence displayed in the construction of these (and innumerable other) sentences is more abstract than the production of language in a conversational setting. You must step back from an activity (the exchange of sentences) you perform routinely and reflect on the "deep structure" of what you do unreflectively. Peterson obviously cannot rise to that level of intelligence. Whether that amounts to being mentally defective or feebleminded is debatable, but, given the statute, it is not unreasonable or arbitrary to conclude that it does. Of course, we may want to argue against such a law being on the books at all, but, once the law is in place, that argument is philosophical rather than legal. We might think that the "Law for the Prevention of Genetically Diseased Offspring" is a bad law—a bad law modeled, Rolfe points out, on a Justice Holmes-approved American law[17] under which an estimated 70,000 men and women were sterilized—but it is law nevertheless, and Judge Hofstetter should not be put on trial for applying it. Or so it can be reasonably argued.

The same kind of argument could be made in the case of Irene Hoffman-Wallner. A housekeeper testifies that she saw Hoffman-Wallner and her Jewish landlord embracing and kissing while the teenage girl sat on his lap. Hoffman-Wallner does not deny that this happened and happened more than once, indeed several times, but she protests that these expressions of affection and the gifts she received from Mr Feldenstein were not what the prosecution suggests they were. ("Nothing like you are trying to make it sound.") Rolfe presses her to say what else she had done until she becomes incoherent, at which point Ernst Janning (Burt Lancaster), the most distinguished of the defendants, interrupts the process, asking, "Are we going to do this again?" At this moment Hoffman-Wallner has the sympathy of both the court and the movie's viewers, so much so that we lose sight of the legal question of whether she did in fact violate the racial pollution laws. On the evidence she herself provides, she did. According to a 1935 decision of the German Supreme Court, the phrase "sexual relations" in the relevant statute must be understood to include "all natural and unnatural sexual intercourse [as well as] all sexual activity with a member of the opposite sex that is carried out in order to substitute for coitus in satisfying the sexual urges of at least one of the partners."[18] Hoffman-Wallner vigorously denies any sexual urges, but she cannot speak for her friend and benefactor (who had been executed), and one is left to speculate on the dynamics of the situation: a 65-year-old man being kissed repeatedly by a pubescent Judy Garland

(Hoffman-Wallner would have been 16, one year younger than Garland when she starred in *The Wizard of Oz*) while she sat on his lap.

So, as in Peterson's case, the judgment against Hoffman-Wallner and Feldenstein was at least arguably correct. To be sure, Ernst Janning muddies the waters a bit when he confesses that his mind was made up before the trial began. He was going to pronounce the two guilty no matter what. But the fact that Janning had base motives for issuing the judgment does not invalidate it. The measure is whether the judgment accords with the law, not whether it proceeds from a pure heart. In saying this, I have slid into making the case for the defense: those the judges convicted were guilty under existing law. That case has considerable legal force (at least under positivist assumptions), but little or no cinematic force, because, as I have noted, the dramatic framing of the scene, in addition to the appeal of actors with a prior claim to audience sympathy, draws our attention away from nice legal points and toward the monumental crime of the Holocaust. As a result, we are continually alternating between and mixing up two accounts of responsibility, one in which the defendants are accused of documented specific acts and another in which they are accused of every act of the Hitler regime. It is Lawson's strategy to bring these two accounts together by arguing that, merely by participating in the machinery of a corrupt state, the defendants were complicit in that state's crimes, even when they were not physically present at their commission: "These defendants fashioned and executed laws and rendered judgments which sent millions of victims to their destination." Lawson is saying that those who are assigned a role in an institutional structure bear responsibility not only for what they directly do, but for the consequences that follow, inevitably it might be said, from the existence of that structure.

Lawson's contention that in carrying out their duties the defendants initiated a sequence that ended in Buchenwald is confirmed, at least rhetorically, by the very fact of the visual images. They are judged guilty of the larger crime with which they are not directly charged, and, when the "ordinary" courtroom trial resumes, their guilt spills over onto the smaller crimes—applying the laws of sterilization and racial pollution—with which they are actually charged. The spreading of guilt also travels in the opposite direction, from the small to the large. We respond to the heart-rending stories told by Peterson and Hoffman-Wallner and convict the defendants of crimes that were probably not crimes under the relevant law so that they can by extension be convicted of the crimes that were crimes but were committed by someone else. Lawson is going to get them one way or the other, and, in fact, gets them both ways.

In response, Rolfe has a pincer strategy of his own. Like Lawson, he widens the net of responsibility, but he does so in order to extricate his clients from both prongs of the double bind Lawson constructs: if responsibility belongs to innumerable agents, cultures, and countries—including, as he observes, those countries like the United States that allowed what happened to happen—no single agent should be singled out for indictment and trial, and his clients, especially Ernst Janning, should not be in the dock. And, on the other hand, if responsibility can be assigned only to those who actually pulled the trigger or turned on the gas, his clients, especially Ernst Janning, didn't do those things and should not be in the dock. The machinery of guilt demands guilty parties, but, in Rolfe's analysis, either the guilty parties are so large in number that prosecuting them is impossible and nonsensical, or the guilty parties are not in court because as low-level functionaries they could not bear the weight of the trial's accusatory rhetoric. While, in Lawson's account, the defendants are guilty of everything, in Rolfe's account they are guilty of nothing.

The legal/rhetorical maneuvers performed by both men are impressive, but when all is said and done the question everyone asks—who is responsible?—is no closer to receiving an answer. (An inebriated Lawson says sardonically that it must have been Eskimos who did it.) The situation in the courtroom mirrors the situation in the larger society, where the same question is endlessly debated in the streets, in restaurants, and in intimate conversations between persons who are trying to negotiate the postwar moral landscape.

When the camera leaves the court, it wanders out into the city, where the protagonists in the legal drama interact with "ordinary" Germans. Often, the vehicle and background of the interaction are found in the music. (As Mrs Bertholt (Marlene Dietrich) says, Germans love to sing.) The movie opens with a rousing version of a German marching song, "Wenn Wir Marschieren": "When we march | A light shines that shines through the dark and the cloud | . . . Our life is the struggle till Germany awakens." As the music plays, the camera is focused on an impressive building topped by a swastika; suddenly the shot zooms in just as the swastika is destroyed by a missile or a detonated bomb. The scene then shifts, only slightly, to the ruins of the city. As the camera pans devastated building after devastated building, the notes of the marching song are continued, but in a slower, lower, almost funereal register. The song now mocks itself: Germany has awakened to a nightmare of its own making. In the last scene of the movie, after Judge Haywood has once again forced Ernst Janning to confront his guilt, the same song plays as Haywood, an aged, overcoated version of the hero of so many western movies, walks alone away from the camera down the narrow corridor of a prison.

In between this musical book-ending, scenes between Judge Haywood and Mrs Bertholt, in whose house he is quartered, unfold against a background and foreground of song. Mrs Bertholt is the aristocratic widow of a general executed by the allies in the wake of an earlier trial. She and Haywood meet when she comes to retrieve some personal items from her former home. They talk, at first awkwardly and then with more ease. At the end of their conversation, Haywood has his driver take her back to the small apartment she now lives in, and, when they meet again by chance in a restaurant, she invites him to a piano concert to be given by a refugee from Hitler now welcomed back as a sign (we are encouraged to believe) of Germany's reform and regeneration. Haywood has been left a ticket at the box office and, when he enters the concert hall, he looks around for her without success until he looks upward and sees her regally posed in a box high above the stage. The camera pans up to her in a way that accentuates both her commanding presence and her extraordinary beauty. The concert over, they meet outside, and she suggests that he walk her to her apartment, only a few blocks away. The time of their stroll is short, but the number of things that fill it up is large, in part because details of Marlene Dietrich's biography bleed into the narrative. Sixty when *Judgment at Nuremberg* was made, Dietrich had been a great star for many years in her native Germany and America. She spurned efforts of the Third Reich to recruit her as an aide to Nazi propaganda and spent much of the war touring tirelessly in support of allied troops. She was sometimes on the front lines with Patton and other generals, and, when the war was over, she was awarded the Presidential Medal of Freedom. As time went on, she filled a cultural role—the beauty who never ages—and she appeared as that character or persona in celebrated cabaret performances where she sang in several languages and wore gowns and tuxedos designed to show off her still youthful body and especially her legs. *Judgement at Nuremberg* was her last substantial film role.

Viewers in 1961 would have known all this, and their knowledge would have had the effect of blurring the distinction between Mrs Bertholt and the actress who plays her. The distinction pretty much disappears when, as Haywood and Bertholt begin to walk past ruins and a blind man sitting in front of them, they are accompanied by the strains of a song. It is "Lili Marleen," a song associated with Dietrich, whose recording of it was so popular with German soldiers that the regime attempted to ban it, but relented in the face of demands for its return. Bertholt/Dietrich sings a bit of the song and describes its words as "very beautiful, very sad." "I wish," she says to Haywood, "I wish you understood German." The wish has (at least) a double meaning: she wishes he could appreciate the force and delicacy of the lyrics, but her deeper wish is that he might understand Germans and Germany and thereby relax the severity of the judgment made on both by the trials. As they walk, she translates the lyrics and explains that they are being spoken by a German soldier who knows he's going to lose his girl and his life. She is, in fact, the girl whose husband—General Bertholt—lost his life, not in battle but at the hands of a tribunal that sentenced him to death by hanging. They reach her building (a semi-ruin) and climb the steps to her small apartment, which is dominated by a portrait of her husband in full military regalia. "Lili Marleen" is still playing in the background. Their conversation turns inevitably to his fate and her bitterness at his not being granted a soldier's death by a firing squad. "What did he know," she asks, "of the crimes they cited him for?" With that question she joins the ranks of the many Germans Haywood meets who disclaim knowledge of what the Nazis were doing. (It was the Eskimos, of course.) Her husband, she exclaims, was the victim of "political murder," of the "revenge the victors always take on the vanquished." "You see that, don't you," she appeals to Haywood, who can only say, "I don't know what I see," and adds, "I do want to understand, I have to." The scene has come full circle: she wishes that he understood the lyrics of "Lili Marleen"; he wants to understand everything. But the distance between them is more than linguistic, and there is no hint in their conversation that it will ever be bridged.

In a later scene, the gulf between them widens, again while music plays in the background. Haywood and Mrs Bertholt meet in a restaurant/beer garden one day after the concentration-camp films have been shown in court. For a while, the words they exchange are lighthearted. Haywood muses that, if this were a magazine article, the two of them would be acting out familiar roles, "the rapidly aging jurist and the beautiful widow who transcend their differences." (Hard as it may be to believe, Dietrich was just one year younger than Tracy.) In another movie, that would be their story, especially given the pairing of two celebrated icons. In this one, however, their story is one of differences they cannot transcend, despite a mutual desire to do so. Haywood says that he is not hungry, and Mrs Bertholt guesses that he has been strongly affected by the films. She insists, as do others, that she, her husband, and their friends were unaware of the horrors the films reveal: "Is that what you think we are? Do you think we knew of those things? Do you think we wanted to murder women and children? Do you believe that? Do you? We did not know." Haywood replies, "As far as I can make out, no one in this country knew." She tries another tack: "There are things that happened on both sides." In other words, no one is pure (a point Rolfe makes repeatedly), and judgment has to end sometime: "Dan, we have to forget if we are to go on living." Their back-and-forth takes place as the maestro leads the orchestra and the patrons in a rousing version of the 1820 folk song "Du, Du," a song also associated with Dietrich. The lyrics take Mrs Bertholt's side: "You don't know how good I am for you | . . . I wish so much that we were united in love." As the chorus is repeated, all the people in the room (except for Haywood and Mrs Bertholt) pound their beer steins on the tables to the refrain "Ja, Ja, Ja, Ja." The musical verdict is "yes," but the dialogue says "no," and a final emphatic pounding of the steins merges seamlessly into the pounding of the gavel by Haywood. We are back in court, but of course we have never left it. Judgment is always being delivered in Nuremberg.

This scene, like many others, affirms multiple positions on the film's contested issues. At any moment, one of four perspectives is temporarily ascendant and urged on us as the basis for assessing the past and determining what should now be done:

- The perspective of natural law or human rights—regnant at all times, in all places—affirmed by Haywood and Lawson, in the face of the claims made for
- The positivist perspective—championed by Hans Rolfe and Judge Ives—that refuses to look beyond the laws delivered by the legal

machinery of a municipality or a country; law is what's on the books, and the question of whether the law is good or immoral is a philosophical not a legal one.

- The perspective of entrenched social hierarchies in relation to which persons are divided into classes—the nobility (Mrs Bertholt), the military (General Bertholt), professions (Ernst Janning), servants (Schmidt the chauffeur, Mr and Mrs Halbestadt, the couple tending to Haywood's needs), laborers, prostitutes, beggars. For Mrs Bertholt the tragedy of the Third Reich was that it was led by a bourgeois "little corporal." She spends her days now much as we imagine her spending them before the war—serving on committees, supporting charities, going to concerts. Politics barely registers for her; she floats above it. She is drawn to Judge Haywood because she senses in him a noble nature, akin to her own. She wants things to continue as before; she wants, as she says, to go on living.
- The perspective of current political realities—sometimes known as "realpolitik"—which demands a calculation not of which actions satisfy the criteria of some set of moral principles, but of which actions satisfy the prudential requirements of real live situations with real live consequences. What do we hope will happen and what can we do to maximize the chances of that hope being realized? At various points in the movie, politicians and career soldiers note that (*a*) the public, only three years after the war, is tired of the trials and has lost interest in them, (*b*) there is no appetite for the conviction of the defendants, (*c*) the support of Germany and German citizens is crucial to American interests in the burgeoning cold war, especially now in the early days of the Berlin airlift, and (*d*) history has passed this moment by. Colonel Lawson has this all explained to him by one of his military colleagues, who reminds him, on the eve of the closing arguments: "We need the help of the German people, and you don't get the help of the German people by sentencing their leaders to stiff prison sentences." The important "thing to do," he concludes (echoing Mrs Bertholt), "is to survive." As he exits the room, Lawson pauses to ask sarcastically: "Just for laughs, what was the war all about?"

That is the question Judge Haywood answers in his judgment (a famous one-take tour de force by Spencer Tracy), which is prefaced by a careful consideration of the arguments Defense Attorney Rolfe and others have made. Haywood says of several of those arguments: "There is truth in this." And, indeed, he has heard them made by one of his co-judges just a short time previously. In their final conference, Judge Curtiss Ives succinctly states the issue: "the conflict between allegiance to international law and to the laws of one's own country." Putting it that way would be clarifying if international law were an entity one could point to as one can point to a codified statute. But it is not, which is why Ives prefers the second alternative, the assignment of culpability in relation to laws formally set down and the limiting of responsibility to agents directly performing the criminal act: "In a state organized along modern lines, responsibility is confined to those who act directly for the state." By "along modern lines" Ives means in accordance with the separation of law as a system from the dictates of a universal morality. On the basis of that standard, Ives declares, "[w]e can't make the interpretation that these defendants are really responsible for crimes against humanity." (Whatever they are.) "How in God's name," Haywood replies, "do you expect me to look the other way at the murder of six million people?" Ives responds with an instrumentalist question: "I'm asking what good is it going to do to pursue this policy?" That is, how will it advance American interests?

For Haywood, the good done is not instrumental, but moral. As he delivers the judgment, he opts for a wider definition of responsibility that includes men who are "conscious participants in a nationwide government-organized system of cruelty and injustice in violation of every moral and legal principle known to civilized nations." But Haywood doesn't hang his case on principle alone. He has a legal argument that links the two accusatory structures—they did something particular, they did everything—aimed at the defendants. The judges in the dock, he asserts, were accessories to the crimes shown in the infamous films: "Any person who sways another to commit murder, any person who furnishes a lethal weapon for the purpose of the crime, any person who is an accessory to the crime, is guilty." A classical instance of "accessory" status is the person who knowingly furnishes the gun with which a murder is then committed. He or she wasn't there, "at the scene," but without his or her act the crime would not have occurred. The gun or lethal weapon in this case is the enforcement of decrees whose aim, Haywood says, was the "extermination of human beings." That aim was realized because of what the judges did, as judges.

This is a tricky and uncomfortable argument that provokes the objection Rolfe and Ives have made repeatedly: criminal law depends on the possibility of fixing blame and must therefore artificially restrict the category of culpable act to deeds done in the narrow timeframe of immediate cause and effect. Otherwise (and these are examples currently alive in the law), gun manufacturers could be held responsible for the weapons they sell, and tobacco companies would be liable for the deaths their product causes. The distinction between making the product (guns, cigarettes, laws) and making good or bad use of it must be maintained, many say, lest the imputation of guilt be universally shared. Are we responsible for the long-term, down-the-road effects of every act we perform? Must we calculate the attenuated significance of every choice we make? Haywood would seem to answer "yes" to these questions when he explains that it is because the defendants were not "degraded perverts" or "maniacs" (and therefore eligible for a verdict of "innocent by virtue of mental defect") that we must hold them responsible in an expansive and expanding way for what they have done. And to the argument of survival made by Ives and Mrs Bertholt—we must forget in order to go on living, we must cease dwelling on the past so that we can have a future—Haywood gives a short but pointed response: "Survival as what?" If we are to survive in a way that is more than merely physical—the body is there and still functions—we must stand for something above mere survival. Let it be noted, Haywood concludes, that, by this decision, we stand for "justice, truth, and the value of a single human being."

Were this a movie like Frank Capra's *Mr Smith Goes to Washington* (1939), it would end with these words, but after he has handed down the sentences, Haywood adds, "Judge Ives dissenting," and Ives begins to make once again the arguments Haywood has just rejected. To its very end, the movie refuses to dismiss conclusively any of the perspectives its characters give voice to. One of those perspectives may win the day, but there will be other days, and the vanquished points of view will reassert themselves and be heard again. Indeed, they are heard three more times before the curtain falls. When Rolfe brings Janning's request that Haywood visit him in prison, he also brings news of the verdict in the I. G. Farben case. I. G. Farben was the manufacturer of Zyklon B, the gas used in the mass executions. Placed on trial, its directors, Rolfe reports, were either acquitted or given light sentences. Rolfe's point is that the world is going in a direction different from the direction Haywood has arrived at. Haywood is unimpressed. What you say, he tells Rolfe, may be logical and in tune with the times, but "to be logical is not to be right and nothing on God's earth could make it right." When he visits Janning in the next scene, Haywood hears another of the arguments that failed to move him, the argument from expediency. Yes, justice demanded a certain judgment, but the present and pressing needs of society suggested the wisdom of another. Throughout the trial it had been said that Janning acted in what he thought were the best interests of his country. Referencing the millions who died, Janning protests that he never thought "it would come to that; you must believe it." And Haywood, for his part, must once again make the point so many slide away from: "It came to that the first time you sentenced a man to death you knew to be innocent." Fidelity to truth and justice cannot be put on furlough here and there in response to circumstances and in the expectation that no deep and lasting harm will be done. The rule of law and the beacon of justice are at once strong and precariously fragile. In his *Leviathan*, Thomas Hobbes speaks of laws as "artificial chains"—that is, constraints—that go from the sovereign state to the ears of its citizens. "These bonds in their own nature but weak, may nevertheless be made to hold, by the danger, though not by the difficulty of breaking them."[19] The bonds are weak because their force depends on the constancy of those constrained by them. That constancy lasts no longer than the resolution of the will to maintain it, and nothing is easier than to relax it, just this once. But "just this once," Haywood is saying, won't have effects that are neatly and safely confined. A breaking of this chain will lead to the breaking of another, and after that another, and, before we know it, bodies are being forklifted into mass graves. The door to Janning's cell closes after Haywood delivers this devastating judgment (he convicts Janning twice), which could again be the movie's last word. But it is not. The last word appears on the screen as a script telling us that none of the ninety-five convicted in the Nuremberg trials is still serving his sentence in 1961. Realpolitik triumphs as the movie ends.

I cannot end this analysis of *Judgment at Nuremberg* without remarking, as others have, on the brilliance of the performances. Tracy, Widmark, Lancaster, Dietrich, Clift, Garland, all deserved Academy Awards. Schell deserved his. And honorable mention should go to two uncredited smaller-than-cameo performances. When Haywood walks around Nuremberg on his own, he has a momentary encounter with a well-dressed, attractive young woman at a food stall. She is smoking a cigarette and appraises him. She smiles at him, and he, knowing what she is offering—herself—declines wordlessly with a small shrug of his shoulders. She says (in German) "Goodbye grandpa," the only words spoken in the scene. Only one word is spoken at a later moment when Haywood and Mrs Bertholt are walking toward her apartment. A man well- dressed but shabby in spirit approaches them from the back, his body almost crouching in its effort to insinuate himself into their conversation. He says, "Zigaretten?" and, when neither of the two replies, slinks away, an emblem of the abject and hopeless condition of a people from whom everything has been taken. We may thrill to the eloquence of Tracy's great speech at the end of the trial, but any triumph we are tempted to feel should be tempered by the fleeting appearance of these two lost souls.

6

The Law's Dogma and Religious Dogma

Inherit the Wind

What makes *Judgment at Nuremberg* a compelling movie, worth revisiting again and again, is its refusal to elevate one perspective on its events to the extent that alternative perspectives are entirely discredited. Unfortunately, this is not true of another Stanley Kramer/Spencer Tracy project, *Inherit the Wind* (1960), a dramatization of the conflict between materialist science—a mainstay of the secular state—and the desire of religious believers to have their beliefs reflected in public practices, especially the practice of public-school teaching.

Standing in the way of that desire is the Establishment Clause of the First Amendment. The Establishment Clause says, basically, that no act of government should have the effect of turning the state into an instrument of religious purposes or policies. The strong Establishment Clause position was articulated by James Madison when he declared, in his "Memorial and Remonstrance" (1785), that no citizen should be forced to "contribute three pence only of his property for the support of any one [religious] establishment." Even the expenditure of so small an amount, Madison believed, would be the beginning of a slippery slope and, therefore, "it is proper to take alarm at the first experiment on our liberties."[1]

Given this stringent view, the business of Establishment Clause law should be to detect in legislative or executive actions either the intention to bring a religious perspective to bear on state matters or the realization of that effect even if no one consciously intended it. In fact, the "not even three pence rule" was relaxed and pretty much

Law at the Movies. Stanley Fish, Oxford University Press. © Stanley Fish (2024).
DOI: 10.1093/oso/9780198898726.003.0007

abandoned in the first modern Establishment Clause case, *Everson* v. *Board of Education* (1947). *Everson* turned on a New Jersey statute that authorized reimbursement payments to parents who expended funds in order to bus their children to and from school. The issue was whether parents who sent their children to parochial schools—in this case, and almost every other, Catholic schools—were entitled to be reimbursed. On its face, a "yes" answer would be a violation of Madison's dictum, and that seemed to be the direction Justice Hugo Black was going in when, writing for the majority, he declared that "[n]o tax in any amount, large or small, can be levied to support any religious activities or institutions," and reinvoked Thomas Jefferson's insistence on "'a wall of separation between Church and State'."[2] But a mere moment later, Black breached the wall by performing what was to become a key Establishment Clause move. He changed the question from, Does the state's action amount to supporting with public funds a religious purpose or institution? (Madison's question) to, Is the state treating religious and secular persons equally; is it being evenhanded? In effect, Black transformed the case into a Free Exercise matter and left Establishment Clause concerns aside.[3]

Once the issue is thus reframed, Black can conclude that it would be wrong to "prohibit New Jersey from extending its general State law benefits to all its citizens without regard to their religious belief."[4] The reasoning is dishonest. Were Catholic parents to be denied the benefit of reimbursement, it would not be because they were being discriminated against on account of their beliefs, but because, impelled no doubt by their beliefs, they were asking the state to act in a way that breached the wall of separation that Black has just invoked. And, if the effect of a "no we can't do that" answer would be economically to disadvantage parochial-school parents vis-à-vis their public-school counterparts, that's just what the Establishment Clause demands, not in a spirit of animus toward religious believers, but in the spirit of the very principle it declares: the state should not spend public monies (or any other resource) for religious purposes, lest it contribute to an establishment of religion. The fact that parochial-school parents will have to pay for a service that public-school parents get for free is merely a reflection and consequence of what "public" means. When the state sets up public institutions of learning, no one should be barred from entering them on the basis of religious belief; but there is, before *Everson*, no affirmative right of parents who desire a private, religious education for their children to demand that public monies help pay for it. After all, they have the alternative of enrolling their children in the state-established schools their taxes support. Opting out of that alternative leaves them with the burden they seek to shift to the state and to citizens not of their religious persuasion. It may seem unfair to ask the parents of parochial-school students to pay twice, once when their taxes fund reimbursements to public-school parents and another time when the cost of transporting *their* children comes out of their own pockets. But that is the unfairness that comes along with living in a secular rather than a religious state; it is the unfairness the Establishment Clause encodes. Discrimination against religion whenever it threatens to invade public precincts is what the Establishment Clause enjoins.

In dissent, Justice Wiley Rutledge makes the appropriate point when he observes that, by substituting the promotion of general education and "the welfare of the individual" for the concern to avoid state entanglement with religion, the court "ignores the religious factor . . . thereby leaving out the only vital element in the case."[5] That is, the only reason the case posed a constitutional question the court chose to take up is that it involved religion generally and the relation of religion to state action specifically. In Black's reasoning, Rutledge complains, the "religious factor" is generalized out of existence and is replaced with the "factor" of treating everyone equally.

The fruit of the *Everson* case has been just what might have been expected: the intermingling of the state with religion has been advanced through the doctrine of evenhandedness in combination with the related doctrine of approving state expenditures for religious purposes as long as the funds are dispersed by third-person parties (that is, parents) and not directly by public officials. (I call this a version of money-laundering.) So, as I write, state funds can be expended to purchase educational supplies, to pay for teachers, to construct parochial-school buildings, to support the publishing and distribution of evangelical magazines, to fund vouchers for parents who want to opt out of the public-school system, to refinish the surfaces of parochial-school playgrounds, in short, to do anything that might be done in and for a secular school.

Still, there remains one area where Madisonian Establishment Clause concerns are taken seriously: *direct* professions of religious faith in the public schools in the form of student prayer or school-authored prayer or instruction in religion (as something to be embraced rather than studied) are generally disallowed by the courts, although that may change given cases like Kennedy v. Bremerton School District (2022) in which the Supreme Court sided with a high school football coach who prayed in the middle of the field.[6] The trajectory here is the reverse of the trajectory initiated by *Everson*: instead of a movement toward more and more accommodation of religious interests, there has been a gradually strengthening insistence that secular instruction not be supplanted or diluted by instruction in religion. The vehicle of that trajectory has been the fierce cultural clash between those who place the teaching of evolution at the heart of the science curriculum and those who regard evolution as an attack on the existence of God. The first significant legal playing-out of that clash was the famous "monkey trial," *Tennessee* v. *Scopes* (1925), on which *Inherit the Wind*, the stage play and the film, is based.

A Tennessee law, the Butler Act, made it an offense to teach that man was descended from the lower animals. The then fledgling American Civil Liberties Union wanted to bring a cause of action asserting violations of academic freedom and freedom of speech, and recruited public-school science teacher John T. Scopes to be a test-case defendant. But the presence of three-time democratic presidential candidate William Jennings Bryan as a prosecuting attorney and of famed atheist lawyer Clarence Darrow as the attorney for the defense turned the trial into a God versus Science spectacle. The trial went on for eleven days (July 10–21) and took many a theatrical twist and turn until district court Judge John T. Raulston ruled that the pertinent question was not whether evolution was true or false (the Butler Act did not mention evolution), but whether Scopes had transgressed a law it was in the power of the legislature-as-employer to pass. The answer to that question was undeniably "yes" (the defense did not challenge the fact), and Scopes was convicted and fined $100, a judgment overturned two years later on a technicality.[7]

In *Inherit the Wind* Bryan's and Darrow's names are changed to Matthew Brady (Fredric March) and Henry Drummond (Spencer Tracy), and the *Baltimore Sun* journalist/pundit H. L. Mencken is rebaptized E. K. Hornbeck (Gene Kelly). The town of Dayton becomes Hillsboro, and the tone of the movie is set immediately by a rousing rendition of "Give Me That Old Time Religion." The refrain line, "It's good enough for me," sends a message that is never qualified or complicated: these are ignorant people whose ears and minds are closed to anything that might dispel that ignorance. Hornbeck declares (in a conversation with Drummond as they walk through the town), there's only one thinking man in Hillsboro and he's in jail.

That's not quite right. Rachel Brown (played by Donna Anderson), fiancée of the jailed Bertram T. Cates (the renamed John T. Scopes, played by Dick York), has done some thinking, although, as the daughter of Reverend Brown (Claude Akins), the leader of the anti-evolution, anti-Cates faction, she is, to say the least, conflicted. A number of Cates's students seem to have taken his ideas seriously without necessarily being convinced by them. A farmer, John Stebbins (Noah Beery, Jr), disagrees vehemently with Brown's fire-and-brimstone theology, because, after the death of his son, Brown said publicly and loudly that the young boy, not having been baptized, had lost his chance at salvation. There are also secular reservations. The town banker is wary of a fundamentalist faith that may not be good for business. The mayor has his eye on the next election and is ready to relax the severe dictates of his neo-Calvinist beliefs if it becomes expedient to do so. Yet, on balance, and even though these minority voices are given a hearing, Hornbeck is right. The portrait of the town that predominates in the movie is of women who either march holding signs demanding hellfire, tar-and-feathering, and hanging for Drummond and Cates, or sit in court, Madam Defarge-like, knitting and cheering the prosecution on in the confidence that they are doing the Lord's work. With such images continually foregrounded against the ever-present background of "Give me that old time religion," slightly rewritten ("If it's good enough for Brady, it's good enough for me"), it is easy to identify with the comfortable and familiar common-sense rationality that a pleasantly rumpled Drummond cheerfully dispenses at every opportunity. In a trailer to the movie, Kramer says that he leaves it to the viewer to reach a conclusion about who is right and who is wrong. No, he doesn't.

To put it mildly, the deck is stacked, but far from subtly. The stacking is done right out in the open. This is particularly so in what we are invited to regard as the movie's key scene, where Drummond calls prosecutor Brady as a witness for the defense. (This actually happened in 1925.) Drummond is driven to this strategy, the movie suggests, because the deck has been stacked against *him* when the judge refuses to allow the testimony of the scientific experts he has brought to

Hillsboro. My client, Drummond explains, is on trial for teaching evolution, and the scientists I want to call will explain, authoritatively, just what evolutionary theory really is. At this point, Brady rises to insist that "the very law we are here to enforce excludes such testimony." His point (not fully articulated, but implicit) is that the status of evolution as an appropriate or inappropriate subject for instruction in the public schools has already been decided by the legislature; the questions Drummond now wishes to take up were debated then, and the court's obligation is to enforce the law, not to revisit and perhaps alter the conclusions reached in the course of the political process. The judge immediately agrees and rules that scientific testimony of the sort Drummond wants to elicit "does not relate to this point of law." In effect the trial is over—there is no legal issue to be litigated—and Drummond, stymied and frustrated, asks to withdraw from the case.

Later that evening, as he gazes on a copy of the Bible, the idea comes to him to discredit Brady by making him look foolish in the eyes of the court and the world. As viewers, we are naturally on the side of the lawyer who a moment ago was defeated and without recourse, but now gets a bright notion that might give him room to maneuver where there had seemed to be none. (In many law movies, a moment like this involves the discovery of an obscure precedent that undoes the opponent's key arguments.) We are also on the side of the man of science, even if we take the point that science is irrelevant to the proceedings. We're rooting for him before a word is said.

In the confrontation that follows, two great performers, Tracy and March, demean themselves by acting out the familiar caricatures of the village atheist who smugly ridicules professions of faith and the fundamentalist clown who proves to be inept when his faith is questioned and challenged. Drummond first gets Brady to say that he holds to a literal interpretation of the Bible (although just what "literal" means is not a simple matter). He then springs what he takes to be a series of traps. As the back-and-forth unfolds, the camera cuts periodically to the spectators whose response to each stage of the confrontation is used by the director to guide our own. At first, the response to Brady is positive: enthusiastic nods and occasional cries of "God bless Matthew Brady." But, as Brady is pushed into corner after corner by Drummond's questions, his supporters become uneasy. Finally, as Brady displays increasing agitation, the expressions in the courtroom turn to pity, consternation, and embarrassment. When Brady begins to declaim the names of the Bible's books as an affirmation of what he believes in, the judge adjourns the court. A visibly shaken, indeed broken, Brady is led away by his wife (Florence Eldridge, March's real-world wife).

The structure of the scene is simple. Thumbing through the Bible, Drummond asks a question, and Brady either declines to answer because he rests in his faith or answers in a way that gives Drummond another opening for ridicule. Drummond starts with an easy query, asking Brady if he gives credence to the story of Jonah and the whale. Brady responds, "I believe in a God who can make a man or make a whale and make both do what he pleases." This statement encapsulates the heart of Brady's position: he will not confine God within the categories and capabilities available to man. God is not an item in his own creation and cannot be held to laws he made and can unmake. Next, Drummond turns to the biblical account of Joshua's stopping of the sun. If that is true, Brady asks, why did the earth not stop spinning on its axis, the continents tumble into one another, and the earth fall into the sun and burn to a crisp? How come this bit of news was missed? "Because it didn't happen," Brady replies. Drummond insists that "[i]t had to happen, according to natural law," by which he means physical law, the laws of physics. This is basically the same point he was making with the Jonah-and-the-whale example (empirically, the Bible makes no sense), and Brady's reply is essentially the one he has already given: "Natural law was born in the mind of the heavenly Father and he can change it, use it as he pleases." This is letter-perfect. Brady does not deny the laws of physics any more than the court rejects zoology and geology as practices when it rules out evidence they provide; he is just saying that they are not a constraint on the actions of the God who established them, and he wonders why the apostles of science fail to grasp this simple point. The reason is equally simple: Drummond is so deeply committed to materialist principles (as opposed to biblical principles) that he cannot conceive of entities or actions they do not explain. The dramatized rhetoric of the scene casts Brady as the narrow-minded know-nothing and Drummond as a man with a liberal, capacious mind, but the reverse is true. It is Drummond who can't see past his rationalist/empiricist nose.

Drummond's next move is to pull out an old chestnut: where did Cain's wife come from? If Adam and Eve were alone in Eden with their two children, how is it that Cain found a woman to marry? Brady acknowledges that he doesn't know (some theologians believe that Cain married one of Adam's innumerable children, a solution that has the inconvenience of involving incest). When Drummond asks, Do you ever stop to think about it, Brady replies, "Never tried to find out," which leads Drummond to exclaim: "It frightens me to think of the state of knowledge in the world if everyone had your driving curiosity." The statement is obviously sarcastic, but it touches upon a point of theology. In the Christian tradition, curiosity of a certain kind has been held to be a sin, not curiosity about natural processes, but curiosity about the ways of God. In his book *Intellectual Appetite*, philosopher of religion Paul J. Griffiths speaks of an inordinate appetite for knowledge we do not need to know. It's called "the curious searching of God's secrets."[8] Desiring to explore the workings of God's creations (for example, through zoology and geology) is okay. Desiring to understand how God managed it is not, for it is an act of pride in which the creature attempts to match the power and scope of the creator. The angel Raphael says to Adam in *Paradise Lost*, after he speculates on the construction of the stars and planets: "Solicit not thy thoughts with matters hid; | Leave them to God above . . . | Think only what concerns thee and thy being."[9] George Herbert in his poem "The Pearl" inventories the body of his worldly knowledge, but acknowledges that "through the labyrinths, not my groveling wit | But Thy silk-twist let down from heav'n to me | Did both conduct and teach me how by it | To climb to Thee."[10] Knowledge begins and ends in God, and learning's best service is to lead the learner to its true source. The canonical formulation of the insight belongs to St Augustine, who in his *On Christian Doctrine* distinguishes between using and enjoying a thing: we use things as vehicles or conveyors to something more valuable; but, if we linger on the vehicle and enjoy it for its own sake, we displace the Creator in favor of something he has created, and we commit idolatry. "By means of what is material and temporary we may lay hold upon that which is spiritual and eternal,"[11] but that happy passage will never be negotiated if we are stuck on the means.

I cite Milton, Herbert, and Augustine in order to provide Brady's pronouncements with a pedigree the movie denies them. Brady's lack of interest in figuring out where Mrs Cain came from is not a defect but a virtue (if you are a person of faith), and Drummond's glorification of curiosity marks him as one who has made a god of human intelligence.

This deification of the independent intellect is announced emphatically by Drummond in response to Brady asking: can it be "that there is something holy to the celebrated agnostic?" "Yes, the individual mind, the child's power to master the multiplication table . . . The advance of man's knowledge is a greater miracle than all the sticks turned to snakes and the parting of the waters." The individual mind is the centerpiece of liberalism: to it is ceded the responsibility for assessing truth and value; and constraints on its operations, even the constraint of fidelity to deity, are considered illegitimate. Drummond and Brady are representatives of two great traditions of thought—one centered on a transcendent power that creates, sustains, and judges, and is the source and measure of value; and the other centered on the capacity of unaided reason to determine what is worthy and true. These traditions are irreconcilable, and from within their respective citadels they are impregnable. That is, they are not vulnerable to the arguments offered by their opposites, because, for each, the denial of the other's arguments is a first and founding principle: liberal empiricism/scientism cannot give weight to a faith in the evidence of things not seen, and a commitment to a God beyond earthly knowledge will not be shaken when a piece of earthly knowledge (if Joshua stopped the sun, why was the universe not burned to a crisp?) is brought forward as a disconfirmation. Had Stanley Kramer and the playwrights who first gave us *Inherit the Wind* dramatized the perpetual conflict between two comprehensive and mutually exclusive ways of knowing, Kramer's statement that he left the choice of where the right of it lies to the viewer might ring true. But that is not what he does; it is what he pretends to do, while he systematically and with every resource film provides undercuts one tradition by making its strongest assertion—the primacy of faith—the object of ridicule.

In the course of the scene, Brady six times makes statements that, were they not surrounded by the stage machinery of near-farce, would stand as perfect, not laughable, expressions of his deep and reasoned beliefs. When Drummond picks up a rock and reports that scientists say it is six million years old, Brady responds: "I am more interested in the Rock of Ages than the age of rocks." Brady spoils the moment by a showy piece of wordplay and by delivering the witticism in a self-admiring way, as March no doubt was instructed by Kramer to do. But the force and cogency of his statement remain: speculation about geological matters may be fascinating, but, when push comes to shove, the more important thing to know, and cling to, is not the evidence of geology, but the evidence of things not seen, the evidence, shadowy and fleeting, of a deity who was there before rocks were and whose story rocks cannot tell. Some have speculated that God created a fossil record in order to tempt man to impious conclusions. So Milton's Raphael: "God to remove his ways from human sense, | Placed heaven from Earth so far, that earthly sight, | If it presume, might err in things too high, | And no advantage gain."[12] A double injunction: keep one eye on what concerns you as an earth-bound being, but remember always the higher perspective in relation to which earthly concerns are transitory and do not abide. The thought, in a somewhat debased romantic form, has found its way into the great American songbook: "The Rockies may crumble, Gibraltar may tumble, they're only made of clay, but our love is here to stay."[13]

A bit later, Drummond poses another question. Was the day named in Genesis a literal, twenty-four-hour day? Brady replies, "I don't know." Drummond persists: "What do you think?" Brady purses his lips in an unattractive manner and responds with another *bon mot*: "I do not think about things I do not think about." Drummond receives this as a self-damning admission of willful ignorance: "Do you ever think about things you do think about?" (a crowd-pleasing line tossed off as he moves away from Brady), but it is a statement about the proper expenditure of mental energies: if you are persuaded beyond doubt that a certain form of speculation is useless—will not in the end get you anywhere—why waste your time engaging it in it? Why not instead dwell on what really matters? (It's Augustine's use-and-enjoy distinction all over again.)

Drummond's theatrical victory over Brady—he earns no intellectual points—is abetted by the physical positions of the two: Brady is tethered to his chair (he does stand at the end), where he sweats profusely and tries to cool himself with a fan advertising a funeral parlor; Drummond is free to move around and to punctuate his statements with gestures directed at the spectators and designed to milk applause, which one of them does. The camera of course follows Drummond, who is clearly presented as the master of ceremonies. He gets the good lines like "The bible is a good book, but it is not the only book." To that pat piece of liberal pluralism Brady replies, "It is the revealed word of God," again a statement that has its own power (what can stand against the revealed word of God?), but the power is quickly diminished and dissipated when Drummond begins a new line of attack: "Says who?" That is, who are you to say what God commands? Once again Drummond rehearses the liberal catechism with its emphasis on the plurality of points of view and the unavailability of a mechanism for choosing between them. No, thunders Brady, in what turns out to be his last gasp: "There is only one great truth in the world." Drummond might have said, but didn't say, "Prove it," a demand that would have once more put faith-generated knowledge and conviction to the test of empirical rationality.

"I believe in a God who can make a man and make a whale and make both do what he pleases." "Natural law was born in the mind of the heavenly Father and he can change it, use it as he pleases." "I am more interested in the Rock of Ages than the age of rocks." "I do not think about things I do not think about." "It is the revealed word of God." "There is only one great truth in the world." Lined up like that, Brady's declarations hang together and constitute a coherent statement of his faith. But we only encounter them piecemeal, surrounded and hemmed in by Drummond's playing-to-the-crowd sarcasm ("Say hello to the prophet from Nebraska") and by his ringing affirmation of beliefs a Hollywood audience would be likely to hold. I don't know whether Kramer and the playwrights were aware of the cogency (from the religious point of view) of Brady's stance and deliberately obscured it, or whether they were as blind as Drummond is to the possibility of reasons and explanations orthodox liberal thought cannot take seriously and believed they were being fair; but whichever it is, the result is the same—cheap, shoddy, and dishonest.

None of these pejorative adjectives applies to what is the best scene in the movie: Drummond and Brady sit side-by-side in rocking chairs on the porch of the Mansion House hotel, talking about their long friendship. Their two faces and upper bodies fill the screen as they rock not in tandem but in alternate motions that mirror the distance between them. One effect of the scene is to humanize the two outsized characters. Brady sets the elegiac tone when he asks Drummond: "Why is it, my old friend, that you've moved so far away from me." Drummond replies, perhaps ungenerously, that it might be Brady who has moved away by standing still. The conversation turns to the threats the townspeople direct against Cates, which Drummond finds distressing and potentially "deadly." "Their faith was challenged," Brady explains. "They need to believe in something beautiful; they're seeking for something more perfect than what they have . . . like a golden chalice of hope." The phrase "golden chalice" reminds Drummond of a rocking horse named "Golden Dancer" he admired when he was 7. It was the "something more beautiful" than what he had, and it seemed unattainable because his parents couldn't afford it. But then, on the morning of his birthday, he awoke to find it at the foot of his bed with its red mane and blue eyes, "a dazzling sight to behold." Immediately he "jumped into the saddle and I started to rock." And just as immediately, it broke in half. It had been put together shoddily with "spit and sealing wax." It was "all shine and no substance." (As Drummond recounts the event, the two of them are still rocking in sturdy porch chairs of the type we can still see today.) For Drummond, the story is an opportunity to draw an analogy between the false glitter of his Golden Dancer and the false hopes fostered by an evangelistic rhetoric that promises a "shining Paradise." But we may also see something more psychologically important, an explanation of why Drummond is the rational, commonsensical, no-nonsense man he is: Golden Dancer is his Rosebud (*Citizen Kane*); the dashing of the hopes he had attached to Golden Dancer—he believed, he recalls, that, if he had it, he would have everything he had ever wanted—amounted to a loss of faith, and from that moment on he was on the lookout for things that glitter but lack substance and lead people to entertain hopes that will never be realized. He has found the prime example of a delusive will o' the wisp in the practices of religion, and especially in religions that promise glory and transformation. Like Brady, Drummond is on a mission driven by a faith he mistakes for anti-faith to take away from men and women the seductive illusions that, he believes, will fail and disappoint them.

At the end of this scene, we actually *know* something about these two that goes deeper than the arguments they hurl at each other in court. Brady is no longer just the overeating bible-thumping orator; he is the man who laments the loss of an intimacy he would like to recover. And Drummond is no longer just the bearer of rational liberalism's banner; he is someone whose experience of an early wound has followed him through life and lent him both strength and weakness of mind. There is a delicacy about the scene, a willingness to explore inner landscapes, that contrasts with the often crude theatrical fireworks of the movie's "big" moments.

The final scene of the movie is not crude, but it is shameless. Brady has collapsed and died in the midst of a speech he tried to give after court had been adjourned. Drummond and Hornbeck stand in the courtroom talking about Brady's death. "There was much greatness in the man," says Drummond, and a little later: "A giant once lived in that body, but Matt Brady got lost because he looked for God too high up and too far away." Hornbeck takes this statement as evidence that Drummond believes in God ("You hypocrite!"), but what Drummond means is that Brady looked for God in some extraterrestrial realm rather than in the human spirit and individual mind, where something approximating deity really lives. Drummond is a humanist, someone who believes that whatever divinity there is resides in man's (and woman's) efforts to build communities of sharing and compassion in the wilderness that is the world. The task is arduous and beset by innumerable obstacles—wars, ignorance, petty passions, natural disasters—and in the attempt to achieve it no resource should be dismissed. Both natural science and biblical wisdom have something to contribute, and, therefore, they should be regarded, not as antagonists, but as partners, each bringing what it can to a common enterprise. It is in that pluralist spirit—there are many viewpoints, many perspectives, many goods, many values—that Drummond performs the film's final act just after Hornbeck has left the courtroom. He puts on his jacket and picks up a copy of Darwin's *On the Origin of Species*, looks at it, and then, with his other hand, he picks up a copy of the Bible. He performs a gesture of weighing and balancing the two books and finally, in a decisive motion, slaps them together, puts on his hat, and, more rumpled than ever, walks out of the courtroom with the books under his arm to the rousing words and music of the "Battle Hymn of the Republic": "Mine eyes have seen the glory of the coming of the Lord." The intention is obvious. The superimposition of the song on the courtroom scene matches and reinforces the message sent by Drummond's literal embrace of the two books. Liberal rationalism and religious faith can walk together; neither need condemn or dismiss the other; each can provide aid and solace to us in their different, but complementary and finally compatible, ways. Liberal audiences and critics love this scene, and well they should; for it legitimates their disinclination to take religion's claim to precedence ("I am the way") seriously while complimenting them for according religion a respectable, but not primary, place in the life of American society. "Self-congratulatory" doesn't even begin to describe the complacency of this scene.

Although *Inherit the Wind* is finally not a law-centered movie—the only legal question is, "Did Cates violate the Butler Act?," and everyone, including Cates, acknowledges that he did—in the years since it appeared many courts have pronounced on the issue it foregrounds, the relationship between religious dogma and instruction in public schools. In the movie, the baseline assumption in place is that, if the subject of creation is to be taught, the biblical account is the default one. The theory of evolution is an outlier (at least in Tennessee, where it is one by law), and special arguments must be made for its inclusion. Today, the reverse is true: evolution is a staple of the science curriculum and Creationism, or Intelligent Design as it is now called by its proponents, is taught as an object of sociological inquiry rather than as a legitimate competing account, at least since the landmark decision in *Kitzmiller* v. *Dover Area School District* (2005).[14]

This turnaround is anticipated, inadvertently, by a question Drummond asks Brady: suppose Bertram Cates "had the language and the lung power to railroad through the state legislature a law that only Darwin could be taught in the schools." Brady obviously regards the hypothetical as absurd, and Drummond does not intend it seriously as a prophecy. He is announcing a point of principle: if we allow populist noise ("lung power") to determine what should be taught, we shall elevate prejudice and opinion over authority based on fact. Drummond is making his familiar pitch for open-mindedness and saying that it would be just as wrong to dismiss biblical teaching in advance and out of hand as it is wrong to dismiss the teachings of Darwin. Better to have the two (along with any other candidates) fight it out in the arena of rational argument and present evidence in support of their respective claims. This level playing field where every voice gets to be heard and the voice with the best evidence wins is supposedly what is being dramatized in the movie; but in fact, as I have argued, the field is structured by the assumptions and norms belonging to one of the participants so that the other participant really doesn't have a chance. In the real world of 1925, it was evolution that didn't have a chance; in the 1960 movie, it is biblical creationism that is disadvantaged in every cinematic way available to the director.

By the 1960s, when the place of the biblical account in public schools became a subject of litigation, the real world had caught up with the movie, at least in the courts. In the culture at large, the biblical account still had significant support (as it does to some measure today), but the legal tide turned in a succession of cases from 1968 to 2005 as Establishment Clause concerns, noted but brushed aside by the Scopes court, came to the forefront. In these years, "Creationism" was continually on the defensive, forced again and again to come up with new arguments as the arguments it had traditionally made were rejected. The pattern was established in *Epperson* v. *Kansas* (1968), where the U.S. Supreme Court struck down a 1928 Arkansas law prohibiting teaching in the public schools that man evolved from a lower species because the law "selects from the body of knowledge a particular segment [evolution] which it proscribes for the sole reason that it is deemed to conflict with a particular religious doctrine." There can be no doubt, the court continued, that "the First Amendment does not permit the State to require that teaching and learning must be tailored to the principles or prohibitions of any religious sect."[15]

In the face of this ringing declaration, the creationists formulated a fallback position: allow evolution to be taught, but require that it be taught in the company of what had come to be called "creation science," a label that had been chosen to replace "creationism" because proponents could then say that they were not forcing a choice between science and faith, but asking that the full range of scientific theories be considered. In *Edwards* v. *Aguillard* (1987), the court shut off that avenue, declaring that, while the sponsors of the law claimed for it the secular purpose of enhancing academic freedom by providing students with all the evidence, the history of the legislation showed clearly that an effort to promote religious belief in the classroom was the true reason for passing the so-called Balanced Treatment Act.[16] In dissent, Justice Antonin Scalia argued that the "vast majority" of the Louisiana legislature's members voted for what they believed to be that secular purpose. In addition, Scalia notes, with seeming approval, the contention by creation scientists that "the body of scientific evidence supporting creation science is as strong as that supporting evolution," which is after all not fact but theory and as theory properly available in schools to the challenge presented by rival theories. Moreover, Scalia added, since the court has said in a previous case that "secular humanism is a religion," and secular humanism is what evolution promotes, teaching evolution exclusively could be seen as an

Establishment Clause violation, because the effect would be to prefer one religion over another.[17]

Scalia's dissent forecast the next move the faith community would make. If the teaching of both accounts in tandem cannot be prescribed, at least alert students to evolution's status as something not completely proven so that they can exercise critical thinking and make up their own minds. (This a nice instance of the religion lobby's appropriation of the vocabulary of liberal pluralism.) But a Fifth Circuit decision (*Freiler* v. *Tangipahoa Parish Board of Education*, 1999) rejected this "disclaimer" strategy, because "the disclaimer [denying evolution the status of fact] . . . encourages students to read and meditate upon religion in general and the 'Biblical version of Creation' in particular," and is thus yet again an Establishment Clause violation.[18]

It was in *Kitzmiller* v. *Dover Area School District* (2005) that creationism, now bearing still another new name, Intelligent Design or ID, made what appeared to be its last stand. In 2004, the Dover Pennsylvania Area School Board of Directors passed a resolution stating that "students will be made aware of gaps/problems in Darwin's theory and of other theories including, but not limited to, Intelligent Design." Students in a ninth-grade biology class were read a statement introducing them to an ID textbook, *Of Pandas and People*, and urging them "to keep an open mind."[19] A group of parents brought a cause of action challenging both the resolution and the disclaimer. District Court Judge Jones, after a lengthy trial featuring scientific experts on both sides, ruled that the repackaging of Creationism as Intelligent Design was a strategic response to *Edwards* v. *Aguillard*, and that, when all was said and done, "ID is creationism re-labeled." Any objective observer, Jones declared, would conclude that the intelligent designer at work in the ID account "is God."[20] Jones is careful to say that he is passing judgment not on the truth of ID, only on its claim to be science, and to that claim he says "no." Why? Because "ID has failed to gain acceptance in the scientific community, it has not generated peer-review publications," and it has been rejected by the American Association of the Advancement of Science, "the largest organization of scientists in this country," and by the National Academy of Sciences, which rules out of the scientific community "explanations that cannot be based on empirical evidence."[21]

Now one can view these statements in two ways, either as a practice's stipulation of what belongs to it and what doesn't, or—the difference may seem slight but it isn't—as an effort by a practice's gatekeepers to limit membership to those already in the ranks. Steve Fuller, a noted sociologist of science who testified on behalf of the School District, took the latter view. Science, he said, "is governed by a kind of, to put it bluntly, ruling elite," whose job it is to exclude people who don't already belong to the club. Whether or not this is the case, it is certainly the case that the reasoning Jones accepts and rehearses is circular: since, according to the leading members of the guild, science "is limited to empirical, observable, and ultimately testable data," and since ID puts at the center of its account a designer who cannot be empirically located, ID "is not a scientific theory."[22] Beaten and excluded from the get-go.

Of course, ID proponents do in fact assert that they are engaging in empirical studies, but they have a potentially stronger argument—that the prevailing definition of what counts as science is an artifact of the discipline's history rather than an unalterable fact of nature, and as such should not be protected from challenge. Evidence that a discipline's definition and demarcation of its object emerge from history rather than from an objective identification of the discipline's essence is not hard to come by. Prior to the experiments conducted by Ignaz Semmelweis and Louis Pasteur, washing your hands before performing an operation was not considered a part of medical science; Semmelweis was mocked and persecuted by the medical establishment for insisting that it was. Before the emergence of abstract art in the work of Braque, Picasso, and their impressionist predecessors, painting was thought to be representational; and for many in the early years (and for some today), geometric figures and colors that relate to each other rather than to an object external to the canvas are just not art. Our understanding of what constitutes an activity, of what identifies its essence, is always the product of historical forces; and those who hold the present beachhead are often reluctant to abandon it or even to think about abandoning it, of to think about the possibility that there is more to their practice than its present shape suggests.

In short, the old guard always resists the avant-garde and mocks its practitioners as fakers and charlatans. In a reversal that is truly astonishing when you stop and think about it, evolutionary science is now old guard and creationism is avant-garde, knocking on the door of a liberal rationalist establishment that wields the Establishment Clause as a shield and a weapon. The petitioner at the door says, "Let me in; I'm doing science too," and the response, emanating from those who control access, is, "No you're not and there's nothing more to be said." Mainstream scientists assume as a first principle that ID couldn't possibly be true; it is not accorded the status of a competitor or a contributor. But ID's exclusion, says philosopher Thomas Nagel, seems less a scientific deduction than an article of faith: "both the inclusion of some mention of ID in a biology class and its exclusion would seem to depend on religious assumptions."[23] It's just that the religions are different. Christianity wants to get ID in; the apostles of the faith of scientific reductionism want to keep it out. Like any faith, the scientific liberal establishment clings to a central tenet, a revealed truth—there is nothing in the world that can't be measured empirically. That tenet recognizes no exceptions, and those who reject it are rejected by it in turn, excommunicated, as it were. Once upon a time, the orthodoxy of biblical creation blocked the teaching of evolution; now the orthodoxy of evolution blocks the teaching of biblical creation. *Inherit the Wind* does not tell the story of scientific reason triumphant over religion; it tells the story of one religion displacing another, largely by managing to get its definitions and assumptions into the category of the generally, if not universally, accepted.

In the wake of liberal rationalism's triumph in the courts and in cosmopolitan circles where it is the received wisdom, it may be time to remake *Inherit the Wind* with the roles reversed: scientism as the entrenched orthodoxy and the biblical account of creation as the upstart newcomer. (Everything that comes around goes around.) The town in this version is not "heavenly Hillsboro, Tennessee," but Berkeley, California. A young teacher at the high school (Jennifer Lawrence) introduces her biology class to the arguments of Intelligent Design and is indicted under a state law that prohibits teaching that man did *not* evolve from a lower species. Two outside and outsized lawyers are brought in, one (Robert Duvall) to defend her, and the other (Sam Waterston) to aid the prosecution. The Duvall character invokes academic freedom, diversity, and openness of mind as reasons for including ID in classroom instruction. The Waterston character counters with paeans to rationality and the unimpeachable authority of the scientific method, which can answer all questions about nature without recourse to theological terms. (Open-mindedness is transferred from the agnostic liberal to the religious believer.) A caustic reporter (Chris Rock) provides the Greek chorus, producing biting witticisms that mock the pompous liberal platitudes the Waterston character strews around, as he did when he played Jack McCoy on *Law and Order* for many years. The town folk do not march in the streets singing, "Give me that old time religion"; they assemble at the courthouse wearing designer jeans and T-shirts bearing the names J. S. Mill, Bertrand Russell, and Richard Dawkins; they sing John Lennon's "Imagine" and are particularly animated when they reach the line "and no religion too." In the big courtroom scene, Duvall calls Waterston as an expert on the power and sufficiency of secular reason to explain all things in nature and asks him, how do you explain love? Where does altruism come from? What measures beauty? Why does man aspire and what does he aspire to? Waterston is caught between the unhappy alternatives of admitting that science cannot speak of such matters or declaring, without offering any evidence, that in time science will naturalize them too. He stumbles around increasingly flustered as even he recognizes the emptiness and circularity of his answers. Finally, he is reduced to reciting passages from Mill's *On Liberty* and Rawls's *Political Liberalism* until he is gently led away by his concerned wife (Meryl Streep). The judge (Queen Latifah) reports a jury verdict in favor of the state but reduces the sentence to time already served. In a final scene, the Duvall character is told that the Waterston character has died while drinking a double latte and eating edamame. He says, "Serves the old bastard right," picks up a piece of fried chicken, drops a copy of *On the Origin of the Species* into a wastepaper basket, and strides out with a Bible under his arm humming the "Ode to Joy" from Beethoven's Ninth Symphony. The movie gets bad reviews from the *New York Times*, *The New York Review of Books*, and *The New Yorker*, but is a great popular hit.

7

Visible and Spectral Evidence

The Crucible

Like *High Noon*, *12 Angry Men*, and *The Wrong Man*, *Inherit the Wind* has been interpreted as a commentary on and even an allegory of McCarthyism and the "red scare." One of the film's screenwriters had been blacklisted, and when we read in an introductory note that the time of this play could be "today," we hear a reference to the anti-intellectualism of the McCarthy-led campaign to identify, demonize, and, in many cases, render unemployed left-leaning actors, directors, screenwriters, and composers.

I confess to having little interest in this political perspective on these films. Yes, each presents a single lone figure who stands heroically against the cravenly conforming crowd; in each, that crowd fixes on a scapegoat who will be made to bear the burden of the community's sins and failures; in each, the not-so-silent majority conducts a witch-hunt, convinced that the rooting-out of those few who carry the virus of evil will be followed by the restoration of law and order. But these features are also displayed in *Judgment at Nuremberg* (where the Third Reich, not the House Un-American Activities Committee, is the villain), in Cecil B. DeMille's *The Ten Commandments* (where the God-defying Egyptians persecute the scapegoated Jews led by Moses, a.k.a. Charlton Heston), in Fritz Lang's *Fury* (where frenzied townspeople call for the hanging of a stranger played by a young Spencer Tracy), and in Frank Capra's *Mr Smith Goes to Washington* (where a corrupt band of platitudinous senators is defeated by the one among them—played by Jimmy Stewart—who remembers what America supposedly stands for). Obviously, then, the components of McCarthyism—a herd mentality, scapegoating, demagoguery, faux patriotism, rampant paranoia,

Law at the Movies. Stanley Fish, Oxford University Press. © Stanley Fish (2024).
DOI: 10.1093/oso/9780198898726.003.0008

persecution of the outlier, moral cowardice masquerading as self-righteousness—are not unique to that American phenomenon, and movies produced by men and women who are probably thinking of McCarthy as they made them are not necessarily rendered more resonant if the viewer has that particular association in mind. (Needless to say, this is not the case with films specifically about the blacklist, such as Martin Ritt's *The Front* and Jay Roach's *Trumbo*.)

I would even include in this judgment Nicholas Hytner's *The Crucible* (1996), a screen adaptation of Arthur Miller's play. In a brief *New Yorker* essay titled "Why I wrote *The Crucible*" (1996), Miller recalls his growing resolution to write "about the hunt for Reds in America," a resolution that came into sharp focus when he read a two-volume study of the witchcraft trials written in 1867 by Charles Upham, then mayor of Salem.[1] A footnote in Upham's treatise alerted Miller to the possibility of a relationship between accuser Abigail Williams and John Proctor, one of those she accused. Intuiting that "Proctor had bedded Abigail," Miller found the beginning of a play in the story of "an ambiguously unblemished soul" (Proctor) from whom "a clear moral outcry could still spring."[2] Note the sequence: he begins wanting to write about McCarthyism, is drawn by the parallel between the present moment and seventeenth-century Salem, and finally zeroes in on a good but flawed man beset by conflicting interests who finds in himself the courage to affirm the truth when so many around him have abandoned it. The more Miller settles into his subject, the further away he moves from the details of the McCarthy era, which becomes a possible external reference rather than a reference internal to his play's drama. As he says, "certain processes are universal." The tale he tells has been told before, he notes, in Nazi Germany and in several Communist states. It will do no good and be to no good analytical end to match the characters in *The Crucible* with the *dramatis personae* of the American 1950s. In short, despite its origin in the biographical moment Miller reports, the play is not about McCarthyism.

It is about evidence and the relationship of evidence to moral judgment. Miller finds in Upham a reference to "spectral evidence," which he defines as follows: "If I swore that you had sent out your 'familiar spirit' to choke, tickle, or poison me or my cattle, or to control my thoughts and actions, I could get you hanged."[3] The proof that you did something bad is the absence of proof. You may plead that you were nowhere in the vicinity, but that means only that you have the devil-inspired power to produce effects from a distance; your defense indicts you. This is "the evidence of things not seen" with a (literally) diabolic twist. The verses from Paul's Epistle to the Hebrews say that you exercise faith when you maintain a conviction of God's power and goodness even when the visible events of the world (wars, crimes, holocausts, natural disasters) provide little or no support for it.[4] The doctrine of spectral evidence says that when things turn out badly for you and your adversaries haven't been seen doing anything against you, you can accuse them of being witches who, because they act at a remove, leave no evidence of their crimes; the more innocent they appear to be, the more likely they are guilty. Deputy Governor of the Province Judge Thomas Danforth (Paul Scofield), called to be the chief magistrate at the Salem witch trials, explains how it works: "In an ordinary crime, witnesses are called to prove guilt or innocence; but witchcraft is an invisible crime. Therefore who shall witness it? The witch of course and the victim. We cannot expect the witch to accuse herself. Therefore we only rely on her victims."

The equivocation in this statement is located in the word "victims." A less tendentious and more accurate word would be "accusers." To be sure, the accusers in *The Crucible*—a gaggle of sexually repressed teenage girls—claim they are victims, but the claim is backed up by nothing but their words, except in that one instance when Abigail Williams (Winona Ryder) is able to display her wound because she has inflicted it. The middle step—the confirmation or disconfirmation of the accusation by independent evidence—is missing, and, by the upside-down logic of the spectral, its very absence signifies guilt: the crime is invisible; therefore there is nothing to be seen, and, as I noted above, the fact that there is nothing to be seen proves that it has been committed. The only thing that might tell against an accuser is her insincerity, but sincerity is as invisible as witchcraft, and for some people feigning it is as easy as fabricating an accusation. In effect, Danforth is presiding over two different systems of law, one that foregrounds standards of evidence and protections for the accused, and another that is without procedure and is informed at every point by a non-rebuttable conviction that the Devil is at work, often invisibly. The first system yields procedural rulings in which Danforth is expert after more than four decades on the bench. The second yields rulings based on the hysterical outpourings of girls who are at once afraid of the consequences, should their lies be exposed, and exhilarated by the power those same lies give them over the judgments of men.

The perils of being caught up in this second system are illustrated in a moment when Danforth himself teeters on its abyss. He is questioning Abigail Williams and asks if it is "possible the spirits you have seen may be illusory only." (Just what "illusory" would mean in the context of spirits is a nice question.) She takes offense, leans in, and says threateningly: "Beware Mr Danforth, do you think yourself so mighty that the Devil cannot turn your wits." Taken aback, Danforth is incredulous: "What say you?" In other words, I can't believe what you're suggesting. Williams replies on the half-beat: "Satan is no respecter of persons; he may corrupt anyone." Merely by asking a challenging question, Danforth finds himself a step away from being the object of the kind of accusation he has himself legitimated when he declares that, with respect to diabolic possession, credence must be given to the accusers, especially when they are children. Until this moment, Danforth had been supremely confident in his authority; now he begins to realize that, in a world where anyone can be corrupted and the signs of corruption are hidden, his authority hangs on the whim of a teenage girl who has been scorned (by John Proctor) and will scorch the earth in response. Williams is telling Danforth that no one is safe, and the entire story to this point supports her.

That story and the movie begin when a group of teenage girls led by Williams dance in the woods around a fire built by Tituba, a native of Barbados. As they dance, a chicken is sacrificed, and each calls out the name of a boy she hopes to attract or a person she wishes harmed. Clothes are shed, blood is drunk, and then the increasingly frenzied scene is interrupted by the appearance of Reverend Samuel Parris, Williams's uncle. The girls flee, and two—one of them Parris's daughter—fall into a deep sleep from which they cannot be awakened. Witchcraft is immediately suspected. Interrogated, the girls name Tituba as someone diabolically inspired. Hectored and beaten, she "confesses" an allegiance with the Devil and begins to name those she has seen in his company. Her example prompts the girls to begin naming names too. (It's a contagion.) One of those names is Elizabeth Proctor (Joan Allen), wife of John Proctor (Daniel Day-Lewis), who slept with Williams when she was employed in the Proctor household. Proctor suspects that Williams is behind this ("You'll be clapped in the stocks before you're twenty") and insists to anyone who will listen that the girls are faking their seizures. Two outside authorities are brought in to settle the matter: Reverend John Hale (Rob Campbell) and Judge Thomas Danforth. Danforth is zealous and proudly strict. Hale in time comes to doubt the veracity of the girls' testimony. Meanwhile inquiries are conducted, trials held, and a number of the accused who refuse to confess are hung. Things come to a head when Proctor drags Mary Warren (Williams's replacement in the Proctor household) into the courtroom, where she testifies that she never saw any spirits. But, shortly after, she recants and goes over to Williams's side. With no other recourse available to him, Proctor denounces Williams as a whore and confesses his affair with her. His wife found him out, he tells Danforth, and sent Williams away, and this is now her revenge. Danforth summons Elizabeth Proctor and asks her why she dismissed Williams. Not knowing that her husband has confessed and eager to protect his reputation, she lies, sealing everyone's fate. Proctor joins her in jail and awaits hanging.

This bare narrative leaves out several subplots, several of which serve to furnish the accusers with old-fashioned and all-too-familiar motives. One man has his eye on the land of another; one woman blames another for her having lost so many in childbirth; Reverend Parris finds in the Devil's influence a convenient explanation of the low esteem he is held in by his parishioners. The most important subplot, really a main plot, involves Proctor and his wife, Elizabeth. He feels that she hasn't forgiven him for his sexual transgression. "An everlasting funeral still marches in your heart," he complains. "Look for some goodness in me and judge me not." Her reply speaks to the key issue in the film: "The magistrate sits in your heart." Again and again in the movie someone says, where's the proof, what's the proof, we must have proof. Everyone looks for visible signs that will conclusively determine guilt and innocence. Elizabeth tells her husband that what he seeks—a just verdict on his person—already exists in a place where no one but he can see it, in his heart. The location of true judgment in the heart parallels and is yet different from the location of diabolic possession in the fevered imagination of Salem's citizens. One is real, the other is not; both are invisible. The internalization of value deprives characters and viewers of any easy way to sort out the moral ambiguities that are found everywhere in Salem. Danforth keeps promising to get to the bottom of things, but there is no bottom of things; there is only the truth (or falseness) of the individual heart and no one to certify it but its owner.

This is Elizabeth's lesson, and she repeats it in the final meeting between them. Danforth has been told that the townspeople have grown tired of hangings; Abigail Williams has gone to the well of accusation one too many times and is no longer believed. After being shunned by people in the street and rejected by Proctor yet again when she visits him in prison, she steals £31 from her uncle and disappears. Informed of her disappearance, an exasperated Danforth decides that an end can be called to the proceedings if John Proctor will confess and, by confessing, save himself from hanging. He goes to the prison and asks Elizabeth to persuade her husband. I promise nothing, she says, but I will speak with him.

The two meet on slightly raised ground overlooking the sea. In other films where a couple is silhouetted against a background of water, the effect is to create and enhance a mood of romance. But romance is absent here. The landscape is bleak; a wind is blowing; both John and Elizabeth are covered with grime and wear tattered clothes; their postures indicate resignation; their expressions are grim; his teeth are stained (they were not at the movie's beginning). He asks her about the baby she is carrying and about their sons, and then he says: "I'm thinking I will confess, Elizabeth, what say you . . . what would you have me do?" That is the wrong question because by asking it he cedes his judgment to an external agent; he has not yet learned that the magistrate sits in his heart. He makes the same mistake when he says to Elizabeth, "I would have your forgiveness." She replies, "It is not for me to give it if you will not pardon yourself; it is not my soul, it is yours, John." She keeps trying to push him in the direction of Polonius' famous advice: "to thine own self be true, | And it must follow . . . | Thou canst not then be false to any man."[5] She tries again: "Only be sure that whatever you will do, it is a good man does it." That is, the value of whatever act you perform resides not in the act, but in the spirit with which it is done. You must find your center, and, if you do that, you cannot step falsely. Proctor still doesn't get it, and he cries out to Danforth and Hale: "I want my life." He does not understand yet where his life truly resides.

Proctor returns to the space in front of the prison and is asked by Danforth: "Did you bind yourself to the Devil's service?" He answers yes, but firmly denies that he has seen any others in his company. He then signs the confession, but immediately snatches it away. Signing the confession should be enough, he contends, without displaying it on the church door. Parris exclaims, "The village must have proof," and Danforth adds, "I must have good legal proof." Actually he does have good legal proof, a confession witnessed by many people; what he wants is a legal proof *plus* the assurance—and what would that be worth and how could it be verified?—that Proctor's statement corresponds to what is in his heart. Danforth here straddles and attempts to conflate the two regimes of law he is pledged to support. According to the one—the regime of procedure and outward indicia—he should be satisfied with the public confession he has extracted. Hale and his other associates urge him to "be done with it." But Danforth wants Proctor not only to say it, but to *mean* it; he wants procedural truth—Proctor has said the required words—faithfully to reflect or to stand in for an internal reality, an unimpeachable and unretractable sincerity. His fear is that, once Proctor is freed, he will recant. Why, he asks, do you balk at a signed paper? The question implies that, if Proctors balks, it must be because his verbal confession is belied by an inner conviction to the contrary. By pressing and refusing to take what he has been given, Danforth (unwittingly) does Proctor the favor of making clear what his signing will mean; it will mean the double affirmation of his guilt, an affirmation that will follow him through history. Provoked by his interrogator, Proctor cries out I cannot sign publicly, in front of everyone, "because it is my name, because I cannot have another in this life . . . I have given you my soul, leave me my name." What he doesn't yet see is that, without his soul, his name isn't worth the paper it is or is not written on. It is Danforth who prompts him to the final step. "Is that document a lie? If it is, I will not accept it." Again, he wants both the outward and the invisible truth. "Which way do you go, Mister?" By his question Danforth means only, Are you going to say the word "lie" or not? But Proctor hears it, correctly, as a question about the relationship between his outward acts and his inner compass. In a moment of incredible intensity that seems to go on forever but lasts only a few seconds, he looks down at the paper, and, with his wife by his side, tears it up and in doing so unites the two laws; his inner innocence is matched by his outward act. Both Proctors exhale with what appears to be relief. They embrace with a passion they have never before displayed, and soon after he is taken away in a cart.

Hale begs Elizabeth to go to him. "There's time yet . . . take away his shame." In reply, she pronounces a benediction on all that has transpired: "He have his goodness now. God forbid I should take it from him." To do so—to get him to retract his retraction—would be to restore the shame he has left behind now that he is no longer a divided being. He *is* his goodness now; his soul and his name are one. This is the point to which the movie has been winding. The search for evidence, for moral certainty, ends here in the exultant confidence of a man who goes to his death saying not only that he can die, but that it is "your first marvel that I can." That's the miracle, that someone as flawed as he is can, after struggle and self-recrimination, achieve a moral center so firm that he is able to face his mortal end with perfect, even joyful, equanimity.

The final irony is that the formal and visible proof everyone has sought is given in the movie's last moment, when it is literally too late. Proctor, Martha Corey, and Rebecca Nurse are brought to the gallows; they ascend and form a triptych that recalls the crucifixion of Christ. As the nooses tighten around their necks, they recite the Lord's Prayer, an act witches were thought incapable of performing. As they intone the words "forever and ever," the trap is sprung.

So their reciting of the Lord's Prayer "proves" they were not witches, but as viewers we always knew that. And the reason we always knew that is *not* that witches do not exist. At no point does the movie compel that conclusion; to the contrary, every one of the characters believes in witches. Reverend Hale certainly does; he just doesn't believe that Proctor and Rebecca Nurse and Martha Corey are witches, because everything about their behavior breathes goodness. Belief in witches makes perfect (indeed inevitable) sense if you believe in the Devil, and belief in the Devil follows naturally from a belief in God, Heaven, and Hell. That is the point famously made by Justice Antonin Scalia when, in a 2013 *New York Magazine* interview, he announced (without being asked) that he believes in the Devil. Noting the interviewer's surprise (if not incredulity), Scalia added, "Yeah, he's a real person. Hey, c'mon, that's standard Catholic Doctrine!" And then he really got going: "My God! Are you so out of touch with most of America, most of which believes in the Devil? I mean, Jesus Christ believed in the Devil! It's in the Gospels! . . . Most of mankind has believed in the Devil, for all of history."[6] It's a package. If you believe in God as the creator and sustainer of all things, and the God you believe in granted free will to his creatures, you must have an account of why those creatures disobey and fall away from him. The Christian answer is that they are provoked to disobedience by a malign agent who appeals to the basest of human instincts, instincts whose strength derives from Adam and Eve's original sin. That agent is the Devil, the first of God's creatures to sin, who is bent on recruiting as many as he can to his alienated condition. Scalia notes that in the Gospels the Devil "is doing all sorts of things. He's making pigs run off cliffs." Now, however, he is wilier and succeeds by "getting people not to believe in him or in God." (It's the Devil's finest trick, says Baudelaire.)

A Devil who no longer makes public appearances and works under cover is difficult to detect; there are no sure signs indicating which of our fellows is of his party and which walk in God's ways. Only God knows, and, as Proctor says early on, "God never spoke in my ear, and I can't think of anyone else he's done the favor." Short of revelation (and its claim will always be contested), no one is in a better position than anyone else to discern where the moral virtues or moral fault lines lie. No formula for sorting out the good from the bad, the truth-teller from the liar, is delivered in the movie, despite the fact that everyone is looking for it. *The Crucible* does not give its viewers advice or leave them with a recommendation; it just tells the story, essentially tragic, of human beings whose desires—sexual (Williams, Proctor), political (Parris, Danforth), financial (Putnam)—intersect with a church hierarchy that sees diabolic intervention everywhere. The question of who is and is not a witch is less the center of the tale than a device—a crucible—that activates the antecedent emotions and agendas of the cast of characters. The results are by and large toxic: John Proctor dies, as do Rebecca Nurse and Martha Corey; Elizabeth Proctor is widowed; Abigail Williams runs away; Giles Corey is pressed to death; Reverend Parris is exposed as an ineffectual political schemer; Reverend Hale, initially confident that in the books he carries "the devil stands stripped of all his disguises," ends confident of nothing but the wrongness of the process he has helped to initiate; Judge Danforth overreaches and sees his authority diminished; the church to which everyone is more or less committed becomes the vehicle of deeds its founder would condemn. The crucifixion/hanging scene at the end of the movie lets us out of it and gives some measure of heroism to Proctor, but the disordered lives of those who remain have not been improved or clarified, much less redeemed.

Nor does the movie dispense political wisdom. Don't scapegoat? Don't look for witches to burn and hang? Don't refuse to hire actors, directors, screenwriters, and composers for political reasons? If these were the lessons *The Crucible* teaches, there wouldn't be much reason to see it, never mind to see it again. *The Crucible* works because it dramatizes the choices faced by men and women who must determine, in the light of no evidence or in the light of evidence tainted by its source, how to take the next step in a world where imperatives ("Be ye perfect") abound, but guidelines are largely absent. This is what John Proctor and Corey Giles do at the cost of their lives; this is what Reverend Hale wants to do, but cannot; he comes to know that he's involved in something bad, but can't see what to do about it except urge Proctor to lie; this is what Abagail Williams never even tries to do, driven as she is by lust; this is what Reverend Parris is incapable of doing; this is what Judge Danforth thinks he already does, but doesn't; this is what Elizabeth Proctor has always done. She is the movie's moral center, and her triumph, secured at a great price, is to bring her husband into that center with her.

Is that center religious? Yes and no. The rectitude Elizabeth displays throughout is rooted in a faith that never wavers, but her firmness does not follow from a particular doctrine or article of belief, even a belief in Jesus Christ as her Savior. She stands on her conviction of what is right, no matter what the world and its authorities, including ecclesiastical authorities like Hale and Danforth, tell her. Her faith undergirds her conviction, but does not produce it. She does not consult scripture before she judges and acts, as others in the movie do, usually to disastrous effect. She consults—not quite the right word because it suggests more deliberation than she displays—her own sense of what is the right and good thing to do (she falters only when she lies to Danforth). That sense, to make my point again, is not entirely independent of religious tenets; but, while those tenets provide her with a *general* assurance that the world is finally benevolently ordered, they do not provide her with sure responses to the *particular* crises that confront her and all of us; those responses flow from herself, from the inner equilibrium she long ago achieved. Her husband is not so steadfast. He wavers when he lusts after Abigail Williams (a failing for which Elizabeth holds herself responsible when she admits to keeping a "cold house"); and he wavers more seriously when, after Mary Warren goes over to Williams's side and he is arrested, he cries out to Danforth, "I say you are pulling down Heaven and raising up a whore. I say God is dead!" What he means is that, if a highly placed representative of the church can give credit to the lies of Abigail Williams and put his wife, a model of integrity, in prison, no standard of right and wrong exists and the world is empty of meaning. He says this in what might be called an anti-baptismal moment, half-submerged in water; but, as he utters these apparently damning words, he raises his hands in a gesture that recalls Christ on the cross. He may declare God dead, but his very posture reminds us that, even when all seems dark and God is nowhere in sight, his presence remains and will in time make itself manifest. In the end, Proctor recovers his faith even as he gains possession of his goodness and goes to his death reciting the Lord's Prayer.

So *The Crucible* is and is not a religious movie. Religion is the reference point for everyone's thoughts and actions, but, when the moment of decision comes for the characters, their religious convictions don't tell them what to do; and those like Danforth who believe they can read directly from a scripture to a moral obligation, end up persecuting and hanging innocent people. Rather than being an aid to his judgment, Danforth's zeal clouds it and dooms him to terrible acts. The tragic figure in the movie is Hale. He arrives displaying a Danforth-like zeal. He beats Tituba into a confession and leads the interrogation of the girls; he visits the Proctor household (in a single-horse carriage with the moon hung low on his right side) and inquires into the firmness of their faith, demanding that they rehearse the Ten Commandments from memory. (Proctor forgets adultery.) He points out that twenty-eight Salemites have confessed an allegiance with the Devil and does not flinch when Proctor observes wryly that the statistic is hardly surprising, given that their choice was to confess or be hung. He asks the Proctors if they believe in witches. Elizabeth replies, "I am a good woman. I know it." What she means is that her knowledge of her goodness suffuses her being and needs no support from her ability to recite scripture or prove (how could she?) that she is not a witch. She challenges him: "If you believe that I may only do good work in the world and yet be secretly bound to Satan, then I must tell you I do not believe it." The very fact that Hale entertains the possibility that she is a witch and looks for signs to confirm it is for her a sure sign that his vision is faulty. "If you think I am one, then I say there are none." Notice the care of the statement: she does not say that there are no witches, only that, if Hale's argument for the existence of witches includes and requires her identification as one, there are no witches.

As events unfold, Hale becomes less and less certain that Williams and the other girls are telling the truth, and, by the time Williams flees, he is sure they are not. When even Danforth realizes that things have gotten out of hand, Hale sees a path out of the morass he has helped create. Elizabeth is brought out of the jail by Danforth. As she stares him down, he falters and turns to Hale, who disclaims any connection to the court and its process. I come only, he says, "to save your husband's life," and he asks her to ask him to lie. "We must help John give them a lie they demand." So Hale, who has presented himself throughout as a seeker of the truth, is reduced to urging false witness, not only as a strategy, but as a godly act. "Life is God's most precious gift; no principle, however glorious, may justify the taking of it; it may be that God damns a liar less than he that throws away his life for pride." The name of this reasoning is casuistry—an evasive and over-subtle use of parsed logic that blurs the distinction between right and wrong—and Elizabeth, to her no doubt eternal credit, sees right through it: "I think that may be the Devil's argument." (It is in fact the argument Milton's Satan offers to Eve when he suggests that God may want the Edenic couple to disobey his command not to eat the apple and thereby display a praiseworthy courage.) She does not say so directly, but it is Hale who is now of the Devil's party, and he remains of that party when he begs Elizabeth to intervene as John is being transported to the scaffold. We have already taken note of her magnificent reply—"He have his goodness now." She retains her goodness, John attains his, and Hale is morally ruined when he mistakes religiosity—an exaggerated piety centered on ritual and outward signs—for the real thing; he wanted so much to do good that he couldn't see good when it was right in front of him. He realizes his error too late and compounds it when he urges a course of action that, if taken, would taint everyone—himself, John, Elizabeth, and all those who have already died because they refused to confess.

I return to the question of contemporary political significance. There isn't any. To be sure, there are scapegoats and betrayals, people wrongly accused, false prophets, a contagion of falsehoods; but there is no McCarthy-like figure, and no analogy to the House Un-American Activities Committee. If you watch *The Crucible* intending to match characters and scenes with events in Hollywood and Washington, you will soon become absorbed in the drama of moral choice, and the details of political life in the early 1950s will recede further and further into the background. Generations of high-school children may have been taught that *The Crucible* is about McCarthyism; Arthur

Miller himself may have believed it, at least at the outset, but the eminent historian Edmund S. Morgan had it right when he wrote that the film is "the story of a man who must reckon with himself before he can join the braver souls who step to their martyrdom without a backward look."[7]

8

Man-Made Law as a Refuge from Both the Devil's Assaults and God's Commands

A Man for All Seasons

Martyrdom is also a subject (but not the only one) in another film with religion and law at its center, Fred Zinnemann's Academy Award winner *A Man for All Seasons* (1966). Everyone knows the story. King Henry VIII (Robert Shaw) wants to divorce Catherine of Aragon, whom he had married after receiving a papal dispensation so that he could wed his brother's widow. Childless, he wants the marriage annulled on grounds that it was unlawful in the first place. As Sir Thomas More (Paul Scofield in an Academy Award-winning performance) remarks, he wants a dispensation from the dispensation so that he can marry Anne Boleyn (Vanessa Redgrave). When the Papal See does not cooperate, Henry declares himself the Head of the Church in England, forces the assent of the English bishops, and in 1534 has Parliament pass an Act that declares Anne his lawful wife and her children lawful heirs—to this More could agree—and also repudiates any foreign authority that might pronounce on the matter. To this second declaration More cannot agree, because it requires a renouncing of papal supremacy and subordinates the eternal authority of the Church to the authority of a temporal monarch. More refuses to affirm the Act by oath, and so opens himself up to a charge of high treason. He maintains that not taking the oath stops short of denying the Act's content; at most, it merely signifies silence, and, since in law silence implies assent, his action must legally be construed as an affirmation.

Law at the Movies. Stanley Fish, Oxford University Press. © Stanley Fish (2024).
DOI: 10.1093/oso/9780198898726.003.0009

But, when Richard Rich (John Hurt), of whom no one has ever said a kind word, testifies, falsely, that, in conversation with him, More denied Henry's title as head of the Church, More is imprisoned in the tower, convicted of treason, and beheaded. (A primary source for this account of Rich's duplicity is William Roper's *Life of Sir Thomas More*; Roper was More's son-in-law.)

The beheading is the only physical act in the movie (unless we count Rich's pratfall in the mud as he flirts, politically, with Cromwell), and it is not shown. All we see is the raised axe, and then "The End." It is director Fred Zinnemann's achievement to make drama out of conversation. To be sure, there are interludes of technicolor splendor, most notably the extended scene when Henry and his retinue arrive at More's estate in Chelsea by water early in the evening. It is as if Zinnemann were saying to the viewer, I know what you look for and expect in a period costume drama; well, here it is as opulent as anything you will see in a David Lean movie. Three sleek boats glide to the shore; oars are raised in synchrony; the king, a gold cape around his shoulders, steps out into the mud, and his courtiers obediently negotiate the mud in imitation of him. He is greeted by More and Lady Alice (Wendy Hiller), who must pretend that she is even now completely surprised by his visit while her household staff frantically prepares a meal. There is an amusing and instructive byplay between Henry and More's daughter (Susannah York), when the king addresses her in Latin and finds himself in a mini-competition that he loses when she replies volubly in the same language. He shifts his ground and asks, "Do you dance, too?" and when she says, "Not well," he declares proudly, "I dance superlatively," and shows her his leg. (Henry here displays his many talents, his male ego, and his emotional vulnerability, all at the same moment.) The scene is layered by opposing and complementary anxieties—Henry's, Alice's, Meg's, all the followers who want to do the right thing as soon as they figure out, by watching the king, what it is.

But then, just as the social dynamics generate a narrative energy, that energy is dissipated, intentionally, when Henry asks More to stay behind while the others troop into the house, leaving the two alone on the stage. Henry asks More if he has thought on the divorce. More replies that he has thought of little else, and they settle down in the shade (actually Henry tramps around and shouts) to talk, as everyone in the movies does, about the divorce. Can you see your way to go with me? Henry asks. "No, I cannot come with your Grace," More replies. "It seems to me a matter for the Holy See." "How is it you cannot see your way to me, everyone else does?" "Then why," More comes back, "does your Grace need my poor support?" Henry's answer goes to the heart of the matter. "Because you're honest, and what is more to the purpose, you're known to be honest." Henry proceeds to catalogue the motives of those who are with him. Their support counts for little, because it can be traced to fear, ambition, or habitual obedience; only More's support would mean something, because everyone would know it to be the product not of calculation but of inner conviction. Ironically, Henry is at this moment complimenting More for an honesty and integrity he is asking him to forsake.

More has this conversation, or some version of it, with everyone—opponents, rivals, friends, family, commissions of inquiry, prosecutors, juries. It constitutes the entirety of the movie's action. The conversation in its many iterations has two dimensions: the stringency and complexity of More's stance are laid out in nuanced detail; and, at the same time, there is an effort to educate his interlocutors. In addition to his identities as lawyer, statesman, theologian, poet, political theorist, and philosopher, More is, at least in this movie, a teacher. The lesson is always the same, and it is taught in one key scene to pupils of varying capacities. The king has departed (he never did come in and eat), and the More household settles back into its routines. More and Lady Alice are sitting at table; she is upset that he and the king are at odds. He comforts her, saying first that, if anything can be done by smiling, he will do it; and, second, and more substantively, "This is not the stuff of which martyrs are made." He is not looking to enroll himself in the list of those who have died for their faith; nor is he eager to be brought to the point where any such choice presses in on him. Just at that moment, Meg and her suitor, William Roper (Corin Redgrave), enter, and he reports his latest revolution in religious thinking. (Two weeks previously he was a heretic; now he is a staunch defender of the Church.) Roper says, with some enthusiasm, "You've had a disagreement with his Majesty." More replies, "Have I?" The response is given with a precision we shall see again: he neither says he has had a disagreement nor that he hasn't. In that way, he commits himself to nothing, and, more importantly, should anyone in the room later be asked, perhaps in court, if More disagreed with the king, the answer could only be "I don't know." More always has an eye on what will count as evidence of his views, and he is determined to provide none and therefore be unavailable to legal probing, if it should come to that, as he hopes it will not.

Richard Rich then enters the room. He has been importuning More for a position, and he has also been talking with Cromwell (Leo McKern), who will, he knows, offer him one, but probably at the cost of his honesty. He would much prefer to serve More, and he implores him, "Help me!" More asks, "How?" "Employ me," Rich cries, and Moore says, "No." He makes as if to leave, but turns around for a last try: "I would be faithful." That is, if you employ me, I will be loyal to you—hardly reassuring, since it suggests that his loyalty depends on his having received something for it rather than on an inner disposition to stand by his friends and his commitments. More's reply is devastating: "Richard, you could not answer for yourself even so far as tonight." That is, the very way in which you make your request is evidence of your moral unreliability, a judgment confirmed when, on that very night, Rich goes straight to Cromwell and offers to betray More if the price is right.

After Rich leaves, a succession of rapid-fire exchanges provides an extraordinary lesson in moral reasoning. Lady Alice demands, "Arrest him." More responds, "For what?" You can't arrest someone without evidence that he has committed a crime. Meg chips in, "Father, that man is bad." More: "There is no law against that." This simple statement goes to the heart of what it means to live under a system of laws. The law is concerned with infractions of written and published rules, and not with the content of citizens' hearts. A man (or woman) may harbor all kinds of unsavory attitudes and dispositions—greed, prejudice, lust, selfishness, ruthlessness, duplicity, disloyalty, cruelty, misogyny, vainglory, rage, hatred, excessive self-regard, an unconcern with others; but, if these inner inclinations do not issue in outward acts that violate generally applicable laws (laws formulated with no particular persons or groups in mind), the law will pay no attention. The reasoning is laid out by Immanuel Kant in his essay "Perpetual Peace" (1795). A society, says Kant, can "attain a good level of moral culture" even when many of its citizens are in their nature immoral. All that is required is a set of laws that are understood by each citizen to protect him from the "self-seeking" instincts of others who want in turn to be protected from him.[1] Those laws must be formulated in such a way that no one perceives them to be favorable to some and unfavorable to others; obeying them therefore does not further the interests of any person or constituency; rather, obeying them serves the interest that everyone has to live in peace and maintain possession of whatever has been lawfully gained. The law against stealing protects me against my neighbor and my neighbor against me, irrespective of whether either of us is a good man or a bad man. Indeed, such laws would serve their order-and-peace-ensuring function, even if the heart of every citizen was foul. Anyone, no matter what his innermost desires, can obey these laws and will do so, if only to secure his own safety: "so that man, even if he is not morally good in himself, is nevertheless compelled to be a good citizen."[2] Being a good citizen has nothing to do with being good. By that formal standard, Rich is a good citizen even if he is morally bad.

Roper isn't having any. "It is God's law," he says, that Rich has broken. More comes back like a shot: "Then God can arrest him." Only God can see into the hearts of men and render a true and deep verdict at the Last Judgment. Earthly authorities must confine themselves to infractions that can be empirically defined. If God has seen something that men can only guess at, let Him inflict punishment or bestow rewards in the next life. Impatient, Lady Alice cries, "While you talk, he's gone." And More retorts, "Go he should were he the devil himself until he broke the law." Roper explodes: "So now you'd give the Devil benefit of law." This draws More's longest response, a mini-dissertation that distills the Kantian lesson. (Keep in mind the various dates: More in the early decades of the sixteenth century, Kant in the late eighteenth century, and Robert Bolt and Fred Zinnemann in 1966.) "What would you do?" he asks Roper, "cut a great road through the law to get at the Devil?" When Roper readily admits he would do just that, More becomes animated, a departure from his usual mode of ironic equanimity: "And when the last law was down and the Devil turned round on you, where would you hide, the laws all being flat? This country is planted thick with laws—man's laws, not God's—and if you cut them down, do you really think you could stand upright in the winds that would blow then?" Without the protection of laws indifferent to what is in your heart or in the heart of your enemy, you would be nakedly exposed to the worst your enemy could do and be without a defense, except the feeble defense of declaring, "I'm a good person and you're not." Only man's laws—procedural, not substantive, impartial, not weighted in the direction of anyone's idea of what is right and good—can serve as a buffer between you and those who would do you harm, including the Devil. The law, More insists, is based, not on virtue, but on a system of cooperative, reciprocal checks and balances that, while not delivering salvation, does deliver safety on the level of everyday life, if you adhere to its rules. That is why More ends the scene by saying, yes, "I give the Devil benefit of law for my own safety's sake."

Notice how much longer my explication of More's position is than his presentation of it. More's account of the relationship of God's law to man's law is cryptic, even at times crabbed, and it is never clear that those he is speaking to understand what he is saying. (In this scene, Meg may understand; Lady Alice and Roper likely do not.) We, the movie's viewers, are also his pupils, and that is in part why the key points must be gone over again and again, so that, after hearing him expound so often, we may come to understand. The next version of the lesson is delivered to Lord Norfolk (Nigel Davenport), More's brusque and roughhewn friend, a man of steadfast personal loyalty who is impatient with philosophical and theological niceties. More has resigned the office of Lord Chancellor (which fell to him after Wolsey died) and handed over the golden chain to Norfolk, who, as they walk on More's grounds, entreats him to "make me understand." (He assumes the pupil's posture.) More explains: "The King has declared war on the Pope because the Pope will not declare that our Queen is not his wife." Norfolk asks, "Is she?," which is equivalent to asking More for his views on the proposed divorce and remarriage to Anne Boleyn. More pretends to be ready with a response, but before giving it he leans in and says, "Have I your word that what we say here is between us two?" Norfolk quickly assents, "Oh very well," only to hear More set the trap: "And if the King should command you to repeat what I may say?" (notice the exquisite delicacy of "may"). "I should keep my word to you," Norfolk replies immediately. The trap is sprung: "Then what has become of your oath of obedience to the king?" Keeping your word is not a virtue one can observe piecemeal; it must extend to every relationship, and if it doesn't, every word offered is as suspect as the person who offers it. Integrity must inform every action you take, not just the actions you choose to perform honorably today.

Norfolk tries another tack. More has just said that the Pope is a descendant of St Peter and "our only link with Christ." "So you believe," Norfolk replies, and throws down a challenge: "Will you forfeit all you have . . . for a belief?" The implication is that because beliefs are by definition not dispositive—they may or may not turn out to be true—it may be unwise to hazard everything on one of them, as More seems to be doing. In response, More delivers his most subtle lesson yet: "Because what matters is that I believe it, oh no, not that I believe it, but that *I* believe it. I trust I make myself obscure." No doubt to Norfolk, but if we are good pupils we may receive the lesson: It is More's (or yours or my) conviction that something is so, not the ultimate truth of the conviction, that demands fidelity. Short of absolute knowledge, which belongs only to God, we must rest on and hew to what, given our best lights, we take to be the case. Consistency with one's deeply held convictions rather than having convictions that are true (and how could anyone know?) is what counts in the moral life. Should More be convinced of something, and then go against it, by word or deed, for convenience's sake, or, as later will be suggested to him by Norfolk, for fellowship's sake, he would lose hold of his moral being. He says exactly that to Meg in the Tower when she urges him to take the oath with inward reservations because God regards more the words of the heart than the words of the mouth. More explains why he cannot: "When a man says an oath, he holds his own self in his own hands, like water. And if he opens his fingers, he needn't hope to find himself again." More will not loosen his grip on his integrity for any reason, because he knows that, once relaxed, if only for a second, that integrity will have been wholly lost. (This is the lesson John Proctor finally learns in *The Crucible*.) At the same time, he is reluctant to publish his integrity—share his thoughts on the divorce with the world—because he would be giving ammunition to his enemies, something a would-be martyr eager for public applause might do, but not something he wants to do. That is why his safety lies in silence about the divorce and remarriage: if he says nothing, no one can repeat his words and bring him into danger; if he keeps the sentiments of his heart to himself—if he and only he owns them—they are safely locked in a citadel no one but God can penetrate.

He teaches the same lesson to Lady Alice shortly after his conversation with Norfolk. Now that he is no longer Chancellor, his finances have suffered, and he tells his servants that he will have to let them go. His main servant, Matthew, assures him that all the servants are on his side. More asks, "What side is that?" and is told, "We all know what you think." No, More responds, "None of you knows what I think, and if you guess at what I think and babble it about, you do me no good service." He then retires to his bedroom, where he negotiates the same sequence. Lady Alice says, "If I'm to lose my rank . . . I want to know the reason." He refuses to give it, admonishing her that "it is a point of law" and conducting a thought experiment: "I'm the Lord Chief Justice, I'm Cromwell, I'm Justice of the Tower. I take your hand and clamp it on the Bible . . . and I say 'Woman, has your husband made a statement on these matters?' On peril of your soul, what is your answer?" She can only say, "No," for he has not, and, he adds, "And so it must remain." Not only his silence, but the silence of those who might be questioned about him is required; they can't say anything if he hasn't said anything. (Or, in Rich's case, if something is said, it is a lie and a perjury.)

The obvious question is how can a movie's pace and energy be maintained if it offers nothing more active than a succession of conversations all of which go over the same territory? How many times can More explain himself before viewers lose interest? In order to ward off that possibility, Zinnemann varies the settings in which the same familiar points are made. The setting then provides the narrative interest, while, at least in cinematic terms, the conversation takes second place to a dramatic urgency conveyed by visual and aural cues—the three boats gliding toward More's shore, the dancing and singing at the wedding of Henry and Anne, the dark stormy night when he first learns of the oath from Meg, the gloomy enclosure of the Tower, the ceremonial trappings at More's trial. Often, the narrative will be carried by clothing. An entire story is told by Rich's gown. He is ashamed of it, and, when More gives him a silver cup he had been offered as a bribe, Rich says that he will use it to buy "a decent gown." Later, Rich, now attached to Cromwell, is in attendance at the interrogation of More, who pays him a compliment. "That's a nice gown you have, Richard." (It's a rich gray with what looks like red velvet sleeves.) By the time More is brought to trial, Rich's gown, ever more opulent, is adorned by the signs of his office. After More declares, "I am a dead man," he has one last question for Rich: "That's a chain of office you're wearing?" Cromwell supplies the information: "Sir Richard is appointed Attorney General of Wales." More's response, sad and wry, is one more testimony to the stringent virtue he teaches and exemplifies: "For Wales? Why, Richard, it profits a man nothing to give his soul for the whole world, but for Wales?" Actually, for a better gown.

More's gown is plain throughout, except for the chain of office he wears as if it were a burden. The movie's first close-up zooms in on the massive chest of Orson Welles's Cardinal Wolsey, a vast field of red with the chain of office at its center. Wolsey summons More, and the dialogue between the two is really a dialogue between their garments. The sober dark gray answers tersely, and the seated red robe alternately cajoles and issues pronouncements. At the conversation's end, Wolsey, who has spoken derisively of More's moral scruples, says, "you should have been a cleric." "Like yourself, your Grace?" the gray gown retorts, and exits. In subsequent scenes, it is the bishops who wear red as they ponder their position in relation to the king's desires. When More is finally put on trial, three red-robed bishops, backed by a golden frieze bas relief, preside high above the floor. The commoners and assembled lords sit in banked rows on either side of the trial space. The scene is shot from above, with More, whose back is turned, at the right-front center, a figure much like Will Kane as he walks, alone, down the main street of Hadleyville in Zinnemann's other great movie. This is More's *High Noon*, although in the place of Frank Miller is a resplendent, multi-colored Rich, who vanquishes him, not with bullets, but with lies. In the final scene, as he stands alongside the executioner, More wears what looks like a dirty gray bathrobe; above him is a clear blue sky filled with the sound of birds. We see the scythe raised, but we never see the head drop.

More's personality is almost as muted as his clothing, but with a difference. The calm low voice delivers brief responses that detonate like little bombs ("Like yourself, your Grace?"). His face wears a half smile that broadens only at moments of family intimacy. His gait is measured and deliberate. Despite, or perhaps because of, the lack of movement and outward urgency, the figure radiates an energy from within, an energy quite literally let loose when, at the end of his trial, and in the knowledge that his fate is sealed, More finally proclaims, almost bellows, the views he has for so long kept hidden. He has been convicted, he says, under an Act of Parliament "which is directly repugnant to the law of God and his Holy Church, the supreme government of which no temporal person by any law can presume to take upon him." It is therefore "insufficient in law to charge any Christian to obey it." The law can tell a man what to do and what not to do with respect to his dealings with other men, but the law cannot command a man to believe something he does not, in fact, believe, cannot command a Christian to transfer his allegiance from the pope to Henry.

Not only is this a firm rejection of the king's claim to rule the Church; it is a brief disquisition on the relationship between God's law and man's, a topic that is never far from the edges of any scene. *A Man for All Seasons* has been misread as a movie about a man who lives his life according to the law of God. That is what happens ultimately, but "ultimately" is not the space in which everyday life occurs. For the most part, one obeys the laws set down by temporal authorities, the laws that are on the books, the thick-planted laws More commends to Roper, the laws that regulate behavior in the spirit of maintaining order and security. Such laws remain intentionally on the surface of things; the question of higher commitments is deferred, and it is a point of prudence not to force a choice between those commitments and the ordinary norms of secular life. Indeed, were someone to force such a choice, he would be courting martyrdom and thereby committing an act of pride. More makes just this point when he explains to his daughter why he will take the oath affirming Parliament's Act if he can find a way to do so without violating his deepest principles: "God made the angels to show him splendor as he made animals for innocence and plants for their simplicity; but man he made to serve him wittingly in the tangles of the mind. If he suffers us to come to such a case as there is no escaping, then we may stand to our tackle as best we can." That is, God wants us to serve him, but doesn't require that we seek occasions to demonstrate our fidelity at some great cost. "It is God's power, not our own, to bring ourselves to such a pass." Until he does, "our natural business lies in escaping." More has been escaping wittily (drawing the admiration even of Cromwell) throughout; it is only now, when events have brought him to "such a pass," that he unburdens himself fully and finds the martyrdom he did everything to avoid. The only real action in the movie is More's effort to find a space, no matter how small, that separates him from having to make the stark choice between man's law and God's law. His entire performance—more subtle and sophisticated than either his enemies or his friends comprehend—is summed up in the words of his final, brief statement: "I die his Majesty's good servant, but God's first." I live by the laws the king and his Parliament lay down until to obey them would be to disobey God. Then, and only then, when the pinch comes and I cannot evade it, do I affirm an allegiance to my Creator.

More's is only one of the visions of law on display in the movie. Wolsey, seen briefly in a mesmerizing performance by Welles, views the law, at least the law of the papacy, as an obstacle to his "efforts to secure a divorce." His concern extends beyond a mere wish to give the king what he wants; he fears that, unless there is a son and a clear title to the throne, "we will have dynastic wars again." He is then something of a patriot, and he will pursue the interests of his country as he sees them by any means at his disposal, including, he acknowledges, unnamed "pressures." He scorns what he calls More's "moral squint" and calls on him to come down to earth, where real-world politics, not abstract principles, set the agenda.

For Cromwell, the law is a political tool, one of the resources available to him as he sets about pursuing his strategic goals. He thinks of himself as an administrator whose job, he says, is "to minimize the inconveniences" that stand in the way of his superior's desires. He has no regard for the law as a value in itself; it is an instrument, something he can manipulate, as he manipulates anything that might be of use to him. He is indifferent to the moral status of the means he employs to his ends. He declines to "rack" More only because he knows that the ling would not approve.

One of the means he employs is Rich, for whom the law, like everything else, is a vehicle for his personal ambition. Rich is educated and well read, but no inner compass guides him, and in the end the only emotion he provokes is the contempt More expresses at the moment he is betrayed. Rich wants only to climb the ladder of office, and there is never any hint that his relentless careerism is attached to anything substantive.

Roper, in contrast, is all substance. He wears his passion for justice on his sleeve, and, if the law is an impediment to the realization of just aims, the law must be circumvented, cast aside, cut down, so that justice can be done. He too has no regard for the law as a value in itself (he is the moral mirror image of Cromwell's amorality) and must be taught by More that the decisive triumph over evil is God's work, not man's, and that man-made law is his only security in a world where a conviction that God is on your side—a conviction everyone has—will not shield you from the slings and arrows of outrageous fortune.

Only More is dedicated to the law as a craft, as something that is more than an instrument and less than the vehicle of salvation. He trusts in the law, not because it provides resolutions to all problems, but because it is the space in which the project of civilization—the project of creating a politics that shelters everyone, so long as everyone plays by the rules—can flourish. *A Man for All Seasons* is a testimony to the necessity of law as a system of mutual, reciprocal protections that can do its salutary work even (the words are Kant's) if what it administers is "a nation of devils."[3]

9

Law as Craft

Anatomy of a Murder

If lawyerly craft emerges as a preeminent value in *A Man for All Seasons*, it is the only value in Otto Preminger's *Anatomy of a Murder* (1959). That's not the usual reading of the movie, which has been seen as a contemporary take on honor killing or as an inquiry into the insanity defense or as an early and daring dramatization of rape law or as an example of the lawyer-as-hero genre. There is something of each of these in the narrative, but at its heart is always the prosaic magic of good lawyering. The story is based on an actual case in which the author of the novel and screenplay participated. The beautiful wife (Lee Remick) of Frederick Manion, an army lieutenant (Ben Gazzara), is raped, or so she says, by Barney Quill, the proprietor of a tavern in Thunder Bay, Michigan. An hour after the incident, Manion goes to the tavern and in plain sight kills Quill with five shots. Laura (Mrs Manion) hires Paul (Polly) Biegler (Jimmy Stewart), a former district attorney who spends most of his time fishing, drinking, and playing the piano, to defend him. Every meeting between them plays like a seduction with Polly on the receiving end. In the course of a raucous trial, spiced with erotic moments of its own, Manion is acquitted, having successfully pled that he was gripped by an "irresistible impulse." The small cast of additional characters includes Polly's acerbic office manager Maida (Eve Arden), Claude Dancer, a bright young lawyer brought in by the prosecution from Lansing (George C. Scott), Mary Pilant, the young hostess/manager of the Thunder Bay Inn (Kathryn Grant), and, most importantly, the older—actually O'Connell and Stewart were exactly the same age—non-practicing lawyer who is Polly's Irish drinking companion and fellow lover of the

Law at the Movies. Stanley Fish, Oxford University Press. © Stanley Fish (2024).
DOI: 10.1093/oso/9780198898726.003.0010

law, Parnell Emmett McCarthy (Arthur O'Connell). Two celebrity non-actors invite us to look beyond the film's frame. Duke Ellington wrote the music and appears in one scene as, what else?, a jazz pianist. And Joseph N. Welch, the attorney for the US Army who famously said to Joseph McCarthy, "Have you no sense of decency, sir, at long last? Have you left no sense of decency?,"[1] plays the judge.

The movie is set in Michigan's Upper Peninsula. The landscape is austere, the trees are bare, the light is thin. A percussive beat (reminiscent of "Take the A Train") accompanies a beat-up Pontiac convertible as it drives into the small town of iron City, Polly Biegler at the wheel. Dressed in fisherman's clothes, Biegler hails the bartender at the local watering hole (this tells us that he is a frequent customer) and proceeds to his modest frame house, a somewhat depressing space decorated by very bad wallpaper. Inside, he wraps the fish he has caught in newspaper before putting them in a refrigerator already well stocked with previous catches. He moves into a room lined with law books, just as Parnell McCarthy enters the house and spots a brown paper bag containing the bottle he and Polly will consume that evening. Polly sits down at an upright piano placed against the wall and picks out a few jazz chords. Although Parnell is obviously unemployed, he rebukes Polly for spending all his time fishing. "Polly, you're a good lawyer"; you should be "here waiting for clients." In defense of himself, Polly reminds him that every evening "I sit around and drink bourbon and read law with Parnell Emmett McCarthy, one of the world's great men." McCarthy acknowledges that they share "a love for the smell of the old brown books," and asks, "What shall we read this evening counselor, a little Oliver Wendell Holmes?" The phone rings.

Much is established in this eight-and-a-half-minute scene. Polly is presented as a self-contained person apparently content with his small routines. The car he drives, always top down, is almost a character; it suggests a freer spirit than he typically displays; it promises that at any moment he might unsettle the expectations others have of him. (Laura Manion says to him, "You're a funny kind of lawyer.") He seems to have no ambitions in the wake of his having been turned out of office by the voters. Yet he remains absolutely committed to the law, even though he is barely practicing it. It is the *feel* of the law, its internal operations, that solicit his affectionate, almost obsessive, attention. He could have gone on reading those old brown books forever if the phone had not rung.

On the other end of the line is Laura Manion, who asks Polly to defend her husband and makes an appointment to meet him the next day. As they talk, the camera shifts back and forth between Polly's house and the pool hall Laura is calling from. She wears a belted trench coat and dark glasses. She says, "Will you help him?," but her voice, breathy and entreating, says, "Will you help me?" Her sensuality travels through the telephone line. The alternating shots of his office and the bar display Polly's choices; he can remain cocooned in the comfortable routine of fishing, piano playing, drinking, and reading, or he can step into the unpredictable and volatile world Laura lives in and represents. The choice is made even more stark when they meet, or, rather, when their automobiles meet. His Pontiac is nose to nose with her nondescript sedan, but she supplies the glamour—slacks, tight top, and, again, sunglasses. She says, "Hi," and, indicating her dog, "This is Muff." "Muff" is a slang word for female pubic hair; later, when Muff is described as leading her in the dark with a flashlight on the night of the killing (an action re-created in the courtroom), the sexual suggestiveness is impossible to ignore. Inside the jailhouse, Polly asks her to remove the sunglasses, and when her bruises are revealed, Polly exclaims, "Gee whiz, did Barney Quill do that?" She replies, "You should see all over." She can't say anything that is not a double entendre.

When her husband is brought into the room, the tension between them is obvious. After a few awkward exchanges, Laura leaves, and Polly engages with his client, a compact man with a wary, intelligent, and faintly arrogant face. When Polly expresses some doubt as to whether any lawyer will be able to get him off "scot-free," Manion reminds him that Barney Quill raped and beat his wife and declares, "I have the unwritten law on my side." He is referring to the folklore tradition that holds a man to be innocent of murder if he killed in response to a violation of his wife's honor. Polly responds quickly and with more force than he has so far shown: "The unwritten law is a myth; there is no such thing as the unwritten law." This small exchange establishes one of the key oppositions in the film between cultural/moral sentiments about what is right and wrong and the specification of right and wrong set down in the law. Positivism, you will recall, is a double thesis; an act is not legal simply because it is considered (at least by some people) to be moral; and, conversely, an act widely regarded as immoral is not thereby rendered illegal. Legality is determined, not by popular judgment or traditional mores, but by what is written in the books, the very books Biegler and McCarthy read every evening. It is a matter, not of morality, but of pedigree. That is what Polly means by declaring that the unwritten law is a myth.

He is only partly right. The unwritten law might be a myth in the sense that in the modern world almost no legal code includes it (if it did, it would of course no longer be unwritten), but it is a myth with real power. In the late nineteenth and early twentieth centuries, invoking the unwritten law was a successful legal strategy more than 60 percent of the time. Indeed, "[k]illing a man who trespassed on the sacred rights of husbands was not only justified, it was solid manly behavior,"[2] and those who engaged in it were regarded as heroes. But by the early and middle 1950s, when *Anatomy of a Murder* was written and filmed, the assumptions underwriting this romanticizing of male vengeance—women as an extension of male identity, women as creatures without agency, honor as a commodity the law should protect—were no longer deeply embedded in the culture, and invocations of the unwritten law had diminished to almost nothing.

It is this historical arc that leads Orit Kamir to say that, "[b]y reviving, supporting, and glorifying the unwritten law, *Anatomy of a Murder* reinforces the honor-based value system [and] regresses to nineteenth-century conservative attempts to curb women's nascent rights."[3] This interpretative judgment is wrong in several respects. First, the film is populated by strong women. Laura Manion may be regarded by her husband and the men she flirts with (every man she meets) and the camera (which makes love to her in every frame) as a commodity and an object to be possessed, but it is she who is in possession of the qualities that draw men to her, at least until a superior physical force takes her power of self-determination away. In the wake of that violation—I write as someone who believes Laura's story, but, even if it is a fabrication, her agency is enhanced because she would then be the author of the script everyone is following—it is she who takes charge of her husband's defense, securing Biegler's services, and at a crucial point providing him with the strategic entry he needs. Biegler has been struggling to get the rape, or at least its possibility, on the record; and, as he is questioning the photographer who took pictures of Barney Quill, Laura leans in and tells him that pictures of her were taken too; he immediately asks the photographer about Laura's appearance in those pictures, and, when her bruises are described, the door is open to the introduction of rape. Maida Rutledge is also self-possessed, but in the different style provided by Eve Arden's trademark sarcasm. Anyone on the receiving end of her verbal jabs is immediately on the defensive, playing catch-up, with the odds against ever catching up. On the flow chart, she may be the manager of Biegler's office, but, more often than not, she is calling the tune. Mary Pilant's strength is quieter. She manages a substantial commercial enterprise (inn, food, bar) with efficiency and apparent ease. She is soft-spoken and self-contained and responds to Polly's questions with honesty and dignity. She more than stands up to Dancer's badgering. She does her civic duty, even though her father's reputation (Parnell has discovered that she is Quill's daughter) may suffer as a result. Like Laura and Maida, she is her own woman. In the last moment of the film, Polly and McCarthy are on their way to consult with her about Barney Quill's estate. They are her employees.

So there is no curbing of women's rights in *Anatomy of a Murder*. Nor is the code of the unwritten law revived. Insofar as it is invoked, it is a resource in a legal argument, not an ethic the narrative embraces. The unwritten law emerges as a topic when Manion mistakenly assumes that he can invoke it in court. When Polly replies that there is no such thing as the unwritten law, he means that Michigan law does not recognize it (although in the nineteenth and early twentieth centuries, several states, including Texas and Oklahoma, did), and therefore Manion is going to have to come up with another defense. Fashioning that defense is the work of the early scenes between Polly and his client. In the course of two conversations, Manion finally offers an account of what happened in which he is at once the actor and disassociated from the event. He heard the shots, but "they didn't seem to be connected with me"; they were "far away like someone else was doing the shooting." Immediately after he says this, Polly says, "Lieutenant Manion, I'll take your case." Earlier, Polly had explained that, of the four possible defenses to murder, only one—"legally excusable"—might be applicable in Manion's case. "What you need is a legal peg so that the jury can hang up their sympathy on your behalf. What's your legal peg?" It is when Manion provides one—"I must have been crazy"—that Polly becomes his attorney. He now has a legal defense—the technical name is "irresistible impulse"—and he can deploy it while relying on the sympathy generated by the unwritten code without having to invoke it, as Michigan law does not permit him to do.

Some commentators have faulted Polly for prompting Manion to fabricate a story, but he does nothing of the sort. He merely informs Manion of his legal situation. "I'm not telling you to do anything. I just want you to understand the letter of the law." It is within the letter of the law and not some moral or philosophical code that a defense must be formulated. Polly takes his cue from a conversation with Parnell, who reminds him, "You owe the Lieutenant a chance to find a defense," and "you might guide him a little." This is not cynical advice, but legal advice. Polly and Parnell aren't acting either morally or immorally; they are acting legally by being faithful to the responsibility they have *as lawyers* to provide the client with the best possible—not the truest or the most righteous—defense. The question of Manion's guilt or innocence—did he murder Quill in cold blood or was he gripped by an irresistible impulse?—is never definitively answered, and neither Polly nor Parnell is much interested in it. They are interested only in finding the legal pegs on which to hang their case. Parnell does not accept Polly's invitation to join him because he believes in Manion (he never even talks to him), but because he is being given an opportunity once again to taste the *professional* pleasures of practicing the law: "I've never been in a big murder case. I might manage to be a real lawyer again."

Being a real lawyer—a lawyer who knows the law and can wield its distinctions effectively—is the film's highest value and the standard the characters are asked to meet. That standard is set early on by Judge Weaver (Joseph N. Welch). Weaver is filling in for a judge who is recovering from an illness, and he introduces himself to those assembled in the courtroom. He speaks with a gentle irony: "While I might appear to doze occasionally, you'll find that I am easily wakened, particularly if shaken gently by a good lawyer with a nice point of law." That's what he's looking for, well-made legal points, and, as the trial continues, he totes them up: "You've got your rape in now, Mr. Biegler." "I'd say you're batting one thousand percent." "You've done enough damage." The game being played is thrust and parry: a question pushes the envelope and is then withdrawn, but not before its complications have registered; a precedent is cited triumphantly (in Michigan you can't plead insanity if your client knew right from wrong) and in turn is trumped by another. It's like a musical composition; one chord is laid down, a second is introduced and becomes predominant, a third is heard in the background, but at a moment's notice it can move front and center. No one—neither the players nor the judge who watches them from his high perch—is occupied with moral or philosophical thoughts. Only craft counts.

The obligations and pleasures of craft are on display in a lovely little scene. It's a Saturday. No court. Judge Weaver is walking toward the courthouse. He looks elegant: flower in the lapel of his jacket, a jaunty hat and a cane. The walk is leisurely. As he passes a door marked "Library," he pauses, having heard something. He gently opens the door, peers in, and we peer with him, over his shoulder. What we see is Parnell sitting at a table, books spread all around him. The camera pans to a second story, where Polly is browsing in the stacks and reading intently in one old law book. As he closes the door, Weaver smiles; it is a smile of satisfaction and approval; here is real lawyering at work. We remain with the camera in the interior of the library. Parnell and Polly begin reading excitedly to each other, and then realize that they are quoting from the same Michigan case. It says that the usual rule in law (the McNaughton rule) is that a person is insane if he or she could not tell right from wrong at the time of the accused act. Polly says, "Listen to the 'but.'" "But the fact that one accused of committing a crime may have been able to comprehend the nature and consequences of this act and know that it was wrong, nevertheless . . ." Here Parnell interjects, "Dear sweet endearing word 'nevertheless.'" Polly continues, "Nevertheless, if he was forced to its execution by an impulse he was unable to control, he will be excused from punishment." That is the precedent they need, the legal peg on which they can hang their case. The law moves, not in mysterious ways, but in ways that can be precisely marked by two adversative conjunctions, by small words that turn out to be legally dispositive.

The precedent they have found makes one more appearance in a scene that gives the final imprimatur to craft. The prosecuting attorneys have been trying to establish that Manion appeared to be cool and direct and fully in possession of his faculties when he shot Quill. He was therefore, they imply, not out of control and acting insanely. This would be a good strategy if Biegler were arguing that Manion was legally insane—that is, unable to tell the difference between right and wrong. But Biegler's contention is that, because he was in the grip of an irresistible impulse, his ability or inability to distinguish right from wrong is irrelevant. A person so gripped would be dissociated from his conscious actions and would appear to be as calm (this is the description offered by a witness) as "a mailman delivering the mail." The defense psychiatrist testifies, "I'm not saying he was legally insane. I'm saying that in his mental state it would not have made any difference if he knew right from wrong. He would still have shot Quill."

The moment he hears this testimony, Dancer, believing that the insanity defense has fallen apart, asks for a conference. District Attorney Lodwick makes what he thinks is the obvious point. Polly, you know that "a guy is not considered legally nuts in Michigan unless he didn't know right from wrong." Polly responds by handing Weaver a book, and Lodwick asks, "What's that?" The judge's gently wry reply is, "It appears to be a law book, Mr Lodwick." The implicit message is, "Shouldn't you know what this is before it's offered? Haven't you done your homework? Aren't you a lawyer?" Weaver begins to read and offers the book to Dancer, who says, "No thank you, your honor, I think I recall the case." Dancer has spent the trial underestimating Biegler, and now, too late, ruefully acknowledges his mistake.

The legal case is over, but the drama is not. The plot turns twice. First, the prosecutors call a jail snitch, "Duke" Miller, who testifies that Manion had said, "I fooled my lawyer, I fooled my headshrinker," and when I get out the first thing I'm going to do "is kick that bitch to kingdom come." Because this surprise testimony undercuts the claim that Manion was acting under a compulsion he could not control, it must be countered with something equally dramatic. And here is where the movie takes a false step. Suddenly, Mary Pilant steps forward with a startling revelation. She has found a torn pair of panties in the laundry of the inn she manages, and she tells the court that the panties must have been thrown down a chute located between her room and Barney Quill's. Her testimony reinstates the case for a violent rape followed by a trauma-induced murder. On cross-examination, Dancer seeks to recover lost ground by suggesting that she is motivated by jealousy: "When you found the panties, was your first thought that Barney Quill might have raped Mrs Manion or was it that Quill might have been stepping out with Mrs Manion?" Pilant is aghast and can only say, "Barney Quill was," before Dancer, his face almost touching hers, interrupts: "Barney Quill was what, Barney Quill was what?" She answers, "Barney Quill was my father," effectively ending the cross-examination and providing Biegler with a just-in-the-nick-of-time triumph.

This is dramatically satisfying, but it substitutes pyrotechnics for Judge Weaver's preferred nice legal points. The best that can be said for it is that it participates in the film's unwillingness to come down on one side or the other. Maida acknowledges after the testimony has concluded that she doesn't know what she would do if she were a juror. Preminger, a lawyer himself, is careful to put us in the same position. He alternates scenes in a way that pushes us first in one and then in the opposite direction. Laura is a shameless flirt who "asked for it"; Laura is an outgoing woman whose attractiveness to men does not justify the assault she suffered. Manion is a cold-blooded avenger of his wife's dubious honor; Manion is a traumatized husband who is unhinged by what happened to his wife. The claim of irresistible impulse is supported by the defense's psychiatrist; but, if you listen to the prosecution's psychiatrist, irresistible impulse is a fiction deployed to excuse a murder committed in plain sight. The detective in charge of the investigation declares under oath that he believes Laura's story; but it is not at all clear that her husband does. Manion insists that he trusts his wife, but she acknowledges, at least to Biegler, that he is jealous by nature, and she swears on a rosary to what happened because, she says, she wanted her husband to believe her. So it goes, back and forth: one piece of evidence striking a blow for the defense, another scoring a point for the prosecution. The "Duke" Miller/Mary Pilant sequence certainly contributes to this pattern, but its double shock—a surprise witness followed by a surprise witness—is blatantly theatrical and threatens to turn the movie into a made-for-TV pot boiler. In the novel by Robert Traver, Mary Pilant is not Quill's daughter and she provides no last-minute testimony. It would have been better if Preminger and Traver had resisted the temptation to melodrama and remained true to the determined irresolution that marks the movie everywhere and is maintained even in its conclusion. As critic Mattie Lucas observes: "The decision reached by the jury makes sense . . . so does the alternative."[4]

The advantage of this irresolution is that it takes the focus away from the usual concerns and questions—Who did what to whom? Who is the hero? Who is the villain? Was justice done?—and puts it on the back and forth of legal tactics, the maneuvering by lawyers within the four corners of the judicial arena. The figure who presides over this arena, noting the outcome of minor skirmishes and major battles, is Judge Weaver, who is at once above the fray and its most important player. The significant thing about the appearance of Joseph N. Welch as Judge Weaver is that it is without any significance. Given his role in bringing down Senator McCarthy, and given director Preminger's long-standing opposition to censorship and his recent public hiring of blacklisted screenwriter Dalton Trumbo for the movie *Exodus*, it would be reasonable to assume that Welch was cast in order to make a political point. But there isn't a whiff of politics in his scenes, nor, for that matter, in any scene. Biegler was defeated by Lodwick in an election, but we never learn anything about what partisan issues may have been in play. There is no hint of any political position taken by Bielger, Parnell, Maida Rutledge, Frederick Manion, Laura Manion, Claude Dancer, Mitch Lodwick, or Mary Pilant. The year is 1959, and there is plenty going on—the still potent red scare, the end of Eisenhower's tenure as president, the anticipated contest between Richard M. Nixon and John F. Kennedy, space probes, the ever-present cold war—but none of it makes its way into the movie. The casting of Welch is a feint: it leads you to expect something that never arrives.

To a lesser extent, the same is true of Laura's sexuality: it smolders and half-erupts, it is the starting point of the whole story, it is a component of every scene between her and Polly, it turns courtroom testimony into an erotic encounter. When Dancer questions her, he moves to within an inch of her face, and the camera frames the two as if it were photographing a seduction; he moves in and out, advancing, then retreating, and then advancing a bit further. In the end, one effect of her testimony in this scene is to reinforce the suggestion that her very presence arouses aggressive male ardor. And yet, with all of this, the only legal question is whether Frederick Manion was or was not in the grip of an irresistible impulse, and that question can be asked and answered independently of what his wife did or didn't do. (The fact of a dissociative reaction does not depend on the empirical status of the trauma-producing stimulus.) The sexual byplay between Laura and almost everyone she encounters may fill up many screen moments, but, in the end, it is only tangentially related to the movie's core value—good lawyering.

Another love story (thoroughly sexless) is inextricably bound up with that value. It is identified when Polly says that there are two things he loves, fishing and an old man named Parnell Emmett McCarthy. The love is reciprocated, and what cements it is a dedication to the law; not to legal outcomes, or to legally engineered policies, but to the study and performance of a craft. In the beginning of the movie, it is mostly study: Polly has no practice to speak of and McCarthy is a long-time drunk for reasons never explained. The importance to both of the "big" case is not the fee they may earn (of course there is none; Manion lights out for parts unknown) or the justice they might do, but the chance to be once again in the arena. The success that crowns their efforts is not the verdict, but what has happened in the course of their effort to achieve it: they have become a team. As they ride to the trailer park in Polly's convertible (somehow more jaunty than it was in the opening scenes), Polly says, "I got one good thing out of this case, a new law partner, if it's all right with him?" This is, in effect, a marriage proposal, and the response is immediate. "He'd be proud to have his name on a shingle with yours." *Anatomy of a Murder* is not usually classified as a "romance of marriage" movie (a genre defined by Stanley Cavell[5]), but it is. What we know as it ends is that Polly and Parnell will live happily together forever after. (In the novel, Polly and Mary Pilant are in the early stages of a romantic involvement; in the movie she is just the new firm's first client.)

Polly and Parnell's union will be well defined and bounded: it occupies the area of a shingle that says this is where we are and who we are. Neither is going anywhere; one can't imagine the small-town Polly moving to Detroit or even to Lansing. Their relationship, then, stands in contrast to, and as a defense against, the relationship between Laura and Manny, which is volatile, unstable, and always on the wing, as they are. (Laura tells Polly that she was attracted to Manny because he was always ready to "go.") The Manions, singly and together, represent a force that threatens equilibrium and security; equilibrium and security are the values Polly and Parnell finally affirm, and it is best for them that Laura and Manny aren't around, even if it means the loss of a fee; the centrifugal energy they stand for and display is a danger to the contained lives the new partners want to lead. Two small moments illustrate the point. Early on, Polly asks Laura if she wears a girdle. She replies, "I don't need a girdle. Do you think I need a girdle?" That is, do I need to be held in? Later in the trial, the issue of confinement is raised again. This time it is a hat that holds her in. Dancer wants to know what kind of hair she has under the hat. "We'd be pleased," Polly says, "to show the court Mrs Manion's hair," and he asks her to take the hat off. She complies and shakes her hair free with a joyous expression on her face, as if to say, at last I can be myself. (It is a moment that bears comparison with our first sight of Rita Hayworth in *Gilda* (1946) and of Natalie Wood in *Marjorie Morningstar* (1958).) In their last meeting on the courthouse steps, just before the verdict is announced, Laura pulls a girdle out of her handbag and says, "Here's a souvenir for you." Polly hands it back: "You'd better keep that; you might need it sometime." Not likely. She will always be breaking free of confinement, just as he will always wear a girdle; its name is the law.

10

Sex, Class, and Class Action

North Country

In another movie with a breathtakingly beautiful woman at its center, *North Country* (2005), domesticity and settled place are sought-after conditions in a landscape that is both physically harsh and harsh in its limitation of possibilities. The setting is a company-owned town in Northern Minnesota. Everyone lives and works in the shadow of a huge mine; there is no escaping it, visually, commercially, or culturally. The inhabitants' aspirations are modest—a job, a house and enough pocket money to go at night to the local watering hole for a drink or a dance. As the movie opens, Josey Aimes (Charlize Theron) has none of these things. She has just left an abusive husband and moved in with her parents (Sissy Spacek and Richard Jenkins), two young children in tow. Glory, an old friend (Frances McDormand), drives a truck at the mine, and persuades her to apply for a position there. She does so and is hired, only to experience, as do her female co-workers, extensive and sustained sexual harassment. After trying unsuccessfully to enlist others in an organized protest, she goes it alone and files the first class action suit asserting sexual harassment and discrimination against women. (The movie is based on an actual case, *Jenson* v. *Eveleth Taconite Company* (1997).)[1]

In other movies that pit ordinary men and women against large corporations and utilities (*Erin Brockovich*, *Dark Waters*, *A Civil Action*), the everyday lives of the chief protagonists are not front and center. Rather, they are the material of subplots that to some extent put a human face on the abstractions the director is really interested in. Do we really care about Erin's relationship with her sometimes boyfriend. No, what we care about is whether Pacific Gas and Electric will finally be held

Law at the Movies. Stanley Fish, Oxford University Press. © Stanley Fish (2024).
DOI: 10.1093/oso/9780198898726.003.0011

accountable for its crimes by Julia Roberts and Albert Finney. In *North Country*, the relationship between Josey and her children is paramount; her interest in Pearson Mines is instrumental; it is at once the potential means to her stated goal—to have a good job at the local iron mine, to own a house, and to be able to take care of her family—and the obstacle to that same goal as long as its administration allows and even encourages the behavior that undermines her dignity and sense of self. For her, the triumphant moment is not when a judge grants her the class action she seeks, but when, in the movie's final scene, she has the leisure and freedom from anxiety to teach her son Sammy how to drive. At that moment the sun comes out for the first time, the snow is gone, the landscape is inviting, and the road beckons her forward. The mine, visible in some of its effects (denuded hills), does not dominate; its presence, massive though it may be, is not dictating her action or filling up her thoughts. What she has found by persisting in her lawsuit is not freedom from the mine's influence (it will always be there), but the satisfaction of having taken a step no one thought possible and the knowledge that she can in the future take other steps, should she wish to.

It is not the mine that is Josey's enemy; her enemy is the culture of which the mine is a symbol, a culture that uses the mine as a convenient alibi for inaction. The hallmark of that culture is an acquiescence in the conditions one finds oneself in, a conviction, residing deep in one's being, that the way things are is the way things will always be and that there's nothing you can do about it. Everyone, including Josey at the beginning, is gripped by that conviction, no one more so than her high-school boyfriend and now daily tormentor, Bobby Sharp (Jeremy Renner). Bobby is no simple villain; he is someone whose character had been formed and wounded by an act of cowardice. When he and Josey were classmates, he saw her being raped by a teacher, and, rather than coming to her aid, he ran away. Years later, he is her co-worker at the mine, where he alternately harasses her and comes on to her. It is as if he were seeking a response that would retroactively justify his refusal to help her; she's just a whore, after all. When Josey reports him to the union, he denies everything and puts out the word that she has been pursuing him. Mine-owner Pearson has been seeking a witness who will testify to Josey's promiscuity; the reasoning is that she can hardly be the victim of sexual advances if she is and has always been a sexual aggressor. He finds Bobby, who is eager to say on the stand that

Josey was never raped, but initiated and enjoyed the encounter with her teacher.

But then he is cross-examined by Josey's lawyer, Bill White (Woody Harrelson), who challenges not only his testimony, but his manhood. What kind of hockey player are you, he asks (everyone in town plays hockey and White had been a high-school star), a red-ice player or a yellow-ice player? A red-ice player, White explains, leaves everything he has on the arena floor, including his blood. A yellow-ice player wets his pants and runs away when "things get tough." What kind are you? Despite objections by Pearson's attorney—hired, he tells her, because she was the best *woman* lawyer he could find—and admonitions by the Judge, White continues to hammer Bobby. "Why didn't you help her?" "She was your friend." "You want to run right now, don't you?" "Are you going to stand up and be a man?" Battered and defensive, Bobby blurts out, "What was I supposed to do?," a question he repeats a moment later. "What was I supposed to do?" Suddenly we see Bobby, not as the malign agent of a misogynistic culture, but as a victim of that culture. When he runs away from the sight of his friend being raped, he is acting as he has been conditioned to act by a lifetime of seeing women objectified and mistreated by entitled men, a lifetime lived in a place where you are expected to do what those around you have always done. He means his question. He literally doesn't know what else to do. Nothing in his experience pointed to an alternative, and it is only when he has been pushed into a corner by Bill White that he finds that alternative, by accident, as it were. Backed to the wall, he tells the truth.

We never know whether this involuntary outburst of truth leads to a lasting change in his behavior (we never see him again), but we do see its immediate effects on others. The judge had said that he would allow a class action suit to proceed if there were at least three plaintiffs. Up to this point, there has only been Josey. Immediately after Bobby answers "yeah" to the question "He was raping her, wasn't he ?," Josey's friend Glory, now disabled by Lou Gehrig's Disease, has her husband read a statement ending, "I stand with Josey." She cannot stand, but others can. First Sherry (whose porta-potty had been tipped over with her in it), and then Big Betty, and then, in a *Spartacus* moment, many of the female mineworkers and some of the men rise in testimony. (In a nice touch, director Niki Caro has two of the women involved in the actual case stand up, too.) These same women had earlier signed affidavits declaring that they had never seen or experienced harassment. They were doing what they thought they had to do; they were going along with the circumstances they had always endured. They told Josey it was no use, that she was making trouble, that nothing would change, that they needed their jobs. They were acting in the way a supervisor (male, of course) urged on them. "Take it like a man." That's what they knew, what they accepted in ignorance and/or denial of any other course. By their collective inaction in the face of unspeakable abuse, they were saying, "What were we supposed to do?" Now, in the wake of Bobby's forced example, they know.

As it unfolds, we have no context for the strategy White employs in his cross-examination of Bobby, but one is provided in a scene cut, unfortunately, from the finished film. It is the night before the trial's crucial day. Josey and Bill have been prepping, and he is clearly upset. Josey assumes that he is nervous about attempting to do something that had never been done—bring a class action suit based on sexual harassment. No, says Bill, "I haven't tried *any* case before." He was, he tells her "the big settler," adept at explaining to clients (his colleagues' clients as well as his own) why trials, even when the evidence is seemingly favorable to you, are always a risk. He counseled plaintiffs to take the money and run rather than staying the course and perhaps suffering a loss. He has never lost a case, he explains, because he withdrew from the field before hand-to-hand combat began. Chosen by Josey to be the instrument of her unwillingness to settle, he turns out to be a serial settler himself. Suddenly, a question never explicitly asked but hanging around the edges—why has the former hockey star and big-time New York lawyer come back to this stifling little town?—is answered. He has come back to settle once again, to settle down in a chair at the bar with Kyle (Glory's husband) and accept the homage he receives (people ask for his autograph) because of past glories. He has come back to join the women mineworkers (who take it like a man), Josey's father (who only comes to her aid late in the game), her mother (who explains, as if it were a cogent excuse, that Josey's husband beat her because he didn't have a job), Glory (who for most of the movie urges her to have a tougher skin), and of course Bobby (who has spent his entire life until now taking care not to stray from the town's explicit and implicit mores). Although he doesn't ask the question directly, Bill is saying to Josey, "What was I supposed to do?"

Josey, unwilling to settle, answers in no uncertain terms: "You stand up. Whether you win or lose, you stand up." These are the very words Bill utters when Bobby asks for the second time, "What was I supposed to do?" "You stand up. You stand up and tell the truth. You stand up for your friends. You stand up, even when you're all alone." In the version of the movie without the deleted scene, the version sent into the world by the director, Bill comes across as a principled champion of truth-telling, no matter what. But the deleted scene tells us that his dramatically appealing affirmation is borrowed from Josey, who has tutored him the night before and lent him both her language and her courage, the same courage she ends up lending to her parents, to Glory, to Sherry, to Big Betty, and to everyone who rises to be counted.

Just a day earlier, she herself had faced a choice between settling for a *modus vivendi* and taking a step she had long feared. When she and Bobby give opposing accounts of what happened between her and her teacher, the one fact they agree on—intercourse did occur—supplies an answer to a question Pearson's attorney has been asking since the beginning of the movie: "Who is Sammy's father?" The trial runs concurrently with the narrative of the events leading up to it; it is always going on. But for the viewer of the early scenes, the point of the trial is obscure. Why is the question of Sammy's parentage being raised? What does that have to do with violence against women and a class action suit focused on workplace harassment? Such questions assume that the legal fact of abuse in a non-domestic place (the mine) and the private lives of the concerned parties are two different things. But the assumption is false. The attitudes and prejudices that flower in acts of intentional degradation in the mine take seed and grow in the houses, playgrounds, and churches, where gender hierarchies are entrenched and taken for granted. Behavior of a scripted kind follows more or less inevitably. Josey's rape and her treatment at the hands of her male co-workers have the same source, the culture to whose strength Bobby testifies when he cries, "What was I supposed to do?"

Josey folds herself into that same culture when she remains silent about the rape and tells Sammy a story about a soldier-lover who died in the army before they could marry. She is still hiding the truth when Pearson's attorney asks her, "Who is Sammy's father?" and she replies, "I don't know who Sammy's father is." After Bobby's testimony, there is nowhere to hide. The identity of Sammy's father is out in the open, and, in response to the public revelation, Sammy runs away, although only to Kyle and Glory's house. When he comes back, Josey finally has the conversation she has been dreading "since the day you were born." What is surprising is that the conversation is centered, not on the rape, but on the moment when the question of paternity ceased to matter for her. It happened when she first felt Sammy stirring inside her. Then I knew, she says, that "you weren't his; you were mine and we're going to be in it together." "You had nothing to do with that ugliness," she tells him, which means also that *she* had nothing to do with that ugliness. Indeed, the agent of the ugliness is erased without a trace; there is no acknowledgment, no child support, no visitations, no nothing; it is as if he had never existed. She is entirely free of him even as a memory, and that freedom extends to the other men she will no longer rely on. She doesn't need a husband or a boyfriend to take care of her (she bristles when Bill White suggests that, because she is a beautiful woman, some man will drive up and take her away from all this); she doesn't need a father to speak up for her; she doesn't need a supervisor to look out for her; she doesn't need a lawyer to rescue her, and she doesn't need a man to teach her son how to drive. It is as if she has achieved the Amazonian fantasy of doing entirely without men. She has made a place for herself by herself and her children, and that's all she ever wanted.

Sammy will now live in that place where before he was in danger of being appropriated by the town and its ways. To be more precise, he was in danger of turning into Bobby Sharp, whom he very much resembles (they share a "Dutch boy" haircut) and whose public vilification of his mother he has internalized (he repeatedly calls her a whore and a liar). Now, after Josey tells him the whole truth and pledges no more "secrets between us," he accepts her assertion that they are in it together and form a unit that functions independently of anything anyone—Bobby Sharp, her co-workers, their wives, her mother's friends, her ex-husband—might say. Of all the things she can be said to have saved—her job, her house, her reputation—the most important thing she saves is Sammy.

So Josey gets what she wants, and what she wants is not coterminous with her legal victory. Her story is smaller (and yet in a way larger) than the story of the first class action suit alleging sexual harassment in the workplace. It is smaller because it is domestic; the larger stage on which the drama plays out is significant for her only because it is a necessary means to securing the stable family situation she yearns for. The fact that what she did (or to be more precise what the person she fictionalizes did) led to a revolution in workplace relations, and improvements in the status of women, would no doubt please her, but she says nothing about that. She just wants to get in the car with her son. It is director Niki Caro's achievement to make a powerful statement that can be generalized to the lives of all women without sacrificing the delicate and complex life of one woman to an abstraction, no matter how important it may be.

North Country is the only movie I consider in these pages that would meet the requirements of the Bechdel test. A movie passes the test, devised by cartoonist Alison Bechdel in 1985, if (1) it features two women in leading roles, (2) the women engage in conversation with one another, and (3) the conversation is not about a man.[2] With three Academy Award winners (Theron, McDormand, Spacek) in prominent roles, *North Country* easily satisfies the first prong. And conversations between women (Josey and Glory, Josey and her mother, Josey and her female colleagues) occupy much of the screen time. The third prong is a bit problematic. Since Josey, Glory, Big Betty, Sherry, and the rest of the cohort are usually complaining about the abuse they suffer at the hands of Bobby and his friends, they are necessarily talking about men. When Alice Aimes and her daughter talk, it is about the effect of Josey's action on her father's self-esteem. And, when all is said and done, the hyper-masculine values that produce an atmosphere as toxic as the mine's taconite (the mine and the town it dominates are mirrors of one another) are not repudiated or even significantly weakened. To be sure, Josey can get her job back, porta-potties and other accommodations to female anatomy will be provided, Sherry will be able to continue looking after her impaired mother, Alice will have imparted a mild feminist lesson to her husband Hank by staying in a motel until he is properly sympathetic to his daughter's plight. These are gains, steps forward, but they do not amount to anything like an overturning of patriarchy, which is still in charge as the movie ends, albeit with some modifications. One is impressed again by Caro's modesty. Just as she declines to dwell on the global significance of the story she is telling (although on-screen messages at the conclusion of the story declare that significance), so does she decline to dramatize a full-scale feminist awakening or the throwing-off of male-forged shackles. Her lesson is quieter though no less affecting; it is embodied in the simple act of driving down the road on a nice day.

The refusal of *North Country* to be a message-film celebrating the unambiguous triumph of virtue is reflected in the music that fills it, music that seems at times to affirm key elements of the culture the film is critiquing. In the extended bar scene, Big Betty leads the girls in a rousing chorus of "Hit Me with Your Best Shot." The song can be heard as either a feminist anthem—"Knock me down, it's all in vain | I'll get right back on my feet again"—or as a rueful acknowledgment of male domination—"You better make sure | You put me in my place." A similar ambivalence informs the songs of Bob Dylan, which are played throughout. Dylan, a son of the Minnesota North country himself, can't say something nice about a woman without wrapping it in a piece of misogyny: "You know a woman like you should be at home, | That's where you belong | Taking care of somebody nice | Who don't know how to do you wrong." These verses from "What's a Sweetheart like you Doing in a Dump like this?" are sung by Dylan in the movie's last scene and through most of the credits. The image they present of a beautiful woman who finds refuge in the home of a kind man is the very image Josey rejects when Bill White offers it to her. What's a song like that doing in a movie like this? It's no better with "Lay, Lady, Lay," a love song made up of equal parts of desire and the need to possess. "Lay, lady, lay, lay across my big brass bed." In short, submit to me. Even the much admired "Girl from the North Country" is an exercise in objectification: the singer doesn't so much want the girl as he wants the memory of the girl, preserved for ever at a distance and through the filter of someone else's eyes: "See for me," he implores, as the flesh and blood beauty is replaced by a narrated beauty he need not ever meet. The song is Dylan's "Ode on a Grecian Urn." It is that kind of worship performed by the male gaze that Josey never solicits but is always subjected to because she is so beautiful.

This leads me finally to a speculation about casting. What if Theron and McDormand had exchanged roles? Would the movie still work? As a feminist statement, it might even be stronger. It is something of a cheat, after all, to have the woman in distress be a great beauty. The injury done to her would be no less an injury if a less spectacular (a word whose etymology I stress) person suffered it. Or are we to understand, as Josey seems to, that her beauty is a burden that makes her all the more vulnerable to the malign energies that emanate from a male world? I don't know the answer.

11

Speech, Radical Innocence, and the Law

Billy Budd

Another beauty, this time male, takes center stage in Peter Ustinov's 1962 adaptation (he is the co-writer, director, producer, and co-star) of Herman Melville's novella *Billy Budd*. The novella and film tell the story of the "handsome sailor" Billy (Terence Stamp, Academy Award nominee in his first role) who is immensely likeable, truth-telling, hard-working, without artifice, and ready to lend a helping hand. He bears malice toward no one, and his generosity of spirit extends to his moral and characterological opposite, Master at Arms John Claggart (the great Robert Ryan), a dark, brooding intellectual whose deepest conviction is that everyone in the world is rotten and corrupt at the core. Billy's very existence is at once a challenge and an affront to that conviction; a challenge because, if Budd is as innocent and pure as he seems to be, the conviction must be given up, and an affront for the same reason. The old sailor called Dansker, played by Melvyn Douglas, says of Claggart that he "bore malice toward a grace he could not have." Driven by the need to demonstrate to himself and everyone else that Billy is no better than he should be, Claggart contrives to provoke him into rash and subversive acts, but he fails until, in the presence of Captain Vere (Ustinov), he accuses the young foretopman of inciting his fellow sailors to mutiny, a serious charge at any time and made more serious by the recent occurrence of a notorious mutiny aboard a ship named *Nore*. Asked by Vere for his response, Billy falls victim to his only physical defect, a stutter that emerges in moments of stress, and is unable to speak. Instead, he signifies his denial

Law at the Movies. Stanley Fish, Oxford University Press. © Stanley Fish (2024).
DOI: 10.1093/oso/9780198898726.003.0012

of the charge with a blow to Claggart's temple, a blow that immediately kills the Master at Arms, who dies with a smile on his face, pleased because Billy's act, he thinks, has vindicated his view of mankind. At a hastily assembled drumhead court martial, there is agreement that Billy was innocent of any intention to harm Claggart, but Vere argues that, according to the Mutiny Act, the accused's intention is beside the point. The only thing that counts is the fact that a sailor has struck an officer, a hanging offense no matter what damage has or has not been done. Billy is found guilty and then hung to the distress of his fellows who seem about to mutiny when a French man-of-war emerges suddenly from a cove and attacks. The men rally and fight for king and country.

Everything in *Billy Budd* revolves around the person and character of the title figure. The "handsome sailor" has another nickname that draws us into the center of the story's meditation on the relationship between good and evil. He is called "baby" by Dansker in the novella and by foretopman Jenkins in the film, a term of endearment that is also a quite literal characterization of his condition. The Latin word for baby is "infans," without speech. Billy, of course, can speak (except at the fatal moment), but so simple and direct is his speech that it forfeits the capacity that is at once speech's greatest glory and its greatest infirmity, the capacity to detach itself from the referent (the physical world or the interior world of the mind and heart) it supposedly serves and create a world of its own where words, rather than being tied to an object external to them, float free of constraint and go in any direction their user desires. It is in the space opened up when speech is not tethered to a prior reality that lies, deceptions, exaggerations, hyperboles, and artful ambiguities flourish. None of these is in Billy's repertoire. Melville's narrator says of him, "To deal in double meanings and insinuations of any sort was quite foreign to his nature."[1] His physical presence, including his speech, is the unadorned and unmediated expression of his inner being; the captain of *The Rights of Man*, the ship from which Billy was impressed, declares "a virtue went out of him."[2] Every action issues from "the harmony within" (Melville).[3] In a conversation with Claggart (in the film, not the book), Billy is asked, "Is it ignorance or irony that makes you speak so simply?" Billy answers, "It must be ignorance because I don't understand the other word." It is not the word but the practice that he does not understand. Irony is the art of saying one thing while meaning another. Billy can neither engage in that behavior nor recognize it when it is directed at him. He isn't ignorant; he's innocent. He is, says Melville, an "upright barbarian [in the original Greek sense of primitive and uncivilized], much such perhaps as Adam presumably might have been ere the urbane Serpent wriggled himself into his company."[4] In this configuration, his opposite is Claggart, the urbane serpent who can no more understand innocence than Billy can understand evil. In an "aesthetic way," Melville tell us, Claggart sees "the charm of it . . . and fain would have shared it, but he despaired of it."[5]

It is no accident that in Melville's descriptions of Billy and Claggart we hear echoes of Milton. Melville was an ardent Miltonist, and Billy is a composite of several of Milton's characters. The first, obviously, is Adam, described in *Paradise Lost* as the image of his glorious maker in whom shone "Truth, wisdom, sanctitude." He stands in "naked majesty," and "His fair large front and eye sublime declared | Absolute rule; and hyacinthine locks | Round from his parted forelock manly hung | Clust'ring, but not beneath his shoulders broad."[6] The verb "declared" does not mean that he said something, but that his body and presence speak for him, indeed speak him. No one in his presence need guess at his intentions or disposition; they radiate from within. Exactly the same congruence of inner and outer is attributed to Christ in *Paradise Regained* by Satan, who, like Claggart, is admiring despite himself. "Thy actions to thy words accord, thy words | To thy large heart give utterance due, thy heart | Contains of good, wise, just, the perfect shape."[7] There is no distance between what is in his heart and what issues either from his body or from his mouth. The third Milton character who shares with Billy a capacity for virtue (which is at the same time an incapacity) is the archangel Uriel, who in book 3 of *Paradise Lost* fails to recognize Satan when, disguised as a youthful angel, he asks for directions to Paradise. Uriel obligingly replies: "That spot to which I point is Paradise | Adam's abode, those lofty shades his bow'r. | Thy way thou canst not miss, me mine requires."[8] The irony is that the dedicated servant of God has facilitated the potential destruction of God's most recent work. But Milton has already anticipated that judgment and discounted it by characterizing Uriel's failure before it occurs in poem time as a sign of his rectitude. Because he is entirely good and honest, Uriel is incapable of discerning evil and dishonesty in another:

> oft though wisdom wake, suspicion sleeps
> at wisdom's gate, and to simplicity
> Resigns her charge, while goodness thinks no ill
> Where no ill seems: which now for once beguiled
> Uriel, though Regent of the Sun, and held
> The sharpest sighted spirit of all in Heav'n.

The more sharp-sighted he is, the more upright he is, the less able is he to "discern | Hypocrisy, the only evil that walks | Invisible."[9] His virtue demands and assures failure. The same is true for Billy, who, when Dansker tries to warn him of Claggart's malign intentions, dismisses the warning because all he knows are the ready smiles Claggart sends in his direction. The idea that those smiles issue from a foul heart that means him harm never occurs to him, for "goodness thinks no ill | Where no ill seems."

Although *Billy Budd*, like *Paradise Lost* and *Paradise Regained*, is a drama of temptation, there is a difference and a significant one. In both Milton poems, the tempter is the Prince of Darkness, and his target is the upright bearer of virtue. In *Billy Budd*, however, it is Claggart who finds himself responding to the blandishments, innocently offered, of his intended victim. The scene (not in the novella) occurs at night. Billy and Claggart are topside, silhouetted against the dark sky, the sound of water lapping at the ship. Billy begins the conversation by remarking that "the sea is clam and peaceful." A bit later Claggart replies, "Calm above, but below a world of gliding monsters preying on their fellows." Obviously, he is referring to the world in general, not just the world beneath the surface of the sea, and, also obviously, he believes, or, rather, has a stake in believing, that Billy, beneath *his* tranquil surface, is such a monster. On this occasion, however, Claggart is interested not in ensnaring or exposing Billy but in understanding him. He wants to know, first, why Billy contradicted his account of how foretopman Jenkins (sent aloft by Claggart, who knew he was ill) died; and, second, why Billy neither fears nor hates him as the other men do. His query on the first point is answered with the very simplicity that defeats Claggart's wiles: "I only knew the truth and I told it." On the second point, Billy reports that he tells his fellows that the Master at Arms isn't as they think he is, because "no man can take pleasure in cruelty." (The movie has already shown Claggart taking pleasure in the floggings he has ordered.) Where Claggart assumes a general depravity, Billy assumes a general benevolence, and thinks that perhaps Claggart's apparently mean-spirited actions are ones he regrets: "I think that sometimes you hate yourself." Do you dare, asks Claggart, "to understand me?" Billy answers, "I think so, sir," and, after remarking that all men are occasionally lonely, he observes that the nights on board ship are particularly lonely and suggests that perhaps the two of them could meet and "talk between watches." "It would mean a lot to me," Billy says, and Claggart admits, "Perhaps to me too."

But, upon hearing himself say that, Claggart recoils from the exchange and recognizes its danger, a danger already more than half-realized: "Oh no, you would charm *me* too?" It's bad enough that Captain Vere, the other officers, and all the men are seduced by Billy; the boy would also seduce him and seems a fair way to having done so, albeit with no intention. Claggart resists temptation's lure in the classic manner by pushing it away. "Get away," he says twice, and he is overheard by his minion Squeak, who emerges from the shadow he always occupies to ask a question that is more pertinent than he knows: "What's the get-me-behind-thee for?" Claggart shows how well he understands what has just happened: "Which of us is Satan then?" Claggart is wryly noting that the purity of his misanthropy is threatened by Billy who occupies the tempter's role. In this reverse scenario, it is very clear: Claggart is at this moment just like Milton's Satan when he is so taken with the sight of Eve that he stands "abstracted . . . | From his own evil" and is for an instant "stupidly good." That is, good in an unthinking, unreflective way. But the instant passes, and he is returned, Milton tells us, to the "hot Hell that always in him burns."[10] So it is with Claggart: when Squeak reports his failure to draw Billy into rebellion, he becomes again what he has always been and proceeds immediately to tell lies about Billy to Captain Vere.

In the confrontation that follows (the dramatic centerpiece of the movie), everyone is true to himself. At first Vere doesn't want to hear Claggart out; he has duties to perform and is a stickler with respect to official obligations. Claggart comes quickly to the point and accuses Billy. Vere reminds him of the punishment for false witness—always the rules and regulations in mind—and sends for Billy. Claggart repeats the accusation with embellishments, adding Dansker and Squeak by name to the list of would-be mutineers; as he speaks, the camera cuts to Vere's face; he plainly disbelieves Claggart, and is eager to hear Billy's denial. "Speak, Budd, defend yourself." Billy works his mouth, but nothing comes out. Claggart presses: "it's not that he can't find the words; it is that there are no words to find." In a way, that's right. Words are representations, always one or more degrees removed from the source they convey and with which they are never identical. No words would be an adequate substitute for the speech of one's entire being; and it is that authentic speech or rather that action more authentic than speech that Billy provides when his arm shoots out. Remarking on Billy's incorrupt nature—he seemed "one to whom not yet has been proffered the questionable apple of knowledge"—Melville likens him to "the illiterate nightingale . . . sometimes the composer of his own song."[11] The nightingale's song, of course, is precisely *not* composed; no self-conscious act produces it; it just comes out, as does Billy's arm. Had Billy found the words, had he "composed" an utterance, he would not have been speaking truly. Far from being an act of gratuitous violence that might have found a better expression in words, Billy's blow is an act of authenticity and virtue. His inability to speak is a perfect (non)sign of his radical innocence.

Lieutenant Radcliffe agrees: "You don't hang a man for speaking the only way he could." Lieutenant Seymour says the same thing: "You can't condemn the boy for answering with his arm for lack of words." Seymour insists on a purity of motive that informs Billy's act. Vere counters by severing the act from the spirit/intention that generated it. The Mutiny Act has no concern with the reasons impelling the rule-breaker; if you go by the book, the fact that the rule has been broken is the beginning and end of the matter. Had "fair process of law" been allowed to unfold, Billy would have been acquitted, Claggart would have hung for false witness, and justice would have been done; but by his blow, says Vere, Billy "has prevented that and turned the law against himself." Later, in the court martial when Seymour had been brought around to Vere's position, he says to Lieutenant Wyatt: "We do not deal with justice, but with the law." Wyatt replies: "Was not the one conceived to serve the other?" The answer Vere gives is "no." In his view, the law exists to provide order, and, in a world where the next mutiny is just around the corner, "[w]e must cling to what vestiges of order we have." For Vere, the law is not the reflection of an overarching abstract value, but an artificially created bulwark between us and the gliding monsters Claggart sees everywhere.

The "we" in Vere's statement includes everyone except Billy and Claggart, who have a different relationship to justice and law from that of anyone else. Vere marks the difference precisely when he says to Billy, "You in your goodness are as inhuman as Claggart is in his evil." They are inhuman because the response of each to circumstances is a function of what they carry within them and not of any empirical calculation of outcomes. A mere human being is always calculating, guessing, hazarding, trying to figure out what to do next, hoping that the choices made are the right ones or at least ones that will count on the side of survival. If you are a mere human, nothing can protect you from the awful contingency (the absence of surety and certainty) that is at the heart of fallen life, not wealth or rank or command. Vere admits at the outset that "the fact that I command does not relieve me of doubts; on the contrary, it magnifies them." Billy and Claggart have no doubts because for each of them in different ways the structure and meaning of the universe are clear and stable. They are less characters, confused, ambivalent, and complicated, than they are allegorical creatures, abstract representations of the virtue and vice they figure forth. The *Avenger* is merely the location of their epic opposition: it is not where they live. In fact, it is not known where they live or where they come from. Billy knows neither his age nor his parentage nor his place of birth; he was found (he has been told) "in a pretty silklined basket hanging one morning from the knocker of a good man's door."[12] Claggart's origins are similarly mysterious. Vere asks Seymour, "What do you know about Claggart before he came aboard the ship?" The reply: "Not much, nobody does." Called to testify in the court martial, Dansker identifies Claggart as a demon of pride who just appears one day and whose baleful influence is ever-growing: "Ever since the Master at Arms came aboard *from God knows where* I have seen his shadow lengthen along the deck." (The image is one we might recall from innumerable Dracula movies.) The spreading shadow of Claggart's malignity is the exact opposite of the spreading benevolence that attends Billy's participation in any scene. In the novella, the captain of *The Rights of Man* tells Radcliffe that before Billy came aboard, "my forecastle was a ratpit of quarrels," but simply by the "virtue that went out of him," the ship has been made a "happy family."[13] The effect these two men produce is independent of any specific thing they do; it is their very presence, their mode of being, that is the most powerful of actions. What they are is not dictated by the world; the world they happen to inhabit is configured by what they are. One could say, therefore, that the *Avenger* is a battlefield being fought over by two almost supernatural forces. Victory in either direction will alter the vessel's character. Will the ship be a fear-infested warren where actions issue from avarice, malice, envy, cynicism, fear, and ambition, or will the ship be a happy family, like the family Billy created just by being Billy?

In the end, these questions are mooted when both Claggart and Billy die and can no longer be responsible for what the *Avenger* becomes. That responsibility belongs to Vere and the other officers who are neither angels nor devils, but mere men of the middle sort, now left to their own devices and the resources available to them. The chief resource—the only guarantor of order in their impoverished landscape, the landscape Claggart described as "a world of gliding monsters preying on their fellows"—is the law, identified not with justice (that chimera never appears) but with rules that provide guidance even if that guidance is non-moral or amoral. Early on Vere reacts when a departure from a rule is characterized as a slight or minor infraction: "An infraction of any rule is serious." The infraction of any rule is serious because the social fabric is so fragile that any rent in it, however small, could lead to a general unraveling. Vere steers, both literally and metaphorically, between two related dangers—the ever present possibility of an encounter with a French warship, and the possibility, heightened by the memory of the recent Nore mutiny, that sailors, notoriously discontent, will break discipline and refuse to obey the ship's officers. If he is to be prepared to meet the first danger (which as a Captain in His Majesty's navy he seeks), he must forestall the second; he must, as he says, "forge" the men into a weapon so that "when the time comes" they will be able to perform and he will be able to lead them. "Shall we acquit ourselves well or badly?" he asks. He is in no way confident of the answer—remember, he admits to harboring multiplying doubts—and his actions are driven by his perceived need to maintain control ("I will be obeyed," he declares when *The Rights of Man* flees his pursuit) and his fear that control will be lost. The delicacy of his position with respect to the twin dangers awaiting him is illustrated when he chases after a small French ship he cannot possibly catch. Asked by Seymour why he perseveres nevertheless, he responds, "I know your objection," but "all I can do is lessen the tension on my own ship." So intent is he on tamping down whatever negative energies his men harbor within them, that he will expend military resources for no reason but to distract them from their complaints.

In the middle of this futile operation, the sailor Jenkins, known by both Claggart and his fellows to be seriously ill, falls to his death from the yardarm despite Billy's efforts to save him. At once, the sailor Kincaid turns to Claggart and shouts, "Damn your bloody eyes!" Soon after, Vere abandons the chase, and when the men are ordered by Claggart to hand in their arms, they do not respond. Vere enters and asks, "What is the matter, Master at Arms?" Claggart answers, "These dogs are out of temper," a statement that provokes Vere to assert his authority in no uncertain terms: "One lawless act, one spurt of rebel temper from any of you . . . and I will bend . . . or crush you if I must." He then asks Kincaid why he shouted at Claggart. Kincaid responds to the question with a question, "Why did Jenkins fall?" Claggart says he doesn't know, and Vere turns to the men for an answer. No one speaks, until Vere asks Billy why he left his post. Billy replies, "I knew Jenkins was sick. I saw him sway." Vere asks Claggart in an accusing tone, "Did you send a sick man aloft?" Claggart answers that Jenkins had first said that he was sick, but then changed his mind and went to stand his watch. Billy immediately demurs: "But that's not the way it happened. Don't you remember, Mr. Claggart?" Claggart: "That *is* the way it happened." Faced with two contradictory accounts, Vere must choose. He fills the right side of the screen and looks directly at Claggart and Billy standing side by side in the left side of the shot. A long pause during which Vere's face is expressionless. Finally he says, "I see." What he sees is that if he does not accept Claggart's defiant statement, he will in effect join those of his men (nearly all of them, it seems) who chafe under the Master at Arms' discipline and risk being a contributor to mutiny. So by his silence he casts his lot with Claggart, preferring the maintenance of order—earlier he has said of Claggarrt, "He is a force for order"—to truth and justice.

He does it again in the court martial. In this extended scene, all the arguments are out in the open. The arc they trace is the reverse of the one we saw in *12 Angry Men*. This time there is a near unanimous sentiment for acquittal; but under pressure from Vere's reasoning, his lieutenants come around one by one to a guilty verdict. The legal grounds are clear. Although Billy did not intend Claggart's death and struck him because his stammer left him with only that form of speech,

Budd's intent, declares Vere, is not to the point; according to the military code, the fact of the blow is sufficient to convict. Taking turns, Seymour, Radcliffe and Wyatt plead the case for both mercy and justice. How can we send a cripple to the gallows because he spoke the only way he could? "Can we adjudge to summary and shameful death a fellow creature we believe to be innocent?" "Couldn't we mitigate the penalty?"[14] "I can't sit by and let an innocent man hang?" To all this, Vere says, "Our consciences are private matters, but we are public men. Dare we give our consciences precedent over the code?" The question of conscience is mixed up with the question of what the men will do in the wake of either a conviction or an acquittal. If we judge him guilty, Wyatt speculates, they'll rescue him and string us up in his place. But if we pardon him, it could be seen as an act of weakness and the men could still revolt, answers Vere; and then "how weak our verdict will appear." The conclusion? "There is no escape." Wyatt, the youngest lieutenant, is the last holdout and Vere challenges him to find a better resolution: "Show us a way to save the boy and do our duty." Wyatt acknowledges that there is no way and yields.

The extraordinary thing is that Billy agrees. After the court martial, he asks, "Is there no hope for me?" Vere's answer indicates that he has been undone by his forensic victory: "What hope is there for any of us?" If doing one's duty requires actions like the one he has just set in motion, how is it possible to step correctly in this world. Billy has one additional question: "Why?" Vere muses aloud: "A child and his endless 'whys.' Why are there wars . . . a question to which grown men have lost the answer. The answer went with innocence." Billy, however, is not a grown man (he is the Peter Pan of sailors), and innocence, the inability to do or even think ill, remains the mark of his character even now. Vere tries to bring him over to the dark side where all grown men live by soliciting his hate: "Hate me, hate will help you conquer your fear." Billy's response is amazing and strikes to Vere's heart like a dagger: "I am not afraid. I did my duty and you are doing yours." This is intolerable: the injustice he knows he is doing is compounded by the unwillingness of his victim to feel wounded by it. Billy's generosity of spirit is a blow as fatal to Vere as was the blow that felled Claggart, and if he is only half-slain here, the deed is complete when, just as the noose is placed on his neck, Billy speaks his last words: "God bless Captain Vere," a blessing more magnanimous than "Forgive them, Father, for they know not what they do." (Vere knows.)

As the execution proceeds, Vere discards his hat, and stands in obvious anguish. When Seymour asks for "Permission to dismiss the men," Vere declines to participate any further in the public order to which he has given his soul: "You can do as you wish, Mr Seymour; it is of no further concern to me; I am only a man not fit to do the work of God or the devil." It is of no further concern to him because by removing his hat (a sign of his office) he has divested himself of the authority lent to him by a system—the system of the military and martial law—he now repudiates. No longer given identity and power by that system, he is now merely a man who cannot discern for himself, absent the direction of either godly revelation or diabolic manipulation, what to do; accordingly, he has decided to do nothing.

Seymour then gives the dismissal order, but to no effect; he tells Captain Hallam to fire on the ranks, but as he is about to do so, the French warship appears with cannons booming. After a few moments of hesitation, Kincaid rallies his fellows and the battle is joined. As this is happening, we see Billy's body on the left-hand side of the screen, inert and unattended to; a moment ago, it was the focus of everyone's attention and is now entirely forgotten. The issue of the struggle is uncertain; we see the body of an officer underneath a piece of sail; he is unidentified, but the suggestion is that it is Vere. (In the novella, Vere dies during an engagement that occurs after the events of Billy's hanging.) So the principle actors in the moral/legal drama—Billy, Vere, Claggart—are all dead; the only thing alive is the war which, as Vere says during the court-martial, was there before any of them were born and will still be there when they are dead. It is hard to overstate the degree to which the film presents a negative vision of the human condition. An injustice—Claggart's accusation—is followed by a tragic accident—Billy's blow—which is followed by another injustice—the law-driven outcome of the trial—which is followed by a hanging, which is followed by the wanton destruction attending naval engagement. In the context of these events, the moral drawn by a voice-over is either extraordinarily imperceptive or a joke: "Justice will live as long as the human soul and the law as long as the human mind." This pious statement belongs to another movie, not the one we have been watching or the one the characters live out. I am reminded of D. H. Lawrence's pronouncement: "Never trust the artist. Trust the tale."[15]

12

The Law and Storytelling

Amistad

There are many artists and many tales in Steven Spielberg's *Amistad* (1997), a movie about the relationship between storytelling and truth. There are a large number of stories in the film, most of them claiming to be the true account of the forty-four black men and women who are on trial in a Connecticut court for assault and murder. The opening scene of the film tells the story from the point of view of the accused. We see one of them, a man known as Cinqué, break free of his chains and then release his fellows, who join together to seize the ship transporting them, killing some of their captors in the process. Two of their captors, Ruiz and Montes, promise to take the ship, *The Amistad*, back to Africa, but instead bring the Africans to the coast of Connecticut, where they are captured and imprisoned. Questions abound: Who are they? Where did they come from? What is their status? Where were they being taken? Were their actions justified? What should be done with them? These questions are asked against the background of the many stories being told as the courtroom scenes play out.

- First, there is the national/political story of a presidential election. President Martin Van Buren (Nigel Hawthorne) is running for a second term. He needs the support of the southern states and especially of Senator John C. Calhoun of South Carolina (Arliss Howard). Calhoun and his colleagues would be displeased, to say the least, if the prisoners were acquitted and declared free men.
- Van Buren must also look to the treaty between the United States and Spain, whose ruler, a pre-teenage Isabella (Anna Paquin), claims the prisoners as her property. That's her story.

Law at the Movies. Stanley Fish, Oxford University Press. © Stanley Fish (2024).
DOI: 10.1093/oso/9780198898726.003.0013

- That claim is challenged by the salvage workers who towed *The Amistad* into shore and argue that its "merchandise" belongs to them. That's their story.
- But a prior claim is lodged by Ruiz and Montes, the two survivors of the shipboard rebellion, who tell the court that the slaves were purchased by them in Cuba—that's their story—and therefore are neither Spanish nor African.
- For the abolitionist Lewis Tappan (Stellan Skarsgård), the story is of the duty of Christians like him to save oppressed people. The specifically legal questions do not interest him; they are just "legal minutiae."
- The "legal minutiae" are all that matter to lawyer Roger Baldwin (Matthew McConaughey), for whom the relevant narrative context is property law. "Were they born slaves?" he asks. If they were, the question becomes whose property they are? "If not, they were illegally acquired," and what we have is "the wrongful transfer of illegal goods." Case and story closed.
- As all these stories are being told (and cross-told), one of the prisoners studies, insofar as he can, a Bible he has been given and becomes obsessed with the story of Jesus, who after being crucified "rose again into the sky." Cinqué says, "This is just a story."
- And, of course, there is the backstory of abduction and imprisonment told by Cinqué on the stand and presented by Spielberg as a dramatized flashback complete with babies thrown overboard. Unimpressed, Prosecutor Holabird (Pete Postletwhaite) says, "Quite a tale," and concedes that, "like all good works of fiction," Cinqué's story is "entertaining."
- The overall context for this carnival of stories is provided by ex-President John Quincy Adams (Anthony Hopkins), who, asked by former slave Theodore Joadson (Morgan Freeman) for legal advice, replies that what he has learned in his years as a lawyer is that "Whoever tells the best story wins." (In the end it will be he who tells the best story.)
- And, as a capstone to this battle of stories, the Supreme Court Justice (played by an actual Supreme Court Justice, Harry Blackmun), who in the penultimate scene gets to say who wins and, therefore, who has told the best story, is named, you guessed it, Story.

The movie's sustained meditation on story is intimately related to its meditation on language. In the early scenes, those who want to help the prisoners are unable to communicate with them. Baldwin needs to know where his clients are from, or, even more basically, who they are. They in turn can't make out the identity and function of those who surround them. They see some Christian abolitionists singing psalms and conclude that they are entertainers. (We as viewers are in a privileged position when we are provided with subtitles for the prisoners' conversations.) A linguist teaches Baldwin and Joadson how to count in Mende, the prisoners' language, and they walk around the harbor calling out numbers in that language. A sailor detaches himself from a conversation and identifies himself as James Covey (Chiwetel Ejiofor), a slave rescued by the British Navy who has chosen to stay in the west. He becomes the interpreter who acts as a middleman between the Mende and the Americans.

It would seem that the communication problem is solved. Baldwin is able to talk to his clients through Covey and prepare their case. But the issue of translation returns in a deeper form as the legal process unfolds. In two trials, the court seems sympathetic to the Mende. When Van Buren and his Secretary of State replace the first judge because they fear his verdict, the judge they handpick disappoints them by ruling in favor of the prisoners (now called the Africans) in even stronger terms. The claim of Spain is rejected outright, as is the claim of the salvagers; Ruiz and Montes are judged to be lying and subject to prosecution for having sworn that the forty-four blacks were purchased by them in Cuba; Cinqué and his fellows are declared citizens of their African tribe and set free. But Van Buren, fearful that, if the decision stands, the civil war that Senator Calhoun has been threatening will follow, appeals to the Supreme Court, and it is left to Baldwin to tell the rejoicing Africans (not yet released from prison) that they are rejoicing too soon.

It is when he tries to explain what has happened that language fails. Cinqué makes what is for him the obvious and conclusive point. You said, he reminds Baldwin, that, if there were a judgment for us, we would go free. Yes, replies Baldwin, but "I should have said . . ." Covey, the interpreter, interrupts to say that he cannot translate those words because there is no word for "should" in Mende. "Either you do something or you don't do it." In Mende, what you mean is what you say, and what you say is what you mean. Baldwin tries again,

"What I meant," he begins, but the interpreter stops him. They have no word for "meant" either, at least "not in the way you mean it." Baldwin means it as marking a distinction between what words, literally construed, say and what a speaker intended (meant) by them. In English, these two "realms" of meaning—utterance meaning and speaker's meaning—can come apart, as they do right here when Covey distinguishes between "mean" and "meant," and a speaker can play in the gap between them. In Mende, plain meaning occupies the entire communicative space, and the equivocations of intention (I said X, but I meant Y) are given no room. Baldwin has one more go at it: "What I said is almost how it works here . . . almost not always." But to Cinqué "almost" is just like "should" and "meant": it allows one to avoid responsibility for an assertion or a promise (I almost meant it, I almost did it); it contributes to a world where nothing is hard and fast.

Cinqué's response to that world and the language that reflects it is philosophical and wordless, or philosophical because wordless. In mid-conversation, he strides away, turns around, and, against a background of flames, strips off all his clothes and faces the camera in full frontal nudity. Here, he is saying without saying, is the real thing. No covering, no words, no layers of deception, just the elemental fact of me, naked and incapable of hiding behind clothes or language (Cinque's nakedness is the equivalent of Billy Budd's wordless blow). He does speak, but only to reject the "civilized" use of words: "What kind of place is this where you almost mean what you say, where laws almost work? How can you live like that?" These questions are addressed to everyone in the scene, but especially to Theodore Joadson, the only non-historical main character in the film. Joadson is a former slave who has been educated and has become prosperous. Two things about him stand out. He is well dressed, indeed overdressed—elegant coat and pants, cape, cravat, stylish top hat, cane—and he is the only figure as tall as Cinqué. As a result, when he receives Cinqué's question—"How can you live like that?"—the bodily similarity of the two large black men only accentuates the moral difference between them. One wears the trappings of civilization and plays the role civilization has assigned him, the savage redeemed and made respectable; the other wears only himself. One inhabits several stories, no one of which is his authentically; the other is authenticity itself. One lives in the world of "should have said," "meant," and "almost." The other can't wait to leave that world and its duplicitous ambiguities behind. ("How can you live like that?") He does just that at the film's end. Clad in white robes, Cinqué stands on the deck of a ship taking him back to Africa. And standing behind him is Covey the interpreter, who will no longer have to inhabit a middle world (precisely the world of the interpreter) between his true home and the home made for him by his white rescuers.

But, before this ending (not exactly happy, because Cinqué finds his village destroyed and his family missing) can be effected, another drama must be played out at the Supreme Court. This climactic story belongs for the most part to John Quincy Adams, who, in the course of the film, undergoes a transformation that makes him the appropriate deliverer of Spielberg's lesson. When we first see him, Adams is apparently asleep in his chair as debate on the founding of the Smithsonian unfolds on the House floor. (He does rouse himself long enough to send a pointed barb in the direction of Representative Pinckney while still in a sleeping position). We next see him receiving Joadson and others who urge him to join their cause. He declines and at the same time takes a rose-cutting that will grow into a healthy bush before the movie ends. The bush's health and vigor mirror the revival of his own. A second request for aid also fails, although he does give Joadson the advice I noted earlier: "Whoever tells the best story wins." But, when Baldwin sends him a letter, part plea, part flattery, he is moved and comes to the jail where Cinqué languishes in surly silence. They bond and work together on the case in preparation for the big day.

On that day, Cinqué is dressed in finery that gives him the appearance of a prince, but the spotlight belongs to Adams, who begins by noting that Baldwin has so completely presented the legal arguments that there is nothing left for him to say. Although we do not hear them, we can assume that those arguments are the same ones that served Baldwin well in the two trials: no evidence supports the property claims urged by Spain, the salvagers, or Ruiz and Montes; therefore, the Africans are free men. Relieved of the necessity to make doctrinal points, Adams can tell a broader story, the very story that legal theorist Ronald Dworkin puts at the center of his jurisprudence. Dworkin famously analogizes the unfolding history of American law to a chain novel, each chapter of which is written by a different author who must strive to efface the difference between him and his predecessors by writing in their spirit. The requirement is that each new contribution must extend the story that is serially being told, and not strike out in a new direction. So it is, says Dworkin, with the law:

judges "must regard themselves as partners with other officials, past and future, who together elaborate a coherent constitutional morality, and they must take care to see that what they contribute fits with the rest."[1]

It is just such an effort that Adam mounts, and he begins by evoking Cinqué's very Dworkinian account of his way of dealing with the present crisis. When I am in the courtroom, he says, I will summon the presence of my ancestors, and "I will reach back and draw them into me." He and they will be one. That's exactly what Adams does. Brandishing an administration pamphlet (*The Executive Review*), he reads from it a defense of slavery (probably by John Calhoun) that describes that practice as inevitable and tied to the nature of man. Adams begs to differ. The natural state of mankind, he declares, is freedom, and the proof is "the lengths a man or woman will go to retrieve it once taken." Adams offers Cinqué as an illustration. He asks him to stand and then declares that he is "the only true hero in the room." It is only because he is black, Adams observes, that his name is not known and heralded. If he were white, "songs would be written about him, the great authors of our time would fill books about him, his story would be told and retold in our classrooms, our children would know his name."

I cannot overemphasize the self-referentiality of this moment. The movie imagines a contrary-to-fact condition—a world where Cinqué is as well known as Patrick Henry—which it is in the act of bringing about. No classroom has an audience as large as a movie's. No vehicle is more likely to make Cinqué a household name than a big-budget film directed by Steven Spielberg and starring Anthony Hopkins, Matthew McConaughey, and Morgan Freeman (now there's a name). To the list of celebrations Cinqué would receive in songs and books, we can add the celebration performed by this movie, which in effect calls for, and delivers, the production of itself. Adams is in the course of telling the best story to an audience of nine; but Spielberg, through him, is telling the best story (as he deems it) to hundreds of millions.

That story is pure Dworkin. Adams rehearses the famous phrases of the Declaration of Independence, a copy of which adorns the courtroom wall, and he then strolls past the busts of Madison, Hamilton, Franklin, Washington, and his father. "We have long resisted asking you for guidance," he says, and for a moment it is not clear whether the "you" he addresses are the founding fathers or the members of the

Supreme Court, who are in the background of the shot. But, when he calls on "the wisdom and strength that inspire us," the ambiguity of reference disappears. It is these august forebears he invokes, and what he asks is that their spirit be internalized (inspire means breathe into) to the point where there is no difference between them and those in the courtroom in 1839, just as there is no difference between Cinqué and the ancestors he draws into him. What we now understand, or should understand, Adams says, is "who we are is who we were." This is both a declaration and an appeal. If we want to do the right thing, we need only step into the shoes of the heroes we venerate, and our path will be clear; we will do the right thing because we are not alone in our judgment of what it is; we are one with the American Revolution's inaugural gesture and we will pronounce on matters as they would have were they here, as, in fact, they are when contemporary voices meld with theirs. The danger that language will detach itself from a clear intention and facilitate equivocation—the danger Cinqué laments when he undresses—will be neutralized if the original intention of the framers is hewed to in the present circumstances.

Spielberg may be surprised to hear it, but he is an originalist. One consequence of his originalist understanding is that it makes a virtue of what everyone in the movie fears—civil war. The right decision in this case, the decision that is faithful to the founders' intention, may indeed, says Adams, have that result. But, if civil war is our destination, "let it come and may it be finally the last battle of the revolution," the battle that makes the founders' words ("all men are created equal") true. Justice Story and his colleagues (minus one) do their part when they rule that Cinqué and his fellows "are not slaves and therefore cannot be considered merchandise, but are rather free individuals with certain legal and moral rights." Casting Supreme Court Justice Harry Blackmun to play Supreme Court Justice Joseph Story is more than a nice touch; it reinforces the message of "who we are is who we were." Insofar as the court is faithful to the Constitution, its current members—even when they are retired—speak with the same voice as those who came before them. Blackmun is not just portraying Story; he is, in the deepest sense of the phrase, just like him. He is a faithful co-author of the chain novel we call constitutional interpretation.

That's the end of the narrative proper, but the movie's meditation on the relationship between language and truth continues in the penultimate scene. At the second trial, Secretary of State John Forsyth

(David Paymer) had cast doubt on the existence of the slave fortress to which witness for the defense Captain Fitzgerald of the British Navy had referred. Fitzgerald concedes that the location of the fortress had not yet been identified, but he is sure, he tells a skeptical Forsyth, that it is there, somewhere. Now, as the movie draws to its close, he has found it, and, after evacuating the imprisoned slaves, he methodically destroys it with cannon shot. As the last wall falls, Fitzgerald turns to a subordinate and says, take a letter to John Forsythe: "It is my great pleasure to inform you that you are in fact correct. The slave fortress in Sierra Leone does not exist." Words may depart from the truth, as they did when Forsythe denied there was such a fortress, but in the end truth is stronger than language and redeems even utterances that flout it. What Forsythe said earlier is made true when the fortress whose existence he questioned is destroyed. The now literal truth of his utterance erases the lie that utterance once proclaimed. He speaks the truth ahead of its time.

I have characterized Spielberg as an originalist, someone who insists on hewing to the meanings that an author or authors originally intended. But I have also argued that in *Amistad* he is telling us that, in court and elsewhere, whoever tells the best story wins. These two positions, apparently in tension, can be reconciled. The original meaning is objectively the true one, but there is no objective method for determining what the original meaning is; that is the work of persuasion, of telling the best story. Spielberg knows that there are competing stories about the American Revolution, the Constitution, and what they mean. He sets out to tell the story he believes to be true, but he also knows that getting others to accept it will require art, not just the rehearsal of facts. So he assembles this cast, hires a writer, engages John Williams to compose the music, and takes advantage of the influence and credit he has gained over the years as the producer and director of movies like *Schindler's List*. But he doesn't stop there. In a partnership with co-producer Debbie Allen, he distributes *Amistad* study kits to public schools where young students watch the movie and answer preprepared questions. Some historians have accused Spielberg of falsifying or stretching the facts in these kits. But he isn't doing history; he's using history in an effort to make his story the one millions of his fellow citizens believe in. *Amistad* has been dismissed as one more "white-savior" movie: falsely imprisoned Africans are rescued by Matthew McConaughey and Anthony Hopkins; now white Americans can congratulate themselves. Maybe, but, if self-congratulation is the price for achieving greater awareness of racial injustice, then perhaps Spielberg is willing to pay it, especially if by virtue of his efforts our children know Cinqué's name as they know the names of Patrick Henry and Paul Revere. Critic Jeffrey Lyons (WNBC TV) calls the movie: "Absolutely unforgettable."[2] If that is true, Spielberg has told the best story, and it has won.

13

Free Speech for Good or Ill

The People vs Larry Flynt and *Absence of Malice*

In their different ways, both *Billy Budd* and *Amistad* are centrally concerned with the relationship between speech, innocence, and truth. (Cinqué and Billy are to some extent contrapuntal figures.) That concern is philosophical and serves as a backdrop for the legal issues that impel the plot forward. But speech, of course, is itself a legal issue and has an amendment of its own, and I now turn to two movies that explicitly take the First Amendment as their subject: *The People vs Larry Flynt* (1996) and *Absence of Malice* (1981). The first is an unabashed valentine to the doctrine of freedom of speech; the second is a cautionary tale.

The dramatic structure of *The People vs Larry Flynt* was identified by director Miloš Forman (a Jewish refugee from Czechoslovakia whose parents perished in the Holocaust) when he said in an interview that the film reflected his "admiration for the beauty and wisdom of the American Constitution, which allows this country to rise to its best when provoked by the worst."[1] That, in effect, is the plot. A thoroughly disreputable scoundrel—loud, brash, crude, coarse, and misogynist—is nevertheless the moral center of the movie because it is to him that the resonant values of the First Amendment are attached. Flynt (Woody Harrelson) puts it precisely near the end: "If the First Amendment will protect a scumbag like me, then it will protect all of you."

The first part of the movie gives content to the word "scumbag." Flynt and his brother Jimmy are introduced as pre-adolescent bootleggers in conflict with their father over profits. We next see them as proprietors of a strip joint, complete with sensual dancers and

Law at the Movies. Stanley Fish, Oxford University Press. © Stanley Fish (2024).
DOI: 10.1093/oso/9780198898726.003.0014

a country music jukebox. When Larry gets the idea of printing a newsletter featuring naked women to publicize their establishment, he's told that he can't do that unless the images are attached to a text. The rationale is not stated, but it is easy to tease out: if images are attached to a text that is saying or advocating something, they are redeemed as extensions of the text's message, which, because it is speech, is protected by the First Amendment. This small moment early on leads directly and indirectly to the film's legal climax, the celebrated case of *Hustler Magazine* v. *Falwell* (1988), in which by a unanimous vote the Supreme Court declared Flynt innocent of any legal wrongdoing for having published a scurrilous cartoon vilifying famed evangelist Jerry Falwell and his mother.[2]

But, before the film presents that case, it works very hard to put the viewers on Flynt's side. As unattractive as Flynt is, his adversaries are even less attractive. They are smarmy, self-righteous, high-handed, and mean-spirited. In a showy piece of casting, three of them are played by non-actors who in real life are on the no-censorship, pro-pornography side. The judge in Flynt's first trial is played by Flynt himself. Brusque and biased, he rules out defense evidence, sentences Flynt to twenty-five years (a sentence later overturned), and denies bail. The prosecutor, who belongs to a group called Citizens for Decent Literature, is played by Democratic Party strategist James Carville. And a lawyer for Jerry Falwell, indignant at Flynt's libel of his client and his mother, is played by ACLU stalwart Burt Neuborne, now (in 2023) a First Amendment scholar at NYU Law School. The message sent by this casting is not subtle: you members of the audience know very well that those portraying these characters don't stand behind the words they utter on screen; the fact of their real-life identities and known political persuasions directs you to receive what they say as cameo actors with suspicion and distrust. In effect, viewers are being told not to take the courtroom scenes seriously; it's not a genuine give-and-take, where the question being debated is open. The issue of record is already settled and is being reinforced by the casting. Flynt, with all his warts—no, *because* of all his warts—represents the preeminent American values of freedom and choice; those arrayed against him, no doubt members of Falwell's "moral majority," represent the forces of intolerance and hypocrisy. The point is further underlined when a professional actor, James Cromwell, plays a sanctimonious anti-pornography crusader who says things like "We must prevent the destruction of the soul of our country." After he speaks, the camera zooms in on his name tag. It's Charles Keating, later to be tried and convicted as a central figure in the savings and loan scandal; we are being told that, of course, a slimeball like Keating would work to limit the amount of speech available to American citizens while conspiring to steal their money. As Neuborne has acknowledged, there is only one story being told here: "The pitch was always free speech against narrow-minded bigots. What you never heard was a more thoughtful voice."[3]

The absence of a thoughtful voice on the other side makes the movie go down easily: you don't have to worry about the ideas (they are already ranked and assessed), and you can surrender to the movie's visual pleasures, which are borderline pornographic. This is a movie about pornography that is itself pornographic. The movie presents itself as a test for the audience, a test it passes, not by resisting the impulse to gaze at breasts and vaginas, but by yielding to the impulse and thus demonstrating a healthy appreciation of God's material bounty. (At one point, Flynt observes that, if God created woman, he must also have created vaginas.) Forman takes a familiar trope and stands it on its cinematic head. In movies like *Vertigo*, *Psycho*, *Rear Window*, *American Beauty*, *Blow Up*, *Body Double*, *Dressed to Kill*, *Peeping Tom*, and *Pushover*, the audience (usually imagined as male) becomes complicit in the voyeuristic acts of a protagonist, and involuntarily shares his guilt. The viewer of *The People vs Larry Flynt* is rescued from guilt when the movie celebrates its protagonist *because* he performs and facilitates scopophilia, the sexualized act of looking at and objectifying the female body. The leering member of the audience escapes criticism and becomes a hero who bravely looks when more puritanical others would avert their eyes.

The phrase "avert their eyes" belongs to the vocabulary of familiar, ACLU-style First Amendment arguments. It refers to the moment of choice in which one decides whether to engage with an image or a text or turn away from it. That choice, says standard First Amendment rhetoric, should be made by the individual and not by a state that seeks to legislate what its citizens may view and hear. In the first trial presented in the movie, Flynt's lawyer, Alan Isaacman (Edward Norton), makes the point vigorously. He does not, he tells the jury, like what his client does, but "what I do like is that I live in a country where you and I make that decision for ourselves." That's freedom, and the price for it is that "we have to tolerate things we don't like." "Things we don't like" is more than a specification of the price we pay; it is a diminution of that price. Government, Isaacman is saying, shouldn't be asked to ban something just because we don't like it. Nor should we ask government to criminalize something just because it offends us or makes us uncomfortable. That would be to set up a paternalistic state, a "nanny" state in which the people are assumed to be incapable of standing up for themselves and negotiating the obstacles life puts in their way. To promote choice over enforced regulation is to promote dignity. Censorship, the argument goes, is not only an illegitimate arrogation of power; it prevents the formation of an informed and supple citizenry, a citizenry capable of making distinctions and realizing a life plan not dictated from above.

It all sounds cogent and even irrefutable, until one questions the characterization of the harm speech can inflict as minimal or incidental, a matter merely of personal discomfort, the discomfort of living with things we don't like. What about speech so lacerating that it leaves its target unable to function in everyday life? What about speech that portrays women as willing partners in their exploitation and degradation and thereby creates a presumption in the minds of some men that acts of sexual violence will be welcomed? What about speech that blankets the country with demeaning characterizations of minorities who become afraid to walk the streets in broad daylight lest they be assaulted? What about *those* things we don't like? These are some of the points regularly made by pro-regulation legal theorists such as Catharine MacKinnon and Jeremy Waldron. They are, of course, rebuttable, but they are not rebutted in this movie, because they are never brought forward. ("What you never heard is a more thoughtful voice.")

The closest the movie comes to acknowledging that there is another side to the free-speech question is in its dramatization of the Falwell case. *Hustler* had published a parody ad interview in its "first-time" series depicting Larry Falwell having drunken sex with his mother in an outhouse: "I never *really* expected to make it with Mom, but then after she showed all the other guys in town such a good time, I figured, 'What the hell!'"[4] Falwell sued for libel, invasion of privacy, and the intentional infliction of emotional distress. A district court denied the libel claim on the reasoning that no one would think the parody asserted "actual facts." In a nice dramatic moment, Isaacman questions Falwell and tricks him into undermining his own legal position. "Have you had sex with your mother?" "Have you ever preached when you were drunk?" Falwell answers, "That's absurd," and Isaacman comes back, "So what you're telling me is nobody would reasonably think these statements about you are true?" Falwell answers, "Yes," and thereby removes any basis for a libel suit: if no one could take these statements as serious descriptions of Falwell's conduct, no libelous assertion has been made. Nothing, in effect, has been said.

This leaves the charge of intentional infliction of emotional distress: even if the ad parody is not libelous, one could argue that it is so "gross and repugnant" (the court's words) and damaging that its target should have the protection of law.[5] No, says the Supreme Court, for two related reasons. First, Falwell is a public figure, and, since *New York Times Co.* v. *Sullivan* (1964), public figures cannot successfully claim to have been libeled unless the misstatements about them were made with full knowledge of their falsity or in reckless disregard of the truth. (That is the "actual malice" standard.[6]) The reason for this latitude, the *Sullivan* Court declares, is that the robustness of political debate is so crucial to democracy that its value outweighs the harm done to the reputation of a public person by a falsehood. The *Hustler* v. *Falwell* court follows Sullivan when it declares that "[a]t the heart of the First Amendment is the recognition of the fundamental importance of the free flow of ideas and opinions on matters of public interest and concern." Therefore, the ideas expressed in the parody ad "contribute to the free interchange of ideas and the ascertainment of truth."[7]

But what, one might ask, *is* the idea whose possible contribution to the Marketplace of Ideas counts for more than any harm its expression might cause? Remember, the libel claim has been dismissed because the ad parody could not reasonably be understood as asserting any "actual facts."[8] How then can this empty, not-to-be-taken-seriously, verbal performance have ascribed to it a discursive force that makes it valuable and even essential to political debate? The answer the court gives is that the parody belongs, however tenuously, to the tradition of political cartoons, a satiric genre "based on exploitation of unfortunate physical traits or politically embarrassing events—an exploitation often calculated to injure the feelings of the subject of the portrayal." Examples of "unfortunate physical traits" cited by the court include an "early cartoon portraying George Washington as an ass," and later cartoons depicting "Lincoln's tall, gangling posture, Teddy Roosevelt's glasses and teeth, and Franklin D. Roosevelt's jutting jaw." An example of the "politically embarrassing events" prong is the work of Thomas Nast, "the greatest American cartoonist," who mounted a "sustained attack" on the corrupting influence of New York's Boss Tweed in the pages of *Harper's Weekly*.[9]

But the enumeration of these supposed analogues by the court only deepens the mystery of my question—what exactly is the idea conveyed by the *Hustler* ad that merits protection? There is no doubt about what idea is being conveyed in a Nast cartoon that shows a huge thumb hovering menacingly over the city or another that shows a bloated Tweed whose head is a huge moneybag. You can read directly from the images to the satiric accusation: Tweed wields a malevolent power that cannot be escaped, or Tweed is not a human being but a runaway capitalist engine of total and immoral control. The cartoons work because, although they are not literally true—Tweed's thumb is no bigger than any other man's, and Tweed's head has the usual human protuberances and cavities—they are rooted in known truths about Tweed's behavior. Yes, the viewer thinks, this captures, even if it exaggerates, the kind of thing Tweed is and does.

In the *Hustler* ad, however, the actions depicted do not present an extension or caricature of traits and dispositions Falwell and his mother (we must never forget her, she was real) were known to have. Lincoln was in fact tall and gangling, Teddy Roosevelt did have big and prominent teeth, his cousin Franklin did have a jutting jaw, Tweed did preside over an empire of corruption, but Jerry Falwell did not commit incest with his mother in an outhouse or preach when he was drunk. The image of him doing those things does not produce a shock of recognition: ah yes, that's typical Falwell behavior. No, the ad is unrelated to any behavior he has ever been known to engage in; it is a lie, a calumny, a defamation. So, for the third time, what *is* the idea being conveyed in the ad, the idea that is a contribution to society's political deliberations and therefore worthy of First Amendment solicitude even if reputations and careers are wounded?

Isaacman tries to answer that question in the movie. He begins his address to the court by proclaiming the value of "uninhibited public debate" and identifies the issue before the court as whether "a public figure's right to protection from emotional distress should outweigh the public interest in allowing every one of the citizens of this country to freely express his views." At this point, a Justice interrupts to ask my question: "But what was the view expressed in exhibit A?"

(The exchanges in the film pretty much track the exchanges engaged in by the Justices in court.) Isaacman responds first by explaining that the parody ad is a "satire of a public figure." The Justice says that he understands, but still must ask: "what is the public interest you're describing, that there is some interest in making him look ridiculous?" That is a serious challenge to Isaacman: making someone look ridiculous may cause members of the public to laugh; but laughter is an involuntary physiological reflex; it has no ideational content and cannot be a contribution to substantive debate. It's hard to see what would be the public interest in multiplying occasions for ridicule. Isaacman has a response. It's more than ridicule: there is a public interest in having *Hustler Magazine* "express the point of view that Jerry Falwell is full of BS." So that is what the ad asserts, according to Isaacman, that Jerry Falwell's preacherly performance—his pious exhortations to Christian virtue—is belied and undercut by the actions he performs when not preaching. And it is certainly true that a disparity between one's public posture and one's private acts might be the basis of saying of someone that he is "full of B.S." That, however, won't work in this instance because of the fact I have repeatedly stressed: Jerry Falwell did not perform these actions; he did not sleep with his drunken mother in an outhouse. No piece of his private behavior can be cited to support the ad's representation of him, and the ad's false suggestion to the contrary, rather than demonstrating that Falwell is a bullshitter, demonstrates that Flynt is a defamer with no other purpose than to wound. (Asked in the earlier trial if it was his intention to destroy Falwell's integrity, Flynt replied: "To assassinate it.")

Another Justice re-asks the question that still has not been answered: "What public service does this serve?" Isaacman answers that it serves the same public purpose served when Garry Trudeau, another celebrated American political cartoonist, portrayed President Reagan as having no brain or President George W. Bush as a wimp. But again the analogy does not hold. Were he challenged on the point, Trudeau could have pointed to things Reagan did (Iran-Contra, Star Wars) that might be called brainless, or he could have noted that the Bush, who cheerled war, was accused of avoiding active military service by using his connections to secure a place in the National Guard. To be sure, these characterizations of Reagan's and Bush's actions have been disputed, but the disputes were about interpretations of a matter of fact. There is no matter of fact to be disputed with respect to Falwell's and his mother's incest and no relationship between those non-facts and Falwell's character. The answer, finally, to the questions what idea is being conveyed and what public purpose is being served by the ad parody is: None whatsoever. Isaacson waxes eloquent about the value of "criticizing public figures." But to criticize someone is to enumerate pieces of his or her behavior that merit censure. The behavior ascribed to Falwell and his mother did not occur. The ad parody is no more a criticism than it is a public service or a contribution to democratic debate. It's just an effusion of bile.

Nevertheless, the court decides 8-0 for Falwell, trumpeting (the words are Rehnquist's) "the fundamental importance of the free flow of ideas," which is "essential to the common quest for truth."[10] But what he and his court approve is neither an idea nor the expression of truth. Those words and phrases glorify something that is indistinguishable from a belch or a fart.

Flynt hears the good news in his bed, where he has been watching a semi-pornographic video of his late wife, Althea (Courtney Love). The romance between the two occupies a lot of screen time, and it is affecting, but it intersects only occasionally with the legal issues. Another plot line is more closely tied to freedom-of-speech concerns. During a trial in Georgia, Flynt and Isaacman are shot as they walk out of court. Flynt is paralyzed from the waist down, and he says, "I can't walk again and I can't make love to my wife." The pain is so great that he becomes addicted to painkillers, and Althea joins him in a bad act of solidarity. When an operation relieves the pain, he quits the drugs, but she cannot, and in time she dies afflicted with AIDS. By alternating the scenes that portray Flynt's pain (physical and emotional) with courtroom scenes, Forman turns the sympathy generated by the tragedy into a further indictment of Flynt's ideological opponents. Of course, none of the crusaders who inveigh against Flynt shot him, but the clear suggestion is that the shooter is carrying out their joint intention, which is to destroy brave Larry Flynt, champion of free speech.

So that's the movie—flamboyant, titillating, over-the-top, engaging, brilliantly acted, and intellectually dishonest, not because the case for free speech is weak, but because the movie only pretends to make it.

Although Sydney Pollack's *Absence of Malice* (1981) precedes *The People vs Larry Flynt* by fifteen years, the earlier film can be read, anachronistically, as a critique of its successor. The difference between the two is that *Absence of Malice* asks the questions Forman's film avoids. Is free speech really such a good thing? Can its effects be malign? If they are malign, and you are their victim, what can you do? Another difference is that, in *Absence of Malice*, the doctrinal issues do not operate in the background, but are named and discussed at length by the characters. In an early scene, journalist Megan Carter (Sally Field) is consulting with her newspaper's attorney about the latitude she has or doesn't have when writing a story. The story concerns the disappearance and suspected murder of union activist Joey Diaz. No one knows what happened to Diaz, and various law-enforcement agencies are feeling public pressure because they have come up with nothing. Elliott Rosen (Bob Balaban), head of the FBI's Organized Crime's Task Force, decides to shake a tree to see if anything falls out. For no particular reason, he focuses on Michael Gallagher (Paul Newman), the son of a deceased bootlegger and the nephew of a Mafia boss. Carter finds out accidentally that Rosen and his staff have been watching films of Big Tommy Gallagher's funeral and learns that Gallagher has a son who is a liquor distributor. She suspects that something is up and goes to see Rosen, although she is afraid that the famously tight-lipped investigator will tell her nothing. Rosen sees her entering the building and instructs his secretary to call him out of the office one minute into their conversation. When he exits the room, Carter finds a file on his desk labeled "Michael Gallagher," and she reads it. She then returns to the newspaper prepared to write a story and is advised by her editor to talk to the paper's lawyer.

So that's the set-up. Rosen wants to stir things up and thinks that, were Michael Gallagher to be made nervous, he might reveal something, either directly or inadvertently. As Rosen puts it in a later scene, either he did it, or he knows who did it, or he can find out who did it. Megan Carter is his chosen instrument: he counts on her reportorial instincts and trusts that she will do something useful to him after she reads the file he has left on his desk. The point of all this is that we know from the beginning that the suspicion about to be cast on Michael Gallagher has no basis. The question, then, is how can a story be written that has no foundation in demonstrable fact?

That question is answered by the lawyer who explains to Carter how things work in the world of journalism. First of all, the facts don't concern him one way or the other. He doesn't care whether what

Carter is writing is true. He is interested, he says, only in the law and the protection it affords the newspaper, should her story "prove to be false." He explores the matter by way of a self-catechism. Is Gallagher a public official? No, he is "not a public official, nor is he likely to become one." Next question: "Is he a public figure"—that is, someone whose name and person would be generally known to readers? Not now, but that may change *after* the paper publishes its story. These questions directly track *New York Times* v. *Sullivan*. In that case, an Alabama police official sued the *New York Times*, claiming that he had been libeled by an ad the paper accepted for publication. In that full-page ad, a group of Alabama clergymen, members of the Committee to defend Martin Luther King, Jr, appealed for funds to counter the "wave of terror" waged against civil-rights workers. Some of the actions making up that wave of terror were described, and, although Commissioner L. B. Sullivan was not named, he contended that the actions referred to, had they occurred, would have been performed by the department he supervised. Thus, he claimed, the ad "would be read as accusing the Montgomery police, and hence him."[11] Moreover, he continued, the paragraphs detailing what happened were full of factual errors. Therefore, he concluded, he had been falsely accused and was the victim of libel, traditionally defined as a written and published false statement.

Justice William Brennan, in his opinion for a unanimous court, markedly altered that definition. He acknowledged that "the description of events" in the ad was "not accurate." Nevertheless, Brennan continued, the value to democracy of "uninhibited, robust" public debate is so great that, even when criticism of a public official contains "factual error" and/or "defamatory content," it should receive constitutional protection unless it can be proven that the false or defamatory statement "was made with 'actual malice'—that is, with knowledge that it was false or with reckless disregard of whether it was false or not."[12] In later cases, constitutional protection was extended to a "public figure," an individual who either "injects himself or is drawn into a particular public controversy, and thereby becomes a public figure for a limited range of issues" (*Gertz* v. *Robert Welch, Inc.* [1974]).[13] "Drawn into" is a deadly phrase, because it indicates how public-figure status can be conferred without the figure doing anything to call attention to himself. Clearly, that is what is about to happen to Michael Gallagher. Megan Carter will write a front-page story reporting that he is the subject of an investigation looking into the disappearance of Joey Diaz. The moment the newspaper containing that item is delivered and read, Gallagher is suddenly a public figure—he's been drawn in—and has forfeited (although not by any act of his own) the protection he would be entitled to, were he a private person.

In effect, as the lawyer explains, the newspaper is free of liability for whatever it chooses to say about Gallagher unless malice—intentional publication of assertions known to be false—can be proved and there has been no effort to get his side of the story. With that in mind, the lawyer urges Carter to contact Gallagher or at least attempt to contact him and leave a record of the attempt. If he denies the accusation, "we will include his denial, which will create the appearance of fairness." Should he decline to say anything, "we can hardly be responsible for errors he refused to correct." And "if we fail to reach him, we tried" and thus did our good-faith duty. He then says again that, "as a matter of law, the truth of your story is irrelevant." The newspaper's lack of any knowledge of what actually happened insulates it from a charge of libel: "We have no knowledge that the story is false; therefore, we are absent malice." (This has come to be known as the "ignorance is bliss" defense.) In the context of our strategic ignorance, "we may say anything we like about Mr Gallagher and he is powerless to do us harm. Democracy is served."

The cynicism of this account of the law can hardly be exaggerated, and it is still in the air when we see Gallagher come to the newspaper in an effort to find out why and how he has become the object of suspicion. In a dramatic and comic moment, he strides up to Carter's desk and announces, "I'm Michael Gallagher." The moment is dramatic, because she wasn't expecting to be confronted directly by the subject of her piece. It is comic, because she looks up and sees—as do we—Paul Newman standing there in all his blue-eyed beauty. In response, she spills her coffee and begins a conversation in which she is already awkwardly positioned. "What do you want?" she asks. "Where did your story come from?" is the reply. "I can't tell you that," she says with all the righteousness of a reporter who has been taught never to reveal her sources. In this case, however, she has no source except the file she read surreptitiously and cannot produce. The ignorance-is-bliss defense is in full working order. Meg tries the direct approach—"Were you involved in Joey Diaz's disappearance?"—and receives a curt "no" in response. (Unaware, Gallagher is following the lawyer's script.) Then why, she rejoins, "are you being investigated?" He answers, "I don't know, that's why I'm here," demonstrating that he is fully caught in the circular trap—something bad has been alleged about him, but his efforts to find out who alleged it only seem to confirm the calumny—set by *New York Times* v. *Sullivan*, which allows the newspaper to say anything but bars him from inquiring into the origin of what it has said. Right on schedule, the lawyer pipes up: "To the best of our knowledge, our story is true. We have an obligation to report such things." Are you not obliged "to tell the truth?" Gallagher retorts. "Of course," Meg replies; the lawyer is silent. Gallagher has one more question, and it too fits neatly into the sequence the lawyer has outlined: "How come you don't talk to me before you write what 'they' say?" Meg gives the proper—according to the law—response: "I tried, I called." Gallagher protests that she should have called back—"I'm around"—but she has already satisfied the *New York Times* v. *Sullivan* requirements. This scene ends inconclusively as far as Gallagher is concerned, but it conclusively illustrates the Kafkaesque situation he has somehow (he doesn't know how) wandered into. He describes that situation perfectly when, in a later scene, the two of them have lunch aboard his boat: "You write what 'they' say and then you help them hide. You say you got a right to do that and I have no right to know who 'they' are."

The consequences of what the newspaper does do not stop with Gallagher's discomfort; they ripple out to affect his life in many ways. Two are particularly important. When Gallagher's name is publicly tied to Diaz's disappearance, his workers, union members, strike and leave him unable to conduct business. In effect, he has lost his livelihood. He also loses his closest friend, Teresa Perrone (Melinda Dillon). She knows where he was on the day Diaz disappeared, because he had accompanied her to Atlanta, where she had gone to have an abortion. A deeply serious Catholic, Teresa wants to help Michael, but she is afraid that, if it becomes known that she aborted a child, both her position as an assistant principal at the local church school and the approval of her father will be forfeit. She seeks out Megan Carter in the hope that the reporter, after hearing what she tells her, will write a story exonerating Gallagher.

They meet in the open air. The scene between them (which helped earn Dillon an Academy Award nomination for best supporting actress) is a contrast in styles and motives. Meg is brisk and no-nonsense; she is interested only in documentable facts. Teresa wants to say as little as possible. Initially, she offers only her sincerity as evidence of the truth of what she is saying. That doesn't cut it: "I can't write a story that says someone claims to know Michael Gallagher is innocent and won't say how or why or even give her name." Teresa, looking increasingly anguished, dances around the hard, specific questions put to her. "Couldn't you say you spoke to someone who was with him the whole time?" She tries to bargain: "If I told you, just you, would it have to be in the newspaper?" Meg is honest: "Probably. I can't promise you anything." Teresa doesn't know how deep in she already is. To her credit, Meg tries to tell her: "I'm a reporter; you're talking to a newspaper"—that is, not to a person—"right now. Do you understand?" When she announces she has a deadline to meet and turns to go, Teresa finally blurts it out, "I had an abortion," to which Meg replies, "That's not so bad," thereby betraying her inability to understand Teresa as a human being caught up in a moral dilemma rather than as a source. She is now completely in reporter-mode and asks for ticket stubs and anything else that will document her story. Teresa slinks away.

When we next see Teresa, she is curled up in the fetal position on the front stoop of her father's house, reading the story Meg has written about her. In an act of desperation, she runs from house to house on her block and picks up the newspapers that have been delivered in the morning. The scene shifts to the newspaper's editorial floor, where Meg's editor informs her that Teresa Perrone has killed herself by slashing her wrists in a bathtub. Totally shaken, she goes to Gallagher's warehouse, now empty. Enraged, he assaults her, ripping her blouse. (There is a similar moment of violence in *The Verdict* when Newman decks Charlotte Rampling in the bar of a New York hotel.). He cries, "She must have felt raped," and asks, "Couldn't you see what it was to her? Couldn't you stop scribbling for a second and put down your goddam ballpoint pen and just see *her*?" Knowing she failed to do exactly that, she tries to make it up in the only coin she has—information. "It was Rosen, Elliott Rosen, who leaked the story about you."

Gallagher factors that information into a plan he has already formulated. The timing of that formulation raises a question the movie never answers. It is after his workers strike and before Teresa contacts Meg that Gallagher says to one of his associates, "We're going hunting." The primary targets of his hunting are Rosen and District Attorney Quinn, but Meg Carter may be a target too, for, shortly after announcing his intention, Gallagher goes to a bar she is known to frequent. After that, things take their usual course, and they move toward a relationship. Is that relationship genuine? Is he really attracted to her or is she just one of the people he is manipulating in an effort to undo those who have undone him? We never know.

What we do know is that he sets in motion a sting with multiple moving parts. First we see him coming out of an electronics store. Next we see him recording a message on an answering machine with two side-by-side cassettes. At this point, we do not know what he is doing; as viewers we are, like his intended victims, in the dark. We remain so when we see him getting a cashier's check at a bank teller's window. It is for $3,000 and made out to the Committee for a Better Miami. If we've been paying attention, something clicks. It has been established earlier that the Committee for a Better Miami is a front for D. A. Quinn's political ambitions; when you contribute to it, you are contributing to him. In short order, Gallagher sets up a meeting with Quinn in a spot by the water. Gallagher proposes a deal. He will try to find out what happened to Diaz. In exchange, Quinn will issue a statement clearing him, and that statement, Gallagher insists, will appear in the newspaper. Quinn agrees to call off the investigation, but is doubtful about the newspaper part. Gallagher sticks to his demand, and says, "When I read in the paper what I want, you get in touch." He gives Quinn a phone number. He's already said that he doesn't want to deal with anyone but Quinn, and when asked why replies that he doesn't trust Elliott Rosen.

Now things are beginning to come into focus. Gallagher is setting up a line of communication between him and Quinn and will be recording whatever Quinn says in the confidence that Rosen will be privy to the recording. He has also drawn Quinn into a partnership that explicitly excludes Rosen, who now becomes someone whose interests are separate from, and perhaps hostile to, theirs. Quinn then does his part to further Gallagher's strategy (of which he knows nothing) by announcing to Rosen that he's terminating the Gallagher investigation. "The hell you are," Rosen replies. Yes, Says Quinn, and, if you call Washington, "I'm going to say that you were coercing a private citizen into becoming a federal witness." Rosen tells him to play his cards, and he does so by making the announcement Gallagher had demanded. Rosen is now suspicious of Quinn and orders a tap on his phone as well as taps on Gallagher's phones and surveillance of his activities. Rosen's subordinate Bob Waddell is worried and asks where they will find a judge who will let them tap Quinn. Rosen replies that he is not going to ask a judge. Gallagher's machinations have led Rosen to unauthorized and likely illegal actions. The noose tightens.

Gallagher receives a telephone message from Quinn saying that they have to get together. Gallagher sets up a meeting, but, before it occurs, he draws another check for $6,000, also made out to the Committee for a Better Miami. Rosen listens to their conversations and gets copies of the checks. His men record and photograph the meeting, which takes place in two side-by-side cars; they have been recording and photographing everything Gallagher does, including what he does in Meg's company; the two are now definitely "involved" (a word that will take on resonance at the end of the movie). Waddell is in love with Meg and warns her against continuing to see Gallagher: "He paid off Quinn." When she protests—"I don't believe you"—he shows her the file containing the checks and photographs. "You can't tell anyone where you learned this. You can't use it. It would mean my job." Just "get out."

Meg is now in a quandary. She has seen what appears to be evidence of her lover's criminality, but she doesn't want it to be true. What she doesn't know is that the evidence has been manufactured, not by the FBI, but by Gallagher himself. He has now done to her what Rosen did when he left the file on his desk—presented her with a choice between her reporter's instincts and her human instincts. The drama between the two plays out when Gallagher arrives at her place with a smile and a bottle of wine. She's cooking, he's uncorking. He looks over and asks, "Something bothering you?" She replies, "Quinn cleared you. Did you know he was going to to?" He says, "No," which is technically true since he didn't know if and when Quinn would accede to his demand; he's starting to think like a reporter. She persists, "Why do you think he called that press conference?" His back is up: "What? Are you working?" He wants to know whom he is talking to, Meg the person or Meg the reporter. "You want to ask as a person, I'll tell you. You want to ask me as a reporter, I've got no comment." She asks nevertheless: "Would you answer just one question? Quinn's statement, did you do anything wrong to get it? Tell me." "I'm sorry I won't," he replies (he still doesn't know whom he's talking to), and she says sadly, "I guess you just did." She thinks he has revealed himself by his reticence; but it is she who has revealed herself by regarding him as a source rather than as the man she cares for. She had said earlier, "The truth is the truth," no matter who speaks it to whom. He is saying, no it isn't; what happens to words when they are exchanged in confidence is one thing; what happens to words when they are broadcast to the world is another; the truth in some very abstract way may be a unitary entity that is always the same; but the effects of the truth will vary greatly with the circumstances of its telling, something Teresa Perrone found out to her cost. He turns to leave, and after he does, she picks up the phone and calls her editor. Clearly a reporter and not a person. She files and writes the story; when it appears, we see Rosen reading the headline—"Strike Force Probes Quinn–Gallagher Link"—and Bob Waddell in a bar looking gloomy. He knows the jig is up.

Everything comes together in a denouement that is dramatic, funny, and fast. The scene shifts to the hall of an official-looking building. Striding down that hall is James J. Wells, Assistant US Attorney General for the Organized Crime Division of the US Department of Justice. He is played by Wilford Brimley, who pretty much steals the movie with one of his trademark gruff-but-smart performances. In the room are all the *dramatis personae*: Rosen, Waddell, Quinn, Meg Carter (along with the paper's lawyer), and of course Gallagher. The scene corresponds to that moment in an Agatha Christie-style who-done-it when the omniscient detective assembles all the suspects and one by one reveals their innocence or complicity. Wells announces that, before the sun goes down, two things will be true that are not true now: "The Department of Justice is going to know what in the good Christ is going on here and, the other, at the end of the day I'm going to have someone's ass in my briefcase." Quinn starts things off by stating that Gallagher is a government witness reporting to him. Rosen interrupts: "Does the arrangement include campaign contributions?" Quinn: "What are you talking about?" Wells tells him, reading from the file Quinn didn't know existed. The report, Wells states, says that "you met with Gallagher and didn't report it and that Gallagher gave money to some committee thinks you're pretty." Moreover, there are "phone taps of you—not legal, mind you—talking on Gallagher's answering machine." Quinn defends himself. "Those were Gallagher's rules. He said he wanted to deal only with me." Wells turns to Waddell and asks, "Where did you get the authority to run these taps?" Waddell answers, no place, "I just went ahead and did it," but Rosen interrupts: "He was acting on my instructions."

Wells asks Rosen to make the case that will explain his actions. Rosen responds by interrogating Gallagher, who acknowledges that Quinn had "asked me if I could help him find out what happened to Joey Diaz." Rosen shows him two checks and asks why they were written. "To contribute to the Committee." "Why?" "Because they do good work." But why give anonymously, Rosen asks. "I wanted them to be anonymous." Rosen turns to accusation: "You made these contributions anonymously because you were paying off Quinn." "Prove it!" Gallagher replies. Quinn sees the light, "He's trying to frame me." Wells asks Gallagher, "Are you that smart," and Quinn answers, "You damn right he is."

Then it's Meg's turn. She tells how Rosen left the file on her desk and she read it. "He intended me to read it so I would write a story that made Mr Gallagher look bad." She balks, however, at revealing who gave her the information that led to the latest story about Gallagher and Quinn. (It was Waddell.) Wells takes this moment to reflect on the relationship between journalism and the law, and he brings together many of the issues the movie has raised. He admits that, when reporters act irresponsibly (as Megan has done), "there isn't a hell of a lot we can do about it." But, as for those who use reporters to leak stuff just to cause trouble, "I can stop them" even if "I can't stop you." And so, he asks Meg again, "I want to know where those stories come from?" The newspaper's lawyer protests the question: "Under the First Amendment, my client is not required to reveal her sources." Wells is having none of it. "The First Amendment don't say that and the privilege don't exist." The privilege he refers to is the "press shield" long sought by journalists and denied them by the Supreme Court. The shield, if it were in place, would permit journalists to resist subpoenas requiring them to identify their sources. In *Branzburg* v. *Hayes* (1972), the court is unequivocal: "Newsmen are not exempt from the normal duty of appearing before a grand jury and answering questions relevant to a criminal investigation."[14] (Many states have now enacted press shield laws, albeit with carve-out exceptions, but there remains none on the federal level.) Aware that she could go to jail, Meg decides this time she will choose not hurting someone over telling the truth. "No rules, just me."

Wells sums up: he tells Gallagher that he is a "smart fellow." Gallagher says ruefully, "Everybody in the room is smart; everybody's just doing their job and Teresa Perrone is dead. Who do I see about that?" His question reminds us that the harm done by irresponsible journalism remains after the feckless parties have gone on to the next big scoop. Wells announces that he will be releasing a statement to the media. It will say, "Mr Quinn may not be the smartest DA around, but there is no evidence suspecting him of anything; it's going to say that you [Meg] were suckered by Mr Rosen here, who has some peculiar ideas on how to do his job; it's going to say that it was premature and real wrong that these investigations ever got reported in the first place." Wells then dismisses everyone but Quinn and Rosen. He tells Quinn that he's in a bad place because of the publicity he's already received. Quinn: "You saying I should resign?" "The president appointed you," Wells rejoins, "and I'm not the one to be kicking you out."

Quinn leaves, and Wells asks Rosen: "What're you thinking of doing after government service?" "I'm not quitting," Rosen says testily, but he has no choice: "You ain't no presidential appointment, Elliott. The one that hired you is me. You got thirty days." Rosen's ass is in Wells's briefcase. It's all over but the shouting and a meeting in the hall by the elevator, where Meg congratulates Michael: "Well, you got us all." The reply is terse, "You got yourselves."

When Meg returns to the newsroom, the lawyer has preceded her and provided an account of Wells's "inquiry" (his word). She finds herself in the position she has so often placed others, the subject of an unflattering news story. Sarah, a young reporter she had mentored, sits down and turns the merciless reportorial lens on her. "I need to know how to describe your relationship with Gallagher." "Just say we were involved," she replies. Sarah presses: "That's true isn't it?," and in response Meg delivers, succinctly, the movie's lesson: "No, but it's accurate." The distinction is a subtle one. We usually fold accuracy into truth, but they are not the same at all. Recently, I asked a bank for my credit card and check records for a particular year. "I'm being audited," I explained. That was an accurate statement, but in the context of my request it was not true. I was in fact being audited, but for another year. I told the literal truth, but I deliberately glossed over a crucial fact, and fell short of telling the whole truth. If Meg were to tell the whole truth about her relationship with Gallagher, she would include her part in putting him in jeopardy, her share of the responsibility for the death of his best friend, her manipulation of Bob Waddell, her inability (until very recently) to be true to herself as a person rather than as a reporter. All that and more are the content of the "relationship." The word "involved" doesn't begin to cover it, although it is accurate—that is, does not state a falsehood. Accuracy in that thin sense is all the law requires; the truth in a more robust sense is not something the press need concern itself with. This means, as we have seen again and again, that the press can publish items that are misleading in their implications, so long as the question "are we deliberately retailing lies?" can be answered, "No." Then the newspaper is "absent malice," and, as the lawyer said at the outset, it can say anything it wants about anybody if the subject of the story can be characterized as a public figure or a "limited public figure," a requirement ever easier to meet in the age of the internet.

When it was first handed down, *New York Times* v. *Sullivan* was hailed as a great victory by free-speech advocates. At last, the transcendent value of the free flow of ideas—even of ideas rooted in falsehood—was being recognized by the Supreme Court. There were some reservations. In a dissent to *Gertz* v. *Robert Welch*, Justice Byron White wondered about the wisdom of "scuttling the libel laws of the States in such a wholesale fashion, to say nothing of deprecating the reputation interest of ordinary citizens and rendering them powerless to protect themselves."[15] Others, including Justice Elena Kagan when she was a law professor, have questioned some of the decisions *New York Times* v. *Sullivan* has spawned.[16] It is only recently, however, that a serious case for reconsidering the "landmark" opinion has been made, notably by Justices Clarence Thomas and Neil Gorsuch. Dissenting from the refusal of the court to take up a case (*Berisha* v. *Lawson* (2021)) that would have required revisiting the *Sullivan* ruling, Thomas and Gorsuch make two arguments. One is historical and emphasized by Gorsuch. Given the change in our technological landscape and the ease with which in an internet age persons can become public figures—indeed, one might say that nowadays it's hard *not* to be a public figure—"the actual malice standard has evolved from a high bar to recovery into an effective immunity from liability" for the spreaders of lies.[17] Thomas's challenge is more fundamental and theoretical. He aligns himself with the view (expressed in an earlier opinion) that the "pronouncement that the First Amendment requires public figures to establish actual malice bears no relation to the text, history, or structure of the Constitution."[18] That is to say (and Thomas had already said it in a 2019 concurrence), the *Sullivan* decision is a departure offered without much argumentative justification from libel law as we have traditionally known it. Moreover, and this is the philosophical point, "[t]he proliferation of falsehoods is, and always has been, a serious matter. Instead of continuing to insulate those who perpetrate lies from traditional remedies like libel suits, we should give them only the protection the First Amendment requires,"[19] which means of course that we shouldn't protect lies or the dissemination of lies.

Absence of Malice is an early version of Thomas's brief against *New York Times* v. *Sullivan*, and it is more severe because it fleshes out in dramatic form the consequences of the actual malice doctrine. Not surprisingly, journalists hated it. Lucinda Franks in the *Columbia Journalism Review* complained that the movie "grotesquely distorted" journalistic practices. Good reporters don't sleep with their sources (although, as Roger Ebert observed in a review, they might if the source was Paul Newman); systems of fact-checking and rigorous editing guard against premature and poorly sourced publication; newspapers don't calculate their legal liability before deciding whether to publish a story; they just labor to tell the truth.[20] Franks and other critics of the film obviously prefer movies like *All the President's Men*, *The Post*, *Spotlight*, *The Paper*, *Good Night, and Good Luck*, *Nothing but the Truth*, *The China Syndrome*, and *Call Northside 777*, all portrayals of reporters as heroic figures fighting, often against great odds, to bring to light facts the public needs to know.

The film's screenwriter, Kurt Luedtke, a former reporter and editor himself, acknowledged that not all reporters and editors perform as his characters do, but he is able to cite instances of behavior that do match the events in his script. Journalist Janet Malcom, writing not about *Absence of Malice* but about her profession in general, is less generous and more categorically damning. In a 1989 *New Yorker* article, she wrote a paragraph that hit her colleagues harder than any film: "Every journalist who is not too stupid or too full of himself to notice what is going on knows that what he does is morally indefensible. He is a kind of confidence man, preying on peoples' vanity, ignorance, or loneliness, gaining their trust and betraying them without remorse."[21]

Malcolm goes on to say that journalists defend their actions by talking about freedom of speech and the public's right to know, but these, she says, are just ways of justifying (perhaps to themselves) their "treachery," which remains in place, as do its effects.[22] In a pithy remark worthy of a philosopher, basketball player and media commentator Charles Barkley, responding to published rumors alleging an affair between him and Madonna, crystalized Malcolm's lesson: "The one thing you have to know about reporters is that they're not your friends."[23] I can add my own small testimony. For a brief period (1999–2005), I was a public figure in Chicago, in part because, when I was hired as a dean at the University of Illinois, Chicago, my salary was higher than the university chancellor's. In a big/small town like Chicago, this was news, and after that my every action was scrutinized and reported, including the fact that, as part of a recruitment effort, I had taken six people to a high-end Gold Coast restaurant to the tune of $360.00 (actually an incredible bargain). No doubt the public had a right to know! To me, and I would guess to Janet Malcolm and Charles Barkley, *Absence of Malice* rings true.

One might say that *Absence of Malice* is no less one-sided than *The People vs Larry Flynt*. One movie celebrates the First Amendment as the cornerstone of our democracy; the other details what happens when the First Amendment becomes a shield irresponsible actors can hide behind. What the movies share are two unanimous Supreme Court decisions that are, at the very least, problematic. *Hustler Magazine* v. *Falwell* denies Falwell a libel remedy, because the parody caricaturing him and his mother is not intended seriously and therefore contains no assertion that might prove libelous. And then the court turns around and claims that the same non-serious, non-assertion writing is a serious contribution to the Marketplace of Ideas. Huh? Either the ad parody says something, and we can determine whether the something it says is a libel or a defamation, or is, in fact, true, or it says nothing we can confirm or disconfirm—it's just cruel and irresponsible venting—and therefore cannot be a contribution to anything except the infliction of gratuitous wounds. Logically, you can't have it both ways, but the court does and congratulates itself for defending free speech even when the speech in question is tasteless and disagreeable. (No, it's nothing, by the court's own argument.) The court believes that it is acting on principle, but the only principle in sight seems to be the principle that Supreme Court justices and other graduates of Yale and Harvard don't like Jerry Falwell.

The value protected in *New York Times* v. *Sullivan* is also the marketplace value of "robust, uninhibited" public debate, but it is assumed without much elaboration that the integrity of debate is best served by allowing, and not attempting to cull out, falsehoods, distortions, and blatant character assassinations. If the conversation democracy invites us to contains truth, half-truths, and downright lies in an undifferentiated mix, if filters and gatekeepers are discouraged and pushed away in the name of some utopia (actually hell) of all-inclusiveness, there is no basis on which we might come to a reasoned conclusion, because the very process of reasoning has been deprived of one of its chief mechanisms, the sorting-out of the wheat from the chaff. The result will be, and is, a cacophony, ever louder and more contentious, always moving further and further away from the settling of fact that is supposedly its goal, because the ability even to specify what a fact is has been its first casualty.

We now have a name for the condition cases such as *Hustler Magazine* v. *Falwell* and *New York Times* v. *Sullivan* have brought us to. We call it fake news. One of the things about fake news is that, once in place, it cannot be removed; the assumptions that generated it—nothing is certain, everything is contestable, where there's smoke there's fire, you never know, let the public decide, you can't rule anything out, my opinion is as good as yours—militate against discarding any instance of it. James Wells may have officially cleared Michael Gallagher of wrongdoing, but, in the fictional world of *Absence of Malice*, many, we can assume, will always regard him as tainted. Maybe that's why at the end of the movie he just gets on his boat and motors away.

My analysis of *Absence of Malice* has been heavy on the legal doctrine at its center and light on its cinematic qualities. It's a fine movie, crisply directed and graced with a score by jazz musician Dave Grusin, who also scored Pollack's *The Firm*. The two movies share famously slight leading men (Newman and Tom Cruise) and a structure: both involve protagonists who are caught up in events that threaten to overwhelm them, but rescue themselves by outwitting (and in Cruise's case, outrunning) their adversaries. (Pollack's *Three Days of the Condor* with Robert Redford could make up the third in a triptych.) Both feature scene-stealing performances by Wilford Brimley. Newman was nominated for his performance, but reviewers were critical of Sally Field, whom they found too perky, not sexy enough, and hampered by having to play a lightweight, not very smart bumbler. That's wrong. In fact, the movie is hers. Newman is good as usual, but the script requires from him only a small number of emotions: he is either wry, earnest, or mildly angry (except for the one violent scene referenced above). Most important, his character doesn't learn anything in the course of the movie; he's just victorious. Field's character, on the other hand, learns everything—about her profession and most of all about herself. She is the one with choices and the problems that come from making bad ones. She is the one whose emotions and judgment pull her in different directions. She is the one who must begin all over again, having lost her job, her self-confidence, her integrity, and her romantic life. He disappears down the inland waterway bathed in the glow of his bitter-sweet triumph (still another version of the western hero). She is left on the dock wondering, only half-facetiously, whether her first employer, *The Berkshire Eagle*, will have her back. He is the man he was when he first appeared at her desk. She is no longer the jaunty, accomplished, and sought-after young woman we met at the beginning. And yet, she is, in her own way, indomitable. He's cool throughout, and that's nice to watch, but, in the end, seeing her become a person rather than a newspaper is the movie's true reward.

14

Poetry Is Against the Law

Howl

As we have seen, *The People vs Larry Flynt* and *Absence of Malice* present opposing views of the First Amendment and freedom of speech. In the former, the First Amendment saves us. In the latter, the First Amendment renders us powerless in the face of undeserved verbal assault. Let me split the difference and conclude with a movie that neither worships freedom of speech nor debunks it, but rather displays one aspect of its utility: it makes a space for art. The movie is *Howl* (2010), and it is essentially a piece of literary criticism, an "*explication de texte*" performed on Allen Ginsberg's "Howl," the most famous and most controversial American poem of the second half of the twentieth century.

Literary criticism is an activity that presupposes an object that does not speak for itself (if it did there would be no need for exegesis) and therefore requires the intervention of an interpreter who promises to excavate the riches that lie beneath its surface. The activity takes many forms—a mere list of approaches to literary interpretation would fill many pages—but common to all of them is an attitude of worrying. That is what the critics does—worry the poem by peppering it with questions. What does this word mean? Why is it repeated? Is that an image, and if so what is it an image of? Is the syntax ambiguous? Is the ambiguity intentional and if so to what end? Does the poem satisfy its readers' expectations, or disappoint them or reorient them? Is the experience of reading the poem frustrating, exhilarating, or inconclusive? What lines from earlier poems are incorporated into this one? Are these borrowings a homage, a theft, a repudiation? What is the poem's genre? Does it adhere to the genre's conventions or bend them

Law at the Movies. Stanley Fish, Oxford University Press. © Stanley Fish (2024).
DOI: 10.1093/oso/9780198898726.003.0015

or break through them? Is the poem's voice the voice of the author, or is the speaker a persona, a projected character invented for the poetic occasion? Is it important to know the date of composition, or are the circumstances of history and of the author's biography irrelevant to the meaning of the poem as poem?

The purpose of these and innumerable other questions is to bring the poem into focus as an object one can contemplate, understand, and assess. What is it trying to do? Does it do it? Is it something worth doing? Does the poem help us to negotiate the difficulties of an often-unfathomable world? Are we uplifted or soiled by reading it? Everyone in *Howl* participates in this inquiry, which is pursued in multiple venues. First (although in fact there is no first, because everything is going on at once), there is the venue of the trial, not of Ginsberg as author, but of poet/bookseller Lawrence Ferlinghetti for having published his poem. The legal issue is whether "Howl" is obscene—that is, a writing that appeals to prurient interests and is without social/literary merit. (This definition is taken from *Roth* v. *United States* (1957), which was later amplified and modified in *Miller* v. *California* (1973).[1]) But, in the excerpts presented to us, this trial sounds like no other, for its question is not did Ferlinghetti commit a crime, but did Ginsberg produce a literary work. Determining whether a crime has been committed is a matter of gathering evidence and then arranging it in a sequence that leads to a conclusion. The reasoning is deductive: so-and-so had motive and opportunity and was seen trying to pawn a piece of the stolen jewelry; therefore, he is the perpetrator. No such checklist of dispositive features leads to the identification of something as a literary work. You can't say, it displays a bunch of metaphors, therefore it's literature, or it's about great men, therefore it's literature, or it celebrates important moral values, therefore it's literature, or its lines rhyme, therefore it's literature. Each of these has at some time been put forward as an identifying characteristic, but for various reasons none of them does the job; something unexplained always remains, the literary essence that escapes formal analysis.

The unavailability of some formula for settling the matter exasperates Prosecutor Ralph McIntosh (David Strathairn), who keeps asking what does this word mean? or is this phrase relevant or what are we to understand by this? or if these words taken by themselves are obscene, why aren't they obscene in "Howl"? He wants to nail things down, and he keeps getting answers that are implicitly and sometimes explicitly rebukes to his questions. He asks critic Mark Schorer (my colleague and department chair at Berkeley in the 1960s) what a passage beginning "angelheaded hipsters" means. Schorer (Treat Williams) replies: "Sir, you can't translate poetry into prose; that's why it's poetry." Undeterred, McIntosh persists: "What are angelheaded hipsters?" The closest he gets to a definite (although indefinite) response to his queries is when critic Luther Nichols says of "blew and were blown by those human seraphim, the sailors" that the words "have several meanings." McIntosh doesn't want several meanings; he wants one.

It is the desire for a single, fixed meaning that poetry deliberately frustrates. In his poem "The Anagram," John Donne asks: "If we might put the letters but one way | In that lean dearth of words, what could we say?"[2] If we could proceed only in a strict linear fashion, looking neither to the left nor the right, never pausing for reflection, the meanings we could communicate would be extremely limited. Linear prose, one word after another in a forced march to a waiting single message, is by and large instrumental and disposable; you use it to effect an end—to obtain information, to describe an object, to get someone to do something, to order pizza—and, when the desired result is achieved, the words you've deployed are discarded; they are of no further interest. Poetry, on the other hand, requires you to pay a sustained attention to itself; its words ask to be read in multiple directions, backwards, sideward, up and down, from left to right, from right to left. You don't throw a poem away after a single use; you return to it, and, every time you do, there is something new to notice and savor. Poetry scorns the confines of linear, one-way and only-one-way, thinking; it ranges freely and kaleidoscopically and resists being re-corralled and put back in a box. (One could say the same about this movie, which refuses linearity in ways that mirror the poem that is its subject.)

One of the boxes poetry exceeds is a trial, this trial in particular. "Howl" is quoted from and interrogated in every moment of testimony, but no one ever gets to it. The poem, and indeed every poem, is a reproach to the project trials are engaged in, the project of getting right down to it, of specifying what is exactly the case, of sticking to the straight and narrow. *Poetry is against the law*, not in an outlaw way, but in a way that insists on there always being more, more distinctions, more perspectives, more detours, more meanings. Neither the defense nor the prosecution directly addresses the inappropriateness (not to say futility) of putting poetry on trial, but they implicitly acknowledge it by shifting the question from "What is literature?" (which has proven unanswerable) to the question "Who is to decide?" In short, they punt. Prosecutor McIntosh wants the decision to be ceded to the "general public," to the "average man," rather than to "experts in modern poetry." Defense attorney Jake Ehrlich (Jon Hamm) declares that the decision has already been made, not by the experts or by the common reader, but by the author who has used these words and not others: "It is not for us to choose the words." The judge (Bob Balaban) agrees with Ehrlich: Ginsberg "has used these words because he believed that his portrayal required them . . . and he should be allowed to express his thoughts and ideas in his own words." The trial is over, not because it has been determined what literature and poetry are, but because the court has recognized its incapacity to make that determination. (To legislative deference, ministerial deference, and higher-education deference—all recognized legal categories—we should add poet deference.)

The inquiry the court leaves unsettled is pursued in the course of a 1957 interview between Ginsberg (played by James Franco) and an unnamed *Time Magazine* reporter, who is never seen on screen. Like the trial, the interview is presented piecemeal, bits of it popping up on the screen when viewers have pretty much forgotten about it. Two extended bits give us Ginsberg's answer to the what-is-poetry question. He acknowledges right off that "in the moment of composition I don't necessarily know what [the poem] means." It is, he says, "like a photograph developing slowly." Indeed, the development continues long after the poet's lifetime, for the poem, if it is one, must be "able to be read . . . many centuries later." The poem is less a statement in the present than a "prophecy" or a "hint" that someone will "pick up on in a hundred years." And how do you write a poem that future readers will strain to understand? Ginsberg's answer to that question is negative; he tells us what not to do. Would-be poets go wrong, he says, when they try "to write something that sounds like something else they read before instead of sounding like them." They are composing according to models rather than in response to what is in their hearts. They err by making a distinction "between what you tell your friends and what you tell your muse." The trick is "to break down that distinction," to "approach your muse as frankly as you would talk to yourself or your friends . . . to write the same way you are."[3]

In the intervals between scenes from the trial and moments in the interview, Ginsberg is doing just that, writing as he is, at times in isolation as he speaks to his muse through a typewriter, or at other times in a public setting as he for the first time (1955) declaims "Howl" to a gallery/coffee-house audience of friends, lovers, fellow poets, and modern poetry enthusiasts who respond to each line with delight and knowing nods. In both settings, the poem is presented directly to us, the movie's viewers, who are hearing lines, not once, but many times. Each time a line or passage we have already met is repeated, our understanding of it is subtly altered by our previous experience of it in the context either of the trial, where meanings are continually debated, or of the interview, where Ginsberg stops to do some literary criticism explaining why he wrote "screamed with joy" in an account of anal penetration when a reader might have expected "screamed with pain," and recalling how he came to compose the line "Moloch whose eyes are a thousand blind windows." In effect, we are the beneficiaries of a master class in literary criticism, as the object of interpretation is turned this way and that and then re-presented to us so that we can answer the implicit question: "What do you see in this now?"

As a further aid to our ever-deepening understanding, Ginsberg's reading of his poem is illuminated even as he speaks its words by animated images (created by street artist Eric Drooker) that seem to fly out of his mouth. In contrast to the black-and-white photography of the Six Gallery *mise en scène*, the animations are brilliantly colored, phantasmagoric, endlessly metamorphosing, literal and metaphorical at the same time, at once a gloss on the words and a glance at further meanings that flicker for a moment before they give way to the next image. The movie ends with the recital by Franco of the closing lines of "Howl," followed by on-screen scripts that tell us what happened to the principal players, as Ginsberg—the real one, not James Franco—sings "Father Death Blues." We finish watching the movie, and we finish reading and hearing the poem at the same time. We exit, not with some message, insight, or lesson, but with a desire to open "Howl" to the first page and read it again.

Were I still teaching literature, I would assign this movie as an exemplar of and primer on poetry, what it is and how to read it. That is what it is about. It is not about the trial, for the main business of the trial is, as I have said, to declare its own irrelevance to the movie's urgent questions. It is not about homosexuality, even though "gayness" is everywhere; it's just not a matter of worry or anguished concern. It's about poetry-making and movie-making and the impossibility of putting limits to either. And that's enough.

Conclusion

No More Delivered than Promised

In conclusion, let me return to the beginning and to my admission in the Introduction that this book has no thesis. If it did have a thesis, the movies I discuss would have to be presented as examples of it. In the absence of any pressure to have a film illustrate something, I am free to follow the clues it offers. Yet readers, I know, seek generality. Are there generalizations to be drawn from the analyses I have offered in these pages? Perhaps, but nothing very deep or deeply interesting. It is mildly interesting to note the caliber of the directors: Sidney Lumet, Alfred Hitchcock, John Ford, Fred Zinnemann, Fritz Lang, Stanley Kramer, Nicholas Hytner, Otto Preminger, Billy Wilder, Peter Ustinov, Steven Spielberg, Miloš Forman, Niki Caro, Sydney Pollack. It is also interesting, and perhaps remarkable, that a number of these men (I am leaving Caro out of the equation for a moment) are refugees from fascist and communist regimes and that, with the exceptions of Hitchcock and Ford, all of them are Jewish. (Lang and Ustinov were not raised as Jews, but were of Jewish descent.) I do not know what to make of these facts, but maybe someone else does. It is not at all remarkable that these directors were able to attract an extraordinary roster of actors and actresses, including (and the list is not exhaustive) Henry Fonda, Vera Miles, Jimmy Stewart, John Wayne, Woody Strode, Katy Jurado, Lee Marvin, Edmond O'Brien, Gary Cooper, Grace Kelly, Lloyd Bridges, Dana Andrews, Joan Fontaine, Gene Kelly, Spencer Tracy, Fredric March, Marlene Dietrich, Richard Widmark, Maximilian Schell, Judy Garland, Montgomery Clift, Lee Remick, Eve Arden, Arthur O'Connell, Ben Gazzara, George C. Scott, Daniel Day-Lewis, Joan Allen, Winona Ryder, Paul Scofield, Robert Shaw, Susannah

Law at the Movies. Stanley Fish, Oxford University Press. © Stanley Fish (2024).
DOI: 10.1093/oso/9780198898726.003.0016

York, Orson Welles, Wendy Hiller, Leo McKern, Terence Stamp, Robert Ryan, Melvyn Douglas, Woody Harrelson, Edward Norton, Morgan Freeman, Anthony Hopkins, Matthew McConaughey, Djimon Hounsou, Charles Laughton, Elsa Lanchester, Tyrone Power, Paul Newman, Sally Field, Charlize Theron, Frances McDormand, Sissy Spacek, James Franco. An enumeration of their Academy Awards and Academy Award nominations would require a little book of its own.

I will backtrack a bit on the austere refusal of generalization. Looking back over these pages, I can discern a few predominant themes, not themes pursued (I didn't pursue any), but themes that just emerged. There is a definite preference in these films for a positivist view of the law, a view that looks for guidance to what is on the books rather than to a higher or unwritten law. *Anatomy of a Murder* and *A Man for All Seasons* are obvious examples. Paul Biegler dismisses the idea of an unwritten law and invites his client to find a legal basis for his position. Thomas More prefers the man-planted laws of England to the higher law invoked by his son-in-law. In *Billy Budd*, Vere resists the appeal to Justice with a capital J and insists on adhering to a code that can alone preserve order. In *The Crucible*, the recourse to invisible law with its spectral evidence is disastrous. In *Amistad*, abolitionist zeal is less helpful than Roger Baldwin's narrow attention to property law. In *Inherit the Wind*, Drummond's common-sense emphasis on physical fact trumps Brady's emphasis on the spiritual. Only in *Judgment at Nuremberg* is higher law or the law of human rights celebrated, although the written law of local municipalities is given its due.

There is also an attention paid in many of these films to language, in both its benign and its malign aspects. In *Absence of Malice*, words do damage, in part because of an overvaluation of free speech. In *Amistad*, words are both the vehicle of hope and transformation and the instrument of deception and equivocation. In *Anatomy of a Murder*, little words such as "but" and "nevertheless" become weapons with which lawyers Biegler and McCarthy can save their client. In *The Crucible*, John Proctor will not say the words that would save him, although he is saved, as his wife explains, by not saying them. In *A Man for All Seasons*, More parses the words of the oath in the hope that he can find a way of construing them that allows him to take it. In *Billy Budd*, Billy's wordless act is the purest utterance in the film. In *Inherit the Wind*, the revealed word of God is set against the words spoken by science.

I didn't mind writing the sentences in the previous two paragraphs, and I could write more. But I didn't find them compelling. They belong in the books I didn't write, the books that have something general to say. Having something general to say is the way, I am told, to attract and hold readers. If you have gotten this far, you have learned, as I have, to do without.

Notes

CHAPTER 1. LIBERAL HEROISM AND REASONABLE DOUBT: 12 ANGRY MEN

1. H. L. A. Hart, *The Concept of Law* (Oxford: Oxford University Press), 6.
2. Thomas Hobbes, *Leviathan, or, The Matter, Form, and Power of a Commonwealth Ecclesiastical and Civil* (London: Andrew Crooke, 1651), 50.
3. Reginald Rose, *Twelve Angry Men*, adapted by Sherman L. Sergel (Woodstock, IL: Dramatic Publishing Company, 1955), 5.
4. John Rawls, *Political Liberalism*, expanded edn (New York: Columbia University Press, 2005), 24–5.
5. Christopher Falzon, *Philosophy Goes to the Movies: An Introduction to Philosophy*, 3rd edn (New York: Routledge, 2015), 66.
6. Mike D'Angelo, "Did *12 Angry Men* Get It Wrong?" (Aug. 2, 2012), at https://www.avclub.com/did-12-angry-men-get-it-wrong-1798232604 (accessed July 7, 2022).
7. *Hopt* v. *People*, 120 U.S. 430, 439 (1887) (quoting and approving the trial court's instruction to the jury in a murder case).
8. Ibid. at 439–40.
9. Sidney Lumet, *Making Movies* (New York: Vintage Books, 1996), 81.
10. Ibid.
11. Jeff Saporito, "What Does '12 Angry Men' Say about Democracy and American Civic Duty?" at https://the-take.com/read/what-does-12-angry-men-say-about-democracy-and-american-civic-duty (accessed July 7, 2022).

CHAPTER 2. THE LAW AS BLIND MACHINE: THE WRONG MAN

1. Daniel Morgan, "The Afterlife of Superimposition," in Dudley Andrew with Hervé Joubert-Laurencin (eds), *Opening Bazin: Postwar Film Theory and its Afterlife* (New York: Oxford University Press, 2011), 137.
2. Sabrina Negri, "I Saw, Therefore I Know? Alfred Hitchcock's *The Wrong Man* and the Epistemological Potential of the Photographic Image," *Film Criticism*, 41/1 (February 2017), at https://quod.lib.umich.edu/f/fc/13761232.0041.107 (accessed July 8, 2022).
3. David Humbert, *Violence in the Films of Alfred Hitchcock: A Study in Mimesis* (East Lansing: Michigan State University Press, 2017), n.p.

4. Jean-Luc Godard, "*The Wrong Man*," in *Godard on Godard: Critical Writings*, ed. Jean Narboni and Tom Milne (New York: Viking Press, 1972), 49.
5. Ibid. 55.

CHAPTER 3. THE LAW EMERGES FROM VIOLENCE: THE MAN WHO SHOT LIBERTY VALANCE AND HIGH NOON

1. Robert B. Pippin, "Who Cares Who Shot Liberty Valance?" in *Hollywood Westerns and American Myth* (New Haven, CT: Yale University Press, 2010), n.p.
2. Jacques Derrida, "The Force of Law: 'The Mystical Foundation of Authority,'" *Cardozo Law Review*, 11/5–6 (July–August 1990), 943.
3. Jacques Derrida, *Of Grammatology*, ed. and trans. Gayatri C. Spivak (Baltimore, MD: Johns Hopkins University Press, 1974), 110.
4. William Shakespeare, *The Tragical History of Hamlet Prince of Denmark* (ll. 77–9), ed. A. R. Braunmuller (New York: Penguin, 2016), 23.
5. Christopher Falzon, *Ethics Goes to the Movies: An Introduction to Moral Philosophy* (New York: Routledge, 2019), ch. 4.

CHAPTER 5. NATURAL LAW VERSUS POSITIVE LAW: JUDGMENT AT NUREMBERG

1. Volker Schlöndorff, *Billy Wilder Speaks*, documentary film (2006) (interview with Wilder).
2. H. L. A. Hart, "Positivism and the Separation of Law and Morals," *Harvard Law Review*, 71/4 (February 1958), 595.
3. Ibid.,596 (quoting Austin).
4. Ibid. (quoting Austin).
5. Ibid. 597.
6. Ibid. (quoting Bentham).
7. Ibid. 599.
8. Ibid. 613.
9. Ibid. 614.
10. Ibid. 618–19.
11. Ibid. 619.
12. Lon L. Fuller, "Positivism and Fidelity to Law: A Reply to Professor Hart," *Harvard Law Review*, 71/4 (February 1958), 654 (quoting the German Law of December 20, 1934).
13. Ibid.
14. Ibid. 655.
15. Ibid. 656.
16. German "Sterilization Law," enacted on July 14, 1933 (effective January 1934).

17. See *Buck* v. *Bell*, 274 U.S. 200 (1927) (Holmes, J.).
18. Quoted in Douglas G. Morris, "The Lawyer who Mocked Hitler, and Other Jewish Commentaries on the Nuremberg Laws," *Central European History*, 49/3–4 (December 2016), 385–6.
19. Hobbes, *Leviathan*, 108–9.

CHAPTER 6. THE LAW'S DOGMA AND RELIGIOUS DOGMA: INHERIT THE WIND

1. James Madison, "Memorial and Remonstrance against Religious Assessments," in *Selected Writings of James Madison*, ed. Ralph Ketcham (Indianapolis, IN: Hackett Publishing Company, 2006), 23.
2. *Everson* v. *Board of Education*, 330 U.S. 1, 18 (1947).
3. Ibid. at 19–20.
4. Ibid. at 19.
5. Ibid. at 94 (Rutledge, J., dissenting).
6. Notably, see *Kennedy* v. *Bremerton School District*, No. 21–418 (U.S. Sup. Ct. June 27, 2022), in which the court holds that the Free Exercise and Free Speech Clauses of the First Amendment protect a public high school football coach's decision—for which he had been fired—to kneel at midfield after games to offer a personal prayer.
7. Despite reversing Scopes's conviction on a technicality, the Tennessee Supreme Court held that the Butler Act was constitutional. *Scopes* v. *State*, 154 Tenn. 105 (1927).
8. For the idea that the human appetite for knowledge should be bounded and disciplined, see two works by Paul J. Griffiths: *Intellectual Appetite: A Theological Grammar* (Washington: Catholic University of America Press, 2009), and *The Vice of Curiosity: An Essay on Intellectual Appetite* (Eugene, OR: Wipf and Stock, 2018).
9. John Milton, *Paradise Lost* (bk VIII, ll. 167–8, 174), ed. William Kerrigan et al. (New York: Modern Library, 2008), 264.
10. *The Poems of George Herbert*, intro. Arthur Waugh (London: Oxford University Press, 1907), 90.
11. St Augustine, *On Christian Doctrine*, in *Readings in Medieval History*, 5th edn, ed. Patrick J. Geary (Toronto: University of Toronto Press, 2016), 28.
12. *Paradise Lost* (bk VIII, ll. 119–22), 262.
13. "Love Is Here to Stay" (1938), music by George Gershwin with lyrics by Ira Gershwin.
14. *Kitzmiller* v. *Dover Area School District*, 400 F. Supp. 2d 707 (M.D. Pa. 2005).
15. *Epperson* v. *Arkansas*, 393 U.S. 97, 103, 106 (1968).
16. *Edwards* v. *Aguillard*, 482 U.S. 578, 593–4 (1987).
17. Ibid. at 621, 62, 624 (Scalia, J., dissenting).

18. *Freiler* v. *Tangipahoa Parish Board of Education*, 185 F.3d 337, 346 (5th Cir. 1999).
19. *Kitzmiller*, 400 F. Supp. 2d at 708–9.
20. Ibid. at 722.
21. Ibid. at 735–7.
22. Ibid. at 726, 735.
23. Thomas Nagel, "Public Education and Intelligent Design," *Philosophy and Public Affairs*, 36/2 (Spring 2008), 200.

CHAPTER 7. VISIBLE AND SPECTRAL EVIDENCE: THE CRUCIBLE

1. Charles W. Upham, *Salem Witchcraft; with an Account of Salem Village, and a History of Opinions on Witchcraft and Kindred Subjects*, 2 vols (Boston: Wiggin and Lunt, 1867).
2. Arthur Miller, "Why I Wrote 'The Crucible': An Artist's Answer to Politics," *New Yorker* (October 13, 1996), at https://www.newyorker.com/magazine/1996/10/21/why-i-wrote-the-crucible (accessed July 10, 2022).
3. Ibid.
4. Epistle to the Hebrews, ch. 11.
5. Shakespeare, *The Tragical History of Hamlet Prince of Denmark* (ll. 77–9), 23.
6. Jennifer Senior, "In Conversation: Antonin Scalia," *New York Magazine* (October 4, 2013), at https://nymag.com/news/features/antonin-scalia-2013-10/ (accessed July 10, 2022).
7. Edmund S. Morgan, "Bewitched," *New York Review of Books* (January 9, 1997), repr. in Edmund S. Morgan, *The Genuine Article: A Historian Looks at Early America* (New York: W. W. Norton, 2004), 63.

CHAPTER 8. MAN-MADE LAW AS A REFUGE FROM BOTH THE DEVIL'S ASSAULTS AND GOD'S COMMANDS: A MAN FOR ALL SEASONS

1. Immanuel Kant, "Perpetual Peace," in Virginia A. Hodgkinson and Michael W. Foley (eds), *The Civil Society Reader* (Lebanon, NH: University Press of New England, 2003), 39.
2. Ibid.
3. Ibid.

CHAPTER 9. LAW AS CRAFT: ANATOMY OF A MURDER

1. Special Senate Investigation (June 9, 1954), US Senate, *83rd Congress* (Washington: Government Printing Office, 1954), 2429.
2. Lawrence M. Friedman and William E. Havemann, "The Rise and Fall of the Unwritten Law: Sex, Patriarchy, and Vigilante Justice in the American Courts," *Buffalo Law Review*, 61/ 5 (December 2013), 1043.

3. Orit Kamir, *Framed: Women in Law and Film* (Durham, NC: Duke University Press, 2006), 119.
4. Mattie Lucas, "Streaming Spotlight: *Anatomy of a Murder*" (January 4, 2018), *From the Front Row*, at http://www.fromthefrontrow.net/2018/01/streaming-spotlight-anatomy-of-murder.html (accessed July 10, 2022).
5. Stanley Cavell, *Pursuits of Happiness: The Hollywood Comedy of Remarriage* (Cambridge, MA: Harvard University Press, 1981), 59, 126, 239.

CHAPTER 10. SEX, CLASS, AND CLASS ACTION: NORTH COUNTRY

1. *Jenson* v. *Eveleth Taconite Co.*, 130 F.3d 1287 (8th Cir. 1997).
2. Alice Bechdel's test appeared in her comic strip *Dykes to Watch out for*, in 1985. See Walker Caplan, *The Hub* (September 13, 2021), at https://lithub.com/read-the-1985-comic-strip-that-inspired-the-bechdel-test/ (accessed July 10, 2022).

CHAPTER 11. SPEECH, RADICAL INNOCENCE, AND THE LAW: BILLY BUDD

1. Herman Melville, *Billy Budd, Sailor (An Inside Narrative)*, ed. Michael J. Everton (Peterborough, Canada: Broadview Press, 2016), 59.
2. Ibid. 57.
3. Ibid. 63.
4. Ibid. 62.
5. Ibid. 87.
6. *Paradise Lost* (bk IV, ll. 290, 293, 300–3), 134.
7. John Milton, *Paradise Regained* (bk III, ll. 9–11), in *Paradise Regained, Samson Agonistes, and the Complete Shorter Poems*, ed. William Kerrigan et al. (New York: Modern Library, 2007), 284.
8. *Paradise Lost* (bk III, ll. 733–5), 121.
9. Ibid. (bk III, ll. 682–4, 686–91), 119.
10. Ibid. (bk VIII, ll. 463–4, 465, 467), 297.
11. *Billy Budd*, 62.
12. See also ibid. 61.
13. Ibid. 56, 57.
14. See also ibid. 114, 115.
15. D. H. Lawrence, *Studies in Classic American Literature* (New York: Thomas Seltzer, 1923), 3.

CHAPTER 12. THE LAW AND STORYTELLING: AMISTAD

1. Ronald Dworkin, *Freedom's Law: The Moral Reading of the American Constitution* (Oxford: Oxford University Press, 1996), 10.

2. Quoted in K. Koutta, "*Amistad*: An Unforgettable Film," *New Herald: Online* (September 2, 2013), at https://theheraldonline.wordpress.com/2013/09/02/amistad-an-unforgettable-film/ (accessed July 13, 2022).

CHAPTER 13. FREE SPEECH FOR GOOD OR ILL: THE PEOPLE VS LARRY FLYNT AND ABSENCE OF MALICE

1. "Director Defends 'The People vs Larry Flynt,'" *Christian Science Monitor* (February 12, 1997), at https://www.csmonitor.com/1997/0212/021297.feat.film.1.html (accessed July 13, 2022).
2. *Hustler Magazine, Inc.* v. *Falwell*, 485 U.S. 46 (1988).
3. Quoted in Nina Bernstein, "A Free Speech Hero? It's Not That Simple," *New York Times* (December 22, 1996).
4. "Jerry Falwell Talks about his First Time," *Hustler* (November 1983), inside front cover (ad parody for Campari Liqueur).
5. *Hustler Magazine*, 485 U.S. at 50.
6. Ibid. at 52 (citing *New York Times Co.* v. *Sullivan*, 376 U.S. 254 (1964)).
7. Ibid. at 50, 53.
8. Ibid. at 50.
9. Ibid. at 54–5.
10. Ibid. at 50–1. Justice Kennedy took no part in the consideration or decision of the case.
11. *New York Times Co.* v. *Sullivan*, 376 U.S. 254, 258 (1964).
12. Ibid. at 270, 273, 279–80.
13. *Gertz* v. *Robert Welch, Inc.*, 418 U.S. 323, 351 (1974).
14. *Branzburg* v. *Hayes*, 408 U.S. 665, 685 (1972).
15. *Gertz*, 418 U.S. 370 (White, J., dissenting).
16. Elena Kagan, "A Libel Story: *Sullivan* Then and Now," *Law and Social Inquiry*, 18 (1993), 197–217 (reviewing Anthony Lewis, *Make No Law: The* Sullivan *Case and the First Amendment* (1991)).
17. *Berisha* v. *Lawson*, 141 S. Ct. 2424, 2428 (Mem.) (U.S. July 2, 2021) (Gorsuch, J., dissenting).
18. Ibid. at 2425 (Thomas, J., dissenting).
19. Ibid.
20. Lucinda Franks, "Hollywood Update: *Absence of Malice*," *Columbia Journalism Review*, 20/4 (November–December 1981), 59–63.
21. Reprinted in Janet Malcolm, *The Journalist and the Murderer* (New York: Vintage Books, 1990), 3.
22. Ibid.
23. Quoted in Richard Macintosh, "A Moment of Truth," *Swans* (November 17, 2003), at http://www.swans.com/library/art9/rmac18.html (accessed July 14, 2022).

CHAPTER 14. POETRY IS AGAINST THE LAW: HOWL

1. *Roth* v. *United States*, 354 U.S. 476 (1957); *Miller* v. *California*, 413 U.S. 15 (1973).
2. John Donne, "The Anagram" (ll. 17–18), in *The Complete Poems of John Donne*, ed. Robin Robbins (New York: Routledge, 2013), 336.
3. Ginsberg's statements are found in slightly different form in an interview conducted by Thomas Clark, "Allen Ginsberg: The Art of Poetry No. 8," *Paris Review*, 10/37 (Spring 1966), 12–55.

Index

For the benefit of digital users, indexed terms that span two pages (e.g., 52–53) may, on occasion, appear on only one of those pages.